# Wine Production Technology in the United States

# Wine Production Technology in the United States

Maynard A. Amerine, EDITOR

*Wine Institute*

A symposium sponsored by the
Division of Industrial and
Engineering Chemistry at the
Second Chemical Congress of the
North American Continent
(180th ACS National Meeting),
Las Vegas, Nevada,
August 26, 1980.

ACS SYMPOSIUM SERIES 145

AMERICAN CHEMICAL SOCIETY
WASHINGTON, D. C.    1981

Library of Congress CIP Data
Wine production technology in the United States.
(ACS symposium series; 145 ISSN 0097-6156)
Includes bibliographies and index.
1. Wine and wine making—United States—Congresses.
I. Amerine, Maynard Andrew, 1911-    . II. American Chemical Society. Division of Industrial and Engineering Chemistry. III. Series: American Chemical Society. ACS symposium series; 145.

TP557.W69          663'.22'0973          80-28041
ISBN 0-8412-0596-5
ISBN 0-8412-0602-3 (pbk.)  ACSMC8  145  1-229
                                              1981

# FOREWORD

The ACS SYMPOSIUM SERIES was founded in 1974 to provide
a medium for publishing symposia quickly in book form. The
format of the Series parallels that of the continuing ADVANCES
IN CHEMISTRY SERIES. Papers are reviewed under the super-
vision of the Editors with the assistance of the Series Advisory
Board and are selected to maintain the integrity of the symposia; however, verbatim reproductions of previously published
papers are not accepted. Both reviews and reports of research
are acceptable since symposia may embrace both types of
presentation.

# CONTENTS

# PREFACE

This symposium considers the current technological status of wine-making in the United States—how various types of wine are now actually made. In 1973, a symposium on wine chemistry featured the status of our knowledge of the various constituents of wine, their determination, and their relation to wine technology. ACS ADVANCES IN CHEMISTRY SERIES No. 137, *Chemistry of Winemaking*, A. D. Webb, Ed., is the collected proceedings of that symposium. It is interesting that the new technology discussed from the chemists' point of view in 1973 has now arrived in our wineries and is being used there.

To place the current industry in perspective, there is first a chapter on the period before 1960. The slow growth of the industry over more than 300 years and the disastrous results of national Prohibition from 1919 to 1933 are outlined. The technical and economic problems of the immediate post-prohibition period are also considered.

The post-1960 developments for various types of wine and different regions of the country are the substance of the remaining chapters. White table wines are now the most important wines produced in California's north coastal region, and consumption is increasing. The new technological procedures being used in their production are particularly emphasized. Some indication of future trends is also included.

Red and rosé table wines of high quality are traditionally produced in the north coastal region of California. The importance of grape variety, region, malo-lactic fermentation, blending, and method of aging are noted.

The increasing demand for table wines and the decreasing demand for dessert wines has resulted in the increased production of table wines in the central valley of California. Statistical data to indicate the volume of table wine produced in this region are given. The warm climatic conditions of this region pose special problems in harvesting grapes and making wines. The procedures developed to improve the quality of the wines are discussed in this chapter.

The production of sherry types of wines has been a feature of the California wine industry for about 100 years. The chapter on their production emphasizes the new technology of submerged-yeast culture that has been developed to produce distinctive types of wine. Information on their composition during production is also included.

Sparkling wines are produced in various parts of the United States. The several types produced, the methods used to produce them, and the effect of the various procedures on composition and potential quality are outlined. The importance of labor-saving procedures is emphasized.

Wines have been produced in the state of Washington for a number of years, but the major increase in wine production there is recent. The particular climatic, varietal, and technical problems of producing wines in this region are discussed in detail.

Wines have been produced east of the Rocky Mountains since the sixteenth century. More wine was produced there than in California until 1880. The specific climatic conditions and the varieties used in this region are different from those of California, Washington, or Oregon. Not only are the varieties different but their ripening is, too. This has resulted in a type of wine production that is different from that used elsewhere. These production procedures are evaluated with special regard to the introduction of new varieties and to renewed interest in wine quality.

The authors conceive of the text as being useful to a wide audience: chemists, enologists, viticulturalists, and those interested in wine production and wines. For this wide audience we have used the most familiar measures: acres and gallons, but °C and mg and mL when appropriate. In some cases two systems are given.

It is evident that the American wine industry is now technologically more advanced viticulturally and enologically than most other countries. Thanks to this, the average quality of our wines is high and our finer wines are among the best produced.

The authors and editor wish to thank the staff of the Wine Institute of San Francisco for their assistance in securing statistical data and illustrations, for preparing the figures and slides, and especially for typing of the manuscript.

MAYNARD A. AMERINE
St. Helena, California
July, 1980

# Development of the American Wine Industry to 1960

MAYNARD A. AMERINE[1]

University of California, Davis, CA 95616, and Wine Institute, 165 Post Street, San Francisco, CA 94108

When the European settlers established their colonies along the Atlantic seaboard, they almost immediately turned their attention to harvesting native grapes and producing wine. Adams (1) credits the French Huguenots with making the first wines from the native Scuppernong grapes, sometime between 1562 and 1564 at Jacksonville, Florida. He also reports the Jamestown settlers made wine in Virginia in 1609 (1608 according to Wagner, 2) and the Mayflower Pilgrims at Plymouth in 1623. Presumably, these early wines were made from grapes that the settlers found growing wild.

## Early Experiments East of the Rocky Mountains

Various incentives were offered to encourage winemaking: European vines (*Vitis vinifera*) and vine dressers were brought to Maryland, the Carolinas, Virginia, Pennsylvania, etc. There are numerous records on importation of vines from Europe before and after the Revolution. Plantings also were made in Georgia, Rhode Island, and New York. As the settlers moved into the Ohio Valley, they repeated their attempts to grow *V. vinifera* with no greater success.

Some plantings of the European grapes succeeded for a time but sooner or later most died. It was not for lack of care or interest. The problems were primarily climatic: excessively cold winters for cold-sensitive *V. vinifera* varieties and high humidity during the growing period. The periodic cold winters partially, and sometimes completely, killed the vines. The humid growing seasons fanned the growth of endemic cryptogamic diseases: downy and powdery mildew, anthracnose, black rot, etc. The death of the vine in the South Atlantic states may have been attributable to Pierce's disease, a bacterial disease that we will later find in California. Fungicides to control mildew, etc. were still far in the future. Finally, in many areas the native root louse, phylloxera, probably destroyed the susceptible *V. vinifera* varieties.

[1]Current address: P.O. Box 208, St. Helena, CA 94574.

0097-6156/81/0145-0001$06.75/0

From the latter part of eighteenth century new varieties of grapes began to appear.   Some of these appear to have been domestications of the native American species, *V. labrusca* and *V. rotundifolia*.   Others of the new varieties appear to be inadvertent nursery crosses of local species and *V. vinifera*.   Concord (the most popular) appears to be primarily *V. labrusca*.   See Figure 1.   Alexander (the first new variety) and Delaware were apparently *V. labrusca* × *V. vinifera* crosses. *V. rotundifolia* was not hybridized but a number of different selections of wild grapes were made.

By 1800 there was a great interest in developing the American grape and wine industry.   This was encouraged by state and federal agencies as well as by private interests.   For example, Thomas Jefferson was a great exponent of wine drinking and encouraged the grape industry, even importing and planting vines in Virginia.

**Commercial Success.**   There were local commercial successes with the new varieties, first in Pennsylvania and later in New York and elsewhere.   The first highly successful large-scale development was in Ohio.   This was largely attributable to Nicholas Longworth and his colleagues, who envisaged the Ohio Valley as the Rhineland of America.   Their greatest success was with Catawba, another hybrid (though no one knows how much *V. labrusca* it contains). Largely white table wine was produced and considerable sparkling wine was made.   Ohio also soon planted extensive vineyards along the shores and on some of the islands of Lake Erie.

R. M. Pool

*Figure 1. Cluster of concord grapes*

The New York industry (including sparkling wines) dates from the same period. German settlers in Missouri also developed a large commercial grape and wine industry from about the middle of the century. Later smaller commercial ventures appeared in other states: New Jersey, Georgia, Kansas, Michigan, Tennessee, Virginia, etc. The wines produced were primarily dry table wines.

The advantages of the *V. labrusca* and *V. rotundifolia* varieties were their resistance to the ubiquitous fungus diseases and to winter killing. To a large extent, the *V. labrusca* hybrids had similar characteristics. Their disadvantage was their strong flavor, especially of the *V. labrusca* cultivars and some of its hybrids. These grapes and their wines had what came to be called a "foxy" flavor. The European settlers, accustomed to the milder flavors of the *V. vinifera* varieties, found it difficult to cultivate a taste for this foxy flavor. Some of the *labrusca* hybrids had low resistance to phylloxera.

There was some rivalry between the California and the Eastern wine industry as soon as the transcontinental railroad was completed. This competition involved natural sectional commercial rivalry of the new industries and fundamental differences in winemaking practices.

**Production Practices.** Few of the new Eastern grape varieties produced enough sugar in the grapes to make a balanced (11 percent ethanol) wine. This was caused by the naturally low sugar and high acidity in the fruit of many of these varieties, particularly in the cooler areas and in cooler seasons.

Therefore, sugar was added to make up for the deficiency. Water, to reduce the high acidity, also was used commonly. The water also reduced the foxy flavor of the native varieties. Neither practice was necessary with *V. vinifera* varieties in California. Later in the nineteenth century, Eastern bottlers often blended California and Eastern wine. This reduced the strong labrusca and scuppernong flavors and, of course, reduced commercial rivalry. Later, laws permitted use of sugar and water except in California. This difference in practice still exists.

The native grapes and their hybrids were generally easy to harvest and crush—at first by feet and later with roller crushers. Open wood tanks were used for red wine fermentations and closed tanks for whites. Eastern grapes are difficult to press because the skins slip from the pulp when pressed. Therefore, with the traditional hydraulic presses, it was difficult to secure a high juice yield. Various expedients were used: rack-and-cloth presses, heating the skins and pulp before pressing, etc. See Figure 2.

Little or no cooling was used during fermentation. Sulfur dioxide began to be employed at the end of the nineteenth century, as were pure yeast cultures. Wines were aged in tanks and barrels. Eastern wines are usually, but not always, easier to clarify than California wines. While some wine was bottled for sale, a great deal was sold in bulk to local bottlers or was sold directly to the consumer in barrels (50 gallons) or in demijohns (3–5 gallons).

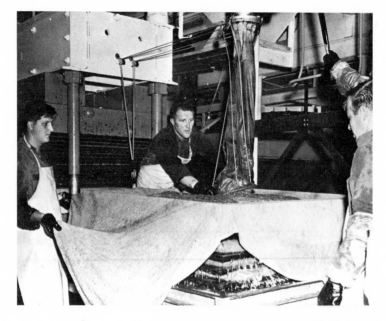

*Figure 2. Old-fashioned rack-and-cloth press*

The cool winters made wine storage in the East easier than in California. Thus, the wines were generally less subject to spoilage during fermentation and storage than in California. Also, the market was close at hand, and there was less spoilage and surreptitious diluting during transportation than occurred in California or during shipment from California to the Eastern markets.

Clarification was by racking, fining, and filtration. With the general use of water, tartrate stabilization was not a major problem. The cold winters also facilitated precipitation of excess tartrates.

Prohibition closed down the Eastern wine industry as quickly and as firmly as it did the California industry. However, the vineyards were partially saved by the increasingly popular grape juice industry, to which Concord was suited admirably. Furthermore, a large amount of grapes were sold to home winemakers, which was legal.

**Post-Repeal.** Following Repeal, many wineries throughout the country were re-established, but by no means all of the pre-Prohibition wineries were reopened. The equipment was similar to that used before Prohibition: roller crushers and crusher–stemmers, sulfur dioxide and pure yeast cultures, etc. In general, larger tanks were used than before Prohibition. Use of pectin-splitting enzymes to facilitate pressing was introduced and used widely. From 1933 to 1960, new and faster filters and bottling equipment and the tank fermentation of sparkling wines were introduced.

The new viticultural development was the introduction of new complex *V. vinifera* interspecific hybrids from France—the so-called French hybrids. These were largely fungus-resistant, but their flavor was less, or not at all, foxy.    A number of these hybrids now are planted widely throughout the East: Aurore, Chelois, De Chaunac, Foch, etc.    Philip Wagner of Riderwood, Maryland, deserves much of the credit for introducing, propagating, and popularizing these hybrids from Europe (*see* Chapter 8).

New methods for training vines and mechanical harvesting of grapes were introduced after World War II.

One other recent development has been a renewed interest in growing *V. vinifera* east of the Rocky Mountains.    This came towards the end of the period under review (1957 to be exact) and will be reviewed more completely in the post-1960 discussion in Chapter 8.

By 1960, there was a decreasing wine industry in all of the eastern states, especially in the number of wineries.    The most successful large wineries were those who used California wine for blending, especially for dessert wines.    See Figure 3.    In Missouri and Ohio, the wine industry decreased dramatically after World War II, in spite of their large local markets.    No one knows the reasons for this decline, but the ubiquitous Concord must bear part of the blame.    It could be made into a dry red wine but the flavor was frighteningly strong.    In sweet wines, the flavor also was

Taylor Wine Company

*Figure 3.  Overhead view of large New York winery*

strong and addition of considerable sugar was required. However, the high-(added)-sugar Concord "kosher" wine was successful and several wineries still produce it.

There was also a small vermouth industry (largely based on California wine). Sparkling wines were produced successfully by a few New York wineries. Sparkling wine production in Missouri and Ohio had nearly ceased by 1960. Probably the competition of low-priced wine from California and Washington was also a factor in the decline.

*California*

Peninou and Greenleaf (3) and Carosso (4) have reviewed the Mission period. When the missionaries came from Baja California to San Diego in 1769, they brought the Mission grape with them, probably by 1770. Its antecedents are not known but the cultivar growing in California is apparently a seedling of some *V. vinifera* variety. The missions south of Point Conception (San Diego, San Juan Capistrano, San Gabriel, and Santa Barbara) were the first to produce wine. Santa Clara and San Luis Obispo were making wines in 1801. By 1806, Langsdorff, the naturalist, had wine from Mission San Jose just south of San Francisco. From 1800, brandy was made at some of the missions, especially San Fernando and Santa Barbara. See Figure 4.

**Early Production Practices.** The methods of making wine were crude. On a platform covered with clean hides, the grapes were heaped and, in the age-old fashion, were crushed by tramping feet. However, the Indians so employed are said to have been "well washed, their hair carefully tied up, and their hands covered with cloth to wipe away perspiration." The juice was caught in leather bags that were emptied into tubs or cemented cisterns, where it fermented under the cover of the skins. After fermentation, the wine was kept in sewed-up hides or large earthenware jugs. Since the missions at first had neither bottles nor casks, the wine was not aged properly, spoiled rapidly, and could not be exported easily.

At one mission at least, there were better methods employed. Father Jose Maria de Zalvidea, who was in charge of viticulture at San Gabriel, increased the planting of vines until by 1830 this mission had 163,000 vines, three wine presses and eight stills. They made between 400 and 600 barrels of wine and 200 barrels of brandy annually. A Father Duran described the wine as being of four kinds: a dry red "very good for the table," a sweet red with a flavor like that of blackberry juice, which he did not like, and two white wines both of which were "delicious for dessert," one from pure grape juice fermented without the skins being used, a second fermented with some grape brandy. The first of these white wines was primarily altar wine, the other "for any use whatever."

No one knows how the padres, with their faulty equipment and methods, prevented their wines from turning into vinegar. One of the main reasons

Wine Institute
*Figure 4. Clusters of Mission grapes*

why the Spanish Californians showed a preference for sweet wines may have been because a sweet vinegary wine is a more palatable wine than a dry sour wine.   Their brandy must have been as crude as their wine considering the low-quality wine and the primitive stills.

The mission vineyards were not planted with any set distance between the vines and a later California winegrower complained in 1851 that the priests and native Californians planted in small patches without regard to locality or a view to improving the vine.   Irrigation was practiced as early as 1793, when Captain Vancouver noted at San Buenaventura, "the grounds were supplied . . . with a few streams, which as occasion required, were conducted to the crop."   By 1835, irrigation was general in the southern vineyards.   At Mission San Antonia de Padua, in southern Monterey County, the padres there under Buenaventura Sitjar, "the passionate conservator of the garden," dug out a ditch—traces of which can be seen still—to San Antonio Creek three miles away to bring in water.

In 1815, under the Spanish regime, prices were fixed by the governor at not more than one dollar per quart for aguardiente or fifty cents for wine in northern California.   In the south, the top price was to be seventy-five cents for aguardiente and twenty-five cents for wine.    See Peninou and Greenleaf (3).

The missions were secularized starting in 1833 and thereafter most of their vineyards were neglected or abandoned.    Even so San Gabriel produced wine and brandy for some time after secularization.

**Early Commercial Developments.**    Privately owned vineyards were planted in the Los Angeles area at an early date and by 1818 there were 55,000 vines there.    Jean Louis Vignes, of Bordeaux, planted vines and made wine commercially, probably the first to do so outside the missions.    According to Carosso (4), he also imported some vines from Europe and shipped wines and brandies to other parts of California.    William Wolfskill, a Kentuckian, also planted vines in the Los Angeles area and made wine by about 1840.    Wine production in California was about 50,000 gallons in 1849 (5).

The discovery of gold resulted in a big increase in the population and increased the demand for grapes for eating and for winemaking.    By 1853 there were over a thousand acres of vines in the Los Angeles area and most of the California wine was produced in this area.    By this time, immigrants from Germany had arrived as well as many French settlers, some of whom planted vines and produced wine.    Later, many Italian immigrants arrived and planted vineyards and developed wineries.

In southern California, the Anaheim development started in 1857 and finally planted over a thousand acres of grapes in that area.    Unfortunately, it was destroyed after 1888 by a mysterious vine disease, now known as Pierce's disease (from a bacterial agent).

Between 1856 and 1862, the number of vines in the state increased from 1.5 million to 10.5 million.    Vines were planted in many new areas during this period.    Wine production on a large scale did not start in northern California until about 1857.    The wines were poor because of the ubiquitous use of the Mission grape, primitive methods of crushing, lack of proper cellars, lack of a California plant for producing bottles (the first one started in 1863), untrained winemakers, etc.    The only important wine merchants of the period were Kohler and Frohling, who started in Los Angeles and later operated primarily from San Francisco.    They exported California wines to eastern United States, Europe, and the Far East.

This brings us to Agoston Haraszthy (Figure 5), a Hungarian immigrant, and his impact on the California grape and wine industry.    He had planted grapes at San Diego by 1850, but his development of the Buena Vista vineyard and winery at Sonoma in northern California starting in 1857 was his major achievement.    He was also a great protagonist for the California grape and wine industry.    He made an observational trip to Europe in 1861 and from it brought back a large collection of grape varieties.    Unfortunately, the vines apparently were distributed poorly, through no fault of his, and did not reach their potential effect in improving the California industry.    The Buena Vista

*Figure 5. Agoston Haraszthy*

Wine Institute

wines won a number of awards, but the vineyards were planted too closely; the sparkling wine venture failed; and phylloxera arrived, whether from its native areas in eastern United States or from infested areas in Europe is not known.    Phylloxera was more devastating at Sonoma than in some other districts.    For these and other reasons, the Buena Vista venture soon failed.    However, the winery survived and is still in operation.

By 1860, there were thirty-two wineries in the state.    Los Angeles was the largest producer, followed by Sonoma and Santa Clara.    Peninou and Greenleaf (3) note that the wines shipped to the eastern United States arrived spoiled "because of faulty methods used in making it."    From 1860 on, vineyards were planted increasingly throughout the state but the poor quality of the wine prevented its achieving a reputation or market.    Immigrants from many countries as well as from the eastern states were involved in this expansion.

Arpad Haraszthy (Agoston's son) wrote a detailed discussion (6) of winemaking in California in 1871.    He deplored the ubiquitous Mission and the attempt to make all kinds of wine from it.    He notes that even at this early date, California winemakers were attempting to reduce manual operations. Even then he complained of onerous federal wine regulations.    He also noted widespread production of artificial wines in eastern United States.    There is little in his report as to how good the best California wines were in 1871.

**University Experiments.**    Eugene Woldemar Hilgard came to the University of California as Professor of Agriculture in 1875.    He was already a prominent soil scientist but he soon took an active interest in the state's struggling and largely unprofitable grape and wine industry.    He wrote a critical pamphlet on the root louse phylloxera as early as 1876.    Amerine (6) has evaluated his many contributions to the California grape and wine industry.    Hilgard helped lobby through the California legislature a bill that on April 15, 1880, created the Board of State Viticultural Commissioners and instructed the Regents of the University of California to provide instruction and research in viticulture and enology.    Both of these provisions of the law had profound and salutary influences on the future California grape and wine industry.    See Figure 6.

Under Hilgard's direction, the University instituted a broad program of research.    Hilgard himself best expressed the objectives of his research: "The plan adopted in this matter is in conformity with my view, expressed in my previous report, and shared by the best vintners in the state, viz: that among the first necessities of the present situation of California wines in the world's market, is the establishment of more definite qualities and brands, resulting from a definite knowledge of the qualities of each of the prominent grape varieties, and of their influence upon the kind and quality of the wine, in blending before, or as the case may be, after fermentation; of the treatment required by each in the cellar, during the time of ripening; and finally, of the differences caused by difference of location, climate, etc. as well as by different treatment of the vines themselves."

Hilgard (7) summarized his results as follows: "I am convinced that, with the proper understanding and utilization of the data given in this report, much

*Figure 6.  Professor Eugene W. Hilgard*

of the uncertainty and haphazard heretofore prevailing will disappear, and that, both in the selection of the grape varieties to be planted, and of the proper blends to be made for particular purposes and types, the data imparted by analyses and the records of vinification will be found of the greatest practical use."

The Board of State Viticultural Commissioners, also organized in 1880, was composed of commissioners from various viticultural regions of the State. They and their executive secretary, Charles A. Wetmore, engaged in a wide range of activities to help the California wine industry: public relations in the press and via exhibitions and conventions (the commissioners and the executive secretary were all engaged in grape and wine production), legal battles (largely with the Federal government on taxes and tariffs), education (directed at growers, winemakers, and consumers), translation of pertinent foreign books, etc. But in 1895, the Board was abolished and the University took over its library and its research functions.

There is no way of measuring the positive effects that the University and the Board had on the California grape and wine industry. Economically, this was not so evident, as wine prices continued to be low. But the whole tenor of the industry gradually changed. By 1900, there was no doubt that California was entering a new period of better wines and greater confidence in its future as a wine-producing state.

Besides phylloxera and grape varieties, Hilgard had many research projects in enology. The most significant was his recommendation of 5.5°–17° C as suitable temperatures for fermenting white table wines. General acceptance in California of this recommendation did not come for seventy-five years. He was correct that lactic spoilage was often caused by stuck fermentations owing to excessive fermentation temperatures.

Hilgard also preached temperance and the importance of wine quality. His famous letter (7) to William Randolph Hearst on what was wrong with the industry was published in the *San Francisco Examiner* of August 8, 1889. In answer to the question "What do you consider the cause of the present depression in the wine market?" he wrote: "Chiefly and fundamentally, the poor quality of the larger part of the wines made, and their immaturity when put on the market. . . . It is high time that the ostrich-like policy of hiding the faults of our winemaking from ourselves were done away with once for all."

He then went on to outline how California wines could be improved. First, the winemakers should either learn how to make sound wine or abandon their occupation. Reprehensible practices that he noted as being prevalent were (1) growing excessive crops on valley lands, (2) attempting to handle such a large acreage that each variety is not harvested at the proper time, (3) carelessness in picking, so that moldy, sunburned, or rotten grapes are not excluded, (4) filling the fermentation tanks too high so that there is no space for a protective cover of carbon dioxide, (5) using excessively large fermenting tanks and hot grapes, (6) stirring up a spoiled cap, (7) leaving the wine too long on the pomace, (8) storing the wines in a cold place too soon, thus preventing the secondary fermentation, (9) defective after-treatment of the wine, such as using tanks that are too large, failure to rack often enough, and not excluding air during racking, and (10) selection of grape varieties unsuited to the local climate.

Hilgard's own evaluation of his research (7) was: "The result of the laboratory work has been to establish a definite basis for rational wine production in this state, by determining both the cultural and winemaking qualities of all of the more important grape varieties in the several regions where our stations were, or are now, located. It is true that the depression under which the wine interests has labored for a number of years past has prevented viticulturists from availing themselves, to any great extent, of the guiding principles established by us; but it is quite certain that in future undertakings of this kind, as well as in any rational winery practice in the immediate future, these facts will have to be taken into definite consideration if the product is to be as good as it can be made under local conditions; as competition as well as critical judging of wines make themselves more plainly felt, such practice must inevitably take precedence of the haphazard, irrational modes of procedure that have so largely prevailed heretofore. Our work in this line represents the largest and most complete systematic investigation of the kind on record thus far in any country."

**Wetmore's View of Winery Practices.** Wetmore (8), of the Board of State Viticultural Commissioners, emphasized the importance of planting the proper variety of wine grape in the climatic region where it would produce its best wine. He also noted that in the period of great experimentation between 1880 and 1885, vines often were planted in the wrong location; in fact, "in many cases large vineyards were separately blocked out for all types from Spain to the Rhine." Wetmore said California has "every condition of soil and climate . . . to compare with Xeres, Malaga, the Mediterranean coast, France, the slopes of the Alps, the valleys of the Rhine and Rhone, and the humid climates on either side of the British channel." The Los Angeles Chamber of Commerce hardly could have improved that.

He also noted that California attempted to produce only cheap wines, which yielded little or no profit. He blamed this on the wine merchants. He found it necessary to describe, as best he could in 1894, the methods of producing the classic types of European wines so that California producers would know the types to "shoot for." He noted the "general complaint that California wines are too strong and lack refreshing qualities." He blamed this also on the demands of New York wine merchants for wines of "heavy body, high color, and strength." This certainly is an indictment of the wine trade of 1894 because such wines could be, and probably were, "stretched." He thought that wines of 8–9 percent might be popular, as German wines were: "Light white wines and clarets, with not exceeding 9 percent alcohol, are greatly needed." This was almost 100 years ahead of its time. The early and excessive ripening of grapes in the warmer regions of California again was noted.

As to California practices in 1894, Wetmore admits that there was bad management in the cellars during the spring and summer. (Again he blamed the wine merchants for delaying their selection of wines for shipment.) Spoilage occurred during aging in warm cellars because of secondary fermentation "to reduce sugar that has not fermented." Wetmore particularly criticized the storage of dry table wines in dry, warm cellars. Lacking such storage, he favored early bottling: "The sooner it is in the bottle after it is ready, the better." He favored not crushing (but noted that most producers used crushers), separation of the wine from the skins, use of "oeno-tannin," anaerobic conditions, complete and early racking, and storage in cool, unventilated, moist, dark cellars. To secure lower alcohol, he believed the vine training system might be changed (to give larger crops?) and "by reducing the must with water" (now prohibited in California.)

He reported red wine fermentations in the skins of five to eight days "until fermentation is completed." He noted that the price of grapes depended on sugar content and that growers of ordinary varieties of high yield (10 tons) got almost as much per ton as growers of quality varieties growing on hillsides with low yield (2–4 tons): $10.00 versus $12.00 per ton.

The development of an oxidized odor in white table wines was common. However, those who burnt sulfur freely in their casks (to produce $SO_2$) had no trouble. Film yeast growth on dry white wines was also a problem, indicating poor cellar practice. The baking of wine to produce sherry was practiced already in California in 1884—in "sherry houses."

About the same time as Wetmore's report, two competent judges evaluated the California wines submitted to the 1893 World's Columbian Exposition in Chicago (9, 10).

Dubois thought the wines had been handled poorly (standing too long upright in the cases). He also found that a number of the wines could have been improved by judicious blending. Specifically, he recommended Merlot and Malbec with Cabernet Sauvignon and Sauvignon vert with Sémillon.

Oldham's report is especially interesting as he was an English wine merchant and had been familiar with California wine "for some years now." In later years, his firm imported large amounts of California wines. He noted that some white wines were fermented on the skins too long and others were left in the wood too long, or both. On the other hand, he criticized some of the reds for "having been kept in large vats in a hot, uneven temperature." Standards of fill were not always up to his standards (excess air space between the wine and the cork). Some wines did not conform to type as much as he would like. His specific comments on the wines were to the point and often very laudatory. The Stanford Angelica of 1892 from the Vina vineyard was "very good indeed; by far the best exhibited." But the ports and sherries were generally poor, he said.    Finally, he was enthusiastic about the future of California, which is "rapidly taking its place as one of the principal wine-producing countries of the world."

A number of imposing wineries were constructed in the state before Prohibition, particularly in the northern part of the state.    See Figure 7.

However, the economics of the wine industry were so precarious that in 1894 (partially because of the national economic depression), seven of the leading wine firms organized the California Wine Association to stabilize wine prices.    As Peninou and Greenleaf (3) state, "From that time on until the coming of Prohibition, the history of winemaking in California is largely the history of the California Wine Association."

The California Wine Association stabilized prices, instituted evaluation of wines as part of wine purchases, established brands by a well-conceived blending program, and instituted chemical control of all of their wines.    There were still several important independent wine producers and merchants but the technological and financial skills of the California Wine Association prevailed.    One of their most important contributions was the Winehaven Winery in Richmond.    This 12-million-gallon winery provided cool storage

Wine Institute

*Figure 7.  Old stone winery in the Napa Valley*

and blending facilities and, after 1911, also made some wine.   By 1918, the California Wine Association controlled directly or indirectly 84 percent of the wine produced in the state, according to Peninou and Greenleaf (3).

**Lachman.**   The description of winemaking in California at the turn of the century by Henry Lachman (*11*) is definitive.   Lachman was the chief enologist of the the California Wine Association.   He notes that until at least 1870, the California wine industry was limited in its ability to produce fine wine by the lack of good wine grape varieties.   The Mission grape, he noted, produced "fine sweet wine, but poor red wine, the chief objections being its strong tannin and earthy taste, due not so much to the ground as to its not being suited for light, dry wines."

Lachman considered that the most rapid progress in improving California wines came in the 1890s when many plantings of new varieties became available, and winemaking was "conducted on more scientific lines."   He also noted the deleterious effects of the phylloxera invasion of California (rampant in the 1880s and 1890s).   In retrospect, this may have been a blessing, as the new vineyards planted on resistant stocks often were grafted to better varieties than the original vines.

Harvesting was, of course, all by hand, by itinerant workers, paid piece work and earning $1.50–$2.00 per day (of which 50 cents had to be paid for meals).   The price paid was adjusted according to the amount of crop.   Harvesting started in Fresno by August 15 and continued to October 20.   Time of harvest was regulated by field sampling.   The minimum sugar desired in this area was 24° Brix (then called Balling).   The grapes were picked into boxes and transported to the nearby winery.   Some grapes were dumped into railway gravel cars.   He notes that "should it take longer, and the grapes arrive in a damaged condition, they can only be used for brandy making."

In the cooler coast areas, the vintage started between September 5 and 10 and continued until mid October.   It is of interest to note, "There is very seldom any crushing done in November in the dry-wine districts, excepting possibly some second-crop grapes or Mission varieties.

The list of varieties grown in the state at that time and their use and yield is interesting.   The original spelling of Lachman is given but modern nomenclature, when different, is given in parenthesis.

> Sweet-Wine Grapes: Trousseau, Sultana, Palamino (Palomino), Thomson's Seedling (Thompson Seedless), Muscat of Alexandria, Sweet Water (Chasselas doré), Feher Szagas, Malaga, and Emperor were grown chiefly on flat land (in the Central Valley) and yielded 6–10 tons to the acre.

> Dry-wine varieties grown in sweet-wine districts and used in the manufacture of sweet wines: Zinfandel, Mataro, Carignan (Carignane), and Burger had yields of 6–10 tons per acre.

Dry-Wine Grapes (red): Zinfandel, Mataro, Grenache, and Charbono produced 4–6 tons in the valley, 2–4 tons on the hills (presumably in the Coastal Valleys and on the slopes of their hills). Cabernet Franc (Cabernet franc), Cabernet Sauvignon, Beclan, Merlot, Gamay, Alicante Bouschet, and Petite Bouschet had yields of 2–3 tons per acre in the valleys, 1–2 tons per acre on the hills. Petite Sirrah (Petite Sirah), Verdot, San Macaire (St. Macaire), Mondeuse, Muenier (Meunier), Barbera, Tenat (Tannat ?), and Chauché noir yielded 3–5 tons in the valleys, 2–3½ tons on the hills.

Dry-Wine Grapes (white): Golden Chasselas (Palomino), Gutedel (Chasselas doré), Johannisberg Riesling (White Riesling), Franken Riesling (Sylvaner), Gray Riesling (Grey Riesling), Traminer, and Sauvignon Vert (Sauvignon vert) had yields of 4 tons per acre in the valley, 2½ tons per acre on the hills. Sauvignon Blanc (Sauvignon blanc), Semillon (Sémillon), and Muscat de Bordelais produced 3–3½ tons in the valley, 1½–2 tons on the hills. Folle Blanche and Colombar (French Colombard) gave yields of 4 tons in the valley, 2 tons on the hills. With Burgers (Burger), Verdal, and Green Hungarian, the yield was 8–12 tons in the valleys, 5–8 tons on the hills.

Red Grapes (used for white wines): Mission, Malvoise (Malvoisie), and Black Pinot produced 4–6 tons per acre in the valley, 3–4 tons on the hills.

Table Grapes (used in winemaking): Rose of Peru, Black Hamburg, Cornichon, Tokay, and Emperor gave yields of 4–6 tons per acre in the valley (in the Central Valley), 3–4 tons per acre on the hills (presumably in the Sierra Nevada foothills).

The crushers were generally located above the fermenting tanks. Roller crushers followed by a stemmer was the usual practice. "As a rule grapes are fermented without the stems in California." The exception noted was when the stems were dry and were then allowed "to pass into the fermenting tanks, so that tannin can be drawn from the stems." This was probably only for red wines.

Daily sugar and temperature readings were made. For red wines, the fermentation lasted 5–7 days and the wine was drawn off the pomace essentially "dry." If raisins or half-dried grapes are present, the fermentation ceased with 1–4 percent residual sugar and lactic bacterial spoilage ensued. Such wine should be distilled, he recommended. He added that if blended with other sound wine, it will contaminate that wine as well.

The late Edmund Henri Twight, who worked for the California Wine Association in the late 1890s, told the writer (about 1936) that he recalled huge amounts of sweet-sour wine in California at that time—perhaps 20 percent, he estimated. There is considerable other evidence that incomplete (stuck) fermentations and unsound faulty wines were common in the early 1900s. This is verified by a letter of 1898 from Frederick T. Bioletti *(12)* of the Berkeley staff of the University to a Fresno winemaker (sic), as follows: "Dear Sir: Your favor of Sept. 15 to Prof. Hilgard has been handed to me for reply.    Mr. Colby and I have examined the wine and find that it contains 13% of alcohol and 3.3% of solid contents which is perfectly normal for a natural wine.

"It certainly has a peculiar taste, in fact, many peculiar tastes.    These tastes are, however, all perfectly easy to produce from good grapes by appropriate methods, such as dirty vats and shoots, hot fermentation, and the use of old and imperfectly cleaned vats and casks that have contained port.    Just how this wine was made of course I cannot say, though I can guess, but it is not necessary to look for any chemical fabrication, for the ordinary methods of producing dry red wine in California are quite sufficient to account for all the 'off' flavors imaginable."

Lachman emphasized the care of the wines.    He recommended weekly examination, storage of whites at 10°–15.6° C, and reds at 15.6°–21° C.    By cleanliness he meant "scrupulously clean": scrubbing with a brush, use of soda and hot water, etc.    Sulfuring (adding $SO_2$) was recommended.    He also recommended that the same kind of wine be kept in the same tanks.

Lachman would limit the fermentors to 5000 gallons, wisely we think because of the lack of cooling facilities.    Production of piquette (pomace wine for distilling) is described.    It should have at least 5–7 percent alcohol.    Extraction with water passed from the bottom of one tank to the top of the next was used.    The washed pomace was still worth $0.75–$1.25 per ton for cream of tartar production.

For white wine production, the grapes usually were not stemmed.    The crushed grapes were left for six to ten hours before the free-run (separated) juice was drawn off.    The pomace was then pressed and the pressed pomace was washed as with red pomace.    The fermentation of white musts was done in 2/3-full oak casks.    The fermentation was watched daily.    The yeast foam was removed.    By the sixth day, the fermentation had slowed down sufficiently to then use a fermenting bung.    "The Italians often use a bag of sand, which they place over the bung-hole."    He recommended fermenting room temperatures of 21°–27° C and cellar temperatures of 15.6°–21° C, preferring 15.6° C after the first year.

Six to ten weeks after the wine was made, it was separated from the sediment (racked).    A further racking occurred between February and October, with another in August or September.    He preferred to store old wines in separate areas from new wines.    Wine storage was often in tanks, 5000–50,000 gallons the first year.    In smaller wineries, 2000–3000-gallon containers were used.

The wines were evaluated and blended at the time of the second racking.    Blending often was done by wine merchants in or near San Francisco.    For export, he noted that a "burgundy" type was blended for England, a "Bordeaux" type for China and Japan, a "vin ordinaire" for New

Orleans, and "Burgundy" light clarets and strong astringent wines (for the Italians) for New York. After blending, the wines were filtered and stored in 1000–4000-gallon casks (ovals).

To clarify (fine) wines, gelatin, white of eggs, and Russian isinglass were used. Curiously, it is recommended that the casks must be filled daily during fining. The fining agents were left in the wine for twenty to thirty days. Wines that did not clarify were re-fined. With gelatin, at least, this was a dangerous practice. Too much filtration was abjured because it "flattens and injures the flavor."

Lachman's recommendations for the chemical composition of blended wines are most interesting. Sweet (dessert) wines should contain about 0.052 g/100 mL of volatile acidity (as acetic) and not used if 0.100 g/mL or over. The total acidity of sherry wines "should not go over 0.50 g/mL free acid." The meaning of this requirement is not clear. Clarets for export "should not exceed 0.12 g/mL volatile acid; at 0.14 g/mL they are considered doubtful, and at 0.16 g/mL they are condemned." These limits are higher than would be tolerated currently (practically or legally). The ethanol content of California red wines was 12.25 percent and of white wines 11.5 percent, but some Burgers and Green Hungarians ran as low as 10 percent (overcropping?) and sauterne types were 13–14.5 percent.

Lachman's recommendations for wines for the market still stand: "Wines should never be put on the market unless they are perfectly clear; that is, they should hold clear and show brilliant before a candle." His recommendation that wines be aged at least eighteen months before bottling simply reflect the inadequacy of the clarification and filtration procedures of his time.

On sensory examination of wines, Lachman was a master. He abhorred still wines of excess carbon dioxide. He writes of "first, second, and third tastes." (But some of these are surely odors, not tastes.) Blending is considered the most difficult branch of the handling of wines. It should, he says, be assisted by chemical analysis. The judge must be in condition. He should be able "to detect any blemish, and tell whether a wine has been corrected by use of lime, chalk, or salt." This tells us a good deal about the poor quality of wines of the period, as does Bioletti's letter (12).

Lachman was far in advance of his time in recommending bottling as the primary means of distributing wines. He recommended bottling reds after three years of aging in the wood and whites after four. For white wines, this is far longer than modern practice would sanction. He was again in advance of his time in recommending test bottling: exposing the bottled wine to heat, light, and a draft for a week or ten days.

As to regional differences, Lachman was familiar with the lighter wines produced in the cooler coastal valleys compared with the heavier wines produced in the warmer interior valley. He believed wines grown in hilly or mountainous country gave higher flavors. He also found the wines of the Livermore Valley to "have a different characteristic altogether from the white wines from our other dry wine districts." Also, the red wines from Livermore grapes were "a different type of red wine from those produced in other districts." Amerine (*13*) agrees with this, particularly for Cabernet Sauvignon.

For California port, practice favored fortifying to 20 percent ethanol with only 6–10 percent sugar, which is lower than now practiced. He also recommended fortifying to 22 percent if the wines were to be held more than three years. For sherry, he recommended fortifying to 20–21 percent at 4 percent sugar. Aging in 50–100-gallon wood cooperage in a shed exposed to morning sun and heated at night to hold at 60° C was recommended. Steam- or hot-air-heated rooms also were used. After heating, the wines were aged five to ten years. At that time, "California is more backward in sherry types than any other types produced in the state, on account of not allowing them sufficient time to develop flavor." The observation might still be made eighty years later. Malaga-type wine was made by adding boiled-down must, baking in the sun, or heating. Tokay types were made from grapes of high sugar content (shriveled or raisined). The California tokay thus appears as a dessert type in contrast to the Hungarian wine called tokay (or tokaj), which is a low-alcohol (usually below 14 percent) type, though it is often sweet.

On sparkling wines, he was less sanguine. He estimated that over one million dollars had been lost in experimenting. He blamed the failure on using too high alcohol wines in the cuvée.

Labor costs were comparatively low: $2.00 per day for the average cellar man, $3.00 for experienced help and $100.00 per month for superintendents or winemakers.

His essay ended on an optimistic note if California producers replanted their vineyards with better varieties and classified their wines according to their virtues. Not a word about Prohibition, which was less than two decades away. In fact, the California industry proceeded blithely along from 1900 to 1918. Not until Prohibition was imminent did wineries bottle wines and try to sell them at whatever price they could get.

There are some progressive developments in the early 1900s, which unfortunately passed largely unused. Bioletti (*14–19*) had noted difficulties of winemaking in hot climates. His bulletins and articles were written clearly and proposed cooling and rational use of sulfur dioxide. Bioletti and Cruess (*20*) and Cruess (*21*) did both laboratory and plant experiments that clearly showed the advantages of the rational use of sulfur dioxide in winemaking. The other was Jordan's (*22*) book on settling, use of pure yeast cultures, cooling, and pasteurization. Jordan was far in advance of his time in these practices, particularly cooling. It is significant that the objective of his experiments was to prevent incomplete fermentations, the bane of the California wine industry at this period. The significance of his book is that he described experiments made over several years in the Repsold winery at Napa. As further evidence of the success of his experiments were the quality of his wines that survived Prohibition.

It is of interest to note the amount of hand labor required in pre-Prohibition wineries.   Crushers often were placed at the highest point in the winery, the fermentors were on the top floor, and storage tanks were on lower floors.   It was not until the 1890s that machine-operated pumps and filters were used commonly.   Grapes, of course, were still delivered in boxes and unloaded by hand and the pomace was removed from the fermentors by hand labor, in a few cases until recently.

The Prohibition period, 1919–1933, was a great one for California grape growers and a disastrous one for the wineries.   Only a few wineries kept their basic permit and produced sacramental or medicinal wines.   The rest were dismantled or kept closed with some minimum attempt to maintain the cooperage and equipment.

The grape growers profited from a huge increase in shipment of red wine grapes to local and eastern markets for the home production of wine (which was legal up to 200 gallons).   There was also an increasing market for raisins and for table grapes.   Prices in the early 1920s were higher than at any previous time.   The demand for red grapes was for those of good shipping quality (thick skins) and high color.   Thus, the finer quality (for wine) varieties were grafted to such varieties as Alicante Bouschet, Carignane, Mataro, Grand Noir, Petite Sirah, Zinfandel, Malvoisie, etc.   These had high yields, some had a fine color, and all could stand up to the 3000-mile, seven-to-fourteen-day trip to New York or Boston.   By 1929, Shear (*see* Amerine and Joslyn, *23*) estimated that home wine production had reached 90 million gallons.   Thus, during Prohibition, the acreage of fine wine-grape varieties decreased sharply (particularly whites) and table-grape and raisin-grape acreages increased.   Prices decreased sharply in the mid 1920s and stayed depressed until World War II.

### 1933 to 1960

Getting the new wine industry started was a major task.   Besides lack of suitable varieties of wine grapes, there were few trained winemakers, little usable equipment, dried-out and leaky containers, little aged wine, and no distribution channels.   The equipment deficiency was largely made up by building the new wineries with concrete fermentors and storage tanks of large size: 25,000–100,000 gallons.   Concrete containers were inexpensive and easy to install.

The first crusher–stemmers were largely modifications of the old Garolla type.   They were made of iron and could handle 50–100 tons per hour.   Excess iron pickup was a major problem until stainless steel was introduced after World War II.

The biggest change after Repeal was the huge demand for fortified dessert wines: angelica, muscatel, port, sherry, and white port.   Prior to

World War II, 75–80 percent of California wine production was of these types. These wines were sold at very low prices, 50–75 cents per bottle. These low prices had a number of unfortunate effects on the California grape and wine industries.

Low prices for wine meant low prices for grapes—so low that surplus table and raisin grapes of lower quality and cost were used widely. The low prices also limited quality. Dessert wines were processed rapidly and seldom aged. At such low profit levels, the larger wineries had an economic advantage so that the number of bonded-wine premises in California dropped from 804 in 1934 to 249 in 1960 and 212 in 1965. But by 1977, it had risen to 373. The number of very large wineries (over 9 million gallons) increased from 9 in 1941 to 36 in 1977. There has been a significant increase in the number of small wineries in recent years, as Table I illustrates.

The dominance of low price dessert wines reduced interest in better grape varieties, improved grape and wine production practices, and properly timed harvesting. The evidence of the turbulent conditions in the industry in this period was the surpluses of low quality wine that developed. Perhaps the most significant effort to solve this problem was the 1938 program to distill surplus wine as it was made and secure loans on the high-proof spirits and brandy this produced. There were other programs to stabilize the industry even up to 1960.

**Table I. Frequency Distribution of Size of California Bonded Winery Premises: December 31, 1941, 1965, and 1977**

| | Number of Wineries | | | | Percentage Change from 1947 | Percentage Change from 1965 |
|---|---|---|---|---|---|---|
| Storage Capacity[a] (gallons) | 1941 | 1947 | 1965 | 1977 | | |
| Less than 10,000 | 201 | 87 | 17 | 115 | + 32.2 | + 576.5 |
| 10,000–25,000 | 22 | 32 | 13 | 34 | + 6.3 | + 161.5 |
| 25,000–50,000 | 28 | 32 | 20 | 32 | 0.0 | + 60.0 |
| 50,000–100,000 | 28 | 30 | 21 | 30 | 0.0 | + 42.9 |
| 100,000–250,000 | 54 | 59 | 27 | 39 | − 33.9 | + 44.4 |
| 250,000–500,000 | 28 | 43 | 23 | 19 | − 55.8 | − 17.4 |
| 500,000–1,000,000 | 20 | 25 | 18 | 18 | − 28.0 | 0.0 |
| 1,000,000–2,000,000 | 31 | 28 | 25 | 21 | − 25.0 | − 16.0 |
| 2,000,000–5,000,000 | 22 | 33 | 30 | 29 | − 12.1 | − 3.3 |
| Over 5,000,000 | 9 | 14 | 18[b] | 36[c] | + 157.1 | + 100.0 |
| Total | 443 | 383 | 212 | 373 | − 2.7 | + 43.6 |

[a] Including fermenters usable as storage as of December 31.
[b] Of 18 wineries with storage capacity in 1965 of over 5,000,000, 11 had 5,000,000–10,000,000 and 7 had over 10,000,000.
[c] Of 36 wineries with storage capacity in 1977 of over 5,000,000, 16 had 5,000,000–10,000,000 and 20 had over 10,000,000.

Source: Compiled by Wine Institute, San Francisco, from unpublished detailed reports.

The production of cheap dessert wines during the depression years also had another unfortunate result: dessert wines were the cheapest source of alcohol. The skid-row alcoholic used wine as his source of alcohol and became known as a "wino."

The high production of dessert wines and brandies required large quantities of high-proof spirits and brandy. The disposal of huge quantities of distillery slops with their high BOD created major problems: killing fish in rivers, malodors from ponding, overloading of commercial sewage disposal systems because of its seasonal character, and possible contamination of underground water supplies. The increasing size of California wineries has increased the problem of winery waste disposal.

Food and Drug agencies, state and federal, even before World War II began efforts to improve the sanitation practices of the industry. From 1958, the Wine Institute employed a sanitation expert. A sanitation handbook that gave detailed instructions on improving winery practices was published and has been kept up to date.

The University of California was called upon for teaching, extension, and research for the new industry. The initial teaching responsibility fell largely on Professor William V. Cruess and his colleagues on the Berkeley campus. They not only developed university-caliber courses, but taught special practical courses. Both at Berkeley and Davis (Professor A. J. Winkler and his colleagues) extensive research programs began and extension work was done through direct contact with wineries, regional meetings, and several statewide conferences. The research was varied: microbiological, biochemical, chemical engineering (distillation), nutritional, and economic (largely by the Giannini Foundation for Agricultural Economics on the Berkeley campus). The results of these studies were the identification and development of control measures for bacterial and yeast disorders, better fining agents, more rational distillation procedures, temperature control (23, 24), flor and submerged culture sherries, better laboratory procedures, climatic zones, varietal recommendations, more rational sensory evaluation procedures, information on the role and mechanism of the malo-lactic fermentation, wine-cooling data and statistical data upon which economic control measures were based (23, 25, 26), and new varieties and viticultural practices.

The Wine Institute, a nonprofit trade organization, was established in San Francisco in 1934. It soon became the authoritative voice of the California wine industry. It was especially effective in numerous legislative and regulatory affairs, not only in California but elsewhere. It collected statistical information and worked on economic measures to stabilize the industry.

One of the extension activities of importance was the regular meeting of the Technical Advisory Committee of the Wine Institute from 1942 to 1973, at which much of the University and other research was first presented. These meetings also provided a mechanism for exchange of ideas for winemakers on a personal basis.

**Table II. Commercially Produced Still and Sparkling Wine Entering Distribution Channels In The United States, By Origin, 1965–1979**

| | United States Produced Wine | | | | | | Foreign Wine[d] | | Total All Wine |
| | California[a] | | Other States[b] | | United States[c] | | | | |
| Year beginning July 1[e] | Total 1 | Percent of Total 2 | Total 3 | Percent of Total 4 | Total 5 | Percent of Total 6 | Total 7 | Percent of Total 8 | 9 |
|---|---|---|---|---|---|---|---|---|---|
| | 1000 wine gallons | | 1000 wine gallons | | 1000 wine gallons | | 1000 wine gallons | | 1000 wine gallons |
| Averages | | | | | | | | | |
| 1950–1954 | 114,457 | 83.2 | 17,300 | 12.6 | 131,757 | 95.8 | 5834 | 4.2 | 137,591 |
| 1955–1959 | 123,767 | 80.5 | 21,184 | 13.8 | 144,951 | 94.3 | 8821 | 5.7 | 153,772 |
| 1960–1964 | 134,817 | 77.1 | 26,351 | 15.0 | 161,168 | 92.1 | 13,836 | 7.9 | 175,006 |
| 1965–1969 | 152,632 | 73.8 | 33,967 | 16.4 | 186,599 | 90.3 | 20,108 | 9.7 | 206,707 |
| 1970–1974 | 228,919 | 71.2 | 48,370 | 15.1 | 277,289 | 86.3 | 44,017 | 13.7 | 321,300 |
| 1975–1979f | 285,518 | 70.6 | 46,330 | 11.5 | 331,848 | 82.0 | 72,737 | 18.0 | 404,584 |

[a] California wine excludes small quantity of California wine exported.
[b] Total U.S. less Total California.
[c] Tax-paid withdrawals.
[d] Imports for consumption.
[e] Prior to 1965, figures are on crop year basis, beginning July 1 of year specified, and including June 30 in following year.
[f] Preliminary figures for 1979.

Sources: Figures prior to 1965 compiled by Giannini Foundation of Agricultural Economics from issues of Wine Institutes' *Annual Wine Industry Statistical Survey*, Part IV. Figures beginning in 1965 compiled by Wine Institute from reports of Bureau of Alcohol, Tobacco, and Firearms, U.S. Treasury Department, and Bureau of the Census, U.S. Department of Commerce.

Table III. Apparent Consumption of Commercial Still and Sparkling Wines in the United States: Tax-Paid Withdrawals of United States and Imported Commercial Still and Sparkling Wines, 1909–1974

| Years beginning July 1[e] | Total, Still and Sparkling[a] | Sparkling Wine | Still Wine, Commercial, Tax-paid Withdrawals | | |
| | | | Total[b] | Dessert, over 14 Percent Alcohol[c] | Table, not over 14 Percent Alcohol[d] |
| | 1 | 2 | 3 | 4 | 5 |
| | | | 1000 wine gallons | | |
| Averages | | | | | |
| 1909–1913 | 68,[f]392 | 867 | 49,445 | 19,196 | 30,247 |
| 1935–1939 | 101,204 | 1185 | 67,525 | 45,399 | 22,126 |
| 1940–1944 | 121,314 | 1674 | 100,019 | 67,196 | 32,823 |
| 1945–1949 | 137,651 | 1935 | 119,640 | 89,584 | 30,056 |
| 1950–1954 | 153,771 | 3260 | 135,716 | 96,986 | 38,730 |
| 1955–1959 | 175,004 | 5365 | 150,511 | 103,861 | 46,650 |
| 1960–1964 | 206,707 | 11,303 | 169,639 | 106,806 | 62,833 |
| 1965–1969 | 321,300 | 21,808 | 195,505 | 103,614 | 91,891 |
| 1970–1974 | 404,584 | 23,992 | 299,492 | 92,309 | 207,183 |
| 1975–1979[g] | | | 380,592 | 77,699 | 302,892 |

a Column 2 plus Column 3; totals differ slightly because of rounding.
b Column 4 plus Column 5; totals differ slightly because of rounding.
c Dessert includes vermouth and other special natural (flavored) wine over 14 percent alcohol. Prior to 1965, dessert wine also includes sake imports.
d Table includes other special natural (flavored) wine not over 14 percent alcohol. Beginning in 1965, table wine also includes sake imports.
e Prior to 1965, figures are on crop year basis beginning July 1 of year specified and ending June 30 in following year.
f The very small consumption of sparkling wine is included in still wine totals 1909–1913.
g Preliminary figures for 1979.

Sources: Figures prior to 1965 compiled by S. W. Shear, Giannini Foundation of Agricultural Economics from reports of Internal Revenue Service, U.S. Treasury Department, and Bureau of the Census, U.S. Department of Commerce. Figures beginning in 1965 compiled by Wine Institute from reports of Bureau of Alcohol, Tobacco and Firearms, U.S. Treasury Department, and Bureau of the Census, U.S. Department of Commerce.

In 1938, the Wine Advisory Board was organized under the Department of Agriculture of the State of California.   It collected a small tax on each gallon of California wine sold and from these funds supported public relations, advertising, and research for the industry.   The research covered a wide field from viticultural and enological research, largely at the University of California, to more than 100 research projects on the possible health values of wine.   The Wine Advisory Board was abolished in 1975 and its functions were assumed largely by the Wine Institute.

The American Society of Enologists was organized in 1950 and continues to function.   This provided an annual meeting for presentation of research papers and for publication of the papers presented (at first through a Proceedings and since 1951 by the *American Journal of Enology and Viticulture*).   The more formal results of the University as well as industry and other research work were published here.   The abstract section of this journal proved helpful to the industry in recording and evaluating new publications on enology and viticulture.

Finally, following Repeal, the University personnel published numerous bulletins, circulars, and books on grape and wine production, incorporating the results of their own and other research and the best industry practices of the time.   These publications were of great value not only to grape growers and winemakers but also to students at the University of California and elsewhere.   They established the reputation of the University of California as one of the most important centers of research in enology and viticulture in the world.

Production of wine increased rapidly after Repeal, as Table II illustrates.   Note the increasing percentage of imported wine and the preponderance of California wine.

The distribution of wine by types is given in Table III.

**Table IV. Indexes of Wholesale Prices For California Wine, 1947–1979[a]**

| Calendar Year Averages | Red Table and Dessert 1 | Red Table 2 | Dessert 3 |
|---|---|---|---|
| | *Percentage of 1957–1959 as 100[b]* | | |
| 1947–1949 | 95.9 | 76.5 | 103.7 |
| 1950–1954 | 79.6 | 74.1 | 82.3 |
| 1955–1959 | 86.2 | 83.7 | 87.1 |
| 1960–1964 | 95.9 | 95.0 | 96.5 |
| 1965–1969 | 101.1 | 101.1 | 101.1 |
| 1970–1974 | 126.1 | 127.6 | 125.2 |
| 1975–1979[b] | 163.9 | 170.1 | 162.5 |

[a] Based on prices f.o.b. California Winery, in cases of twelve fifths or equivalent.
[b] Preliminary figures for 1979.

The changes in indexes of wholesale prices for California wine are given in Table IV.

With increasing production and profits, many new wineries were constructed in architecturally pleasing styles. See Figures 8 and 9.

E. & J. Gallo

*Figure 8. Headquarters of large California winery*

Sterling Vineyards

*Figure 9. New winery in the Napa Valley*

### Literature Cited

1. Adams, L. "The Wines of America," 2nd ed.; McGraw-Hill: Boston, MA, 1978.
2. Wagner, P.M. "Grapes Into Wine. A Guide to Winemaking;" Knopf: New York, 1976.

3. Peninou, E.; Greenleaf, S. "Winemaking in California;" Peregrine Press: San Francisco, CA, 1954.
4. Carosso, V.P. "The California Wine Industry, 1830–1895: A Study of the Formative Years;" Univ. of California Press: Berkeley, Los Angeles, 1951.
5. U.S. Tariff Commission. "Grapes, Raisins and Wine," *U.S. Tariff Comm. Rep* **1939**, *134*, 1–408.
6. Haraszthy, A. "Wine-making in California;" The Book Club of California: San Francisco, CA, 1978.
7. Amerine, M.A. "Hilgard and California Viticulture," *Hilgardia* **1962**, *33*, 1–23.
8. Wetmore, C.A. "Treatise Concerning the Principles Governing the Production of Distinct Types of Wine in Europe and California," Part I of Appendix B, Report of the Board of State Viticultural Commissioners for 1893–94; A.J. Johnston, Supt. State Printing; Sacramento, CA, 1894, pp. 5–42.
9. Dubois, E. "Report on California Wines and Brandies," Part I of Appendix B, Report of the Board of State Viticultural Commissioners for 1893–94; A. J. Johnston, Supt. State Printing; Sacramento, CA, 1894, pp. 44–45.
10. Oldham, C.F. "Report on California Wines and Brandies Exhibited at the World's Columbian Exposition, Chicago, U.S.A, 1893," Part I of Appendix B, Report of the Board of State Viticultural Commissioners for 1893–94; A. J. Johnston, Supt. State Printing; Sacramento, CA, 1894, pp. 50–58.
11. Lachman, H. "The Manufacture of Wines in California," *U.S.D.A. Bur. Chem. Bull.* **1903**, *72*, 25–40.
12. Bioletti, F.T. Univ. of California Archives, Berkeley, CA, personal communication.
13. Amerine, M.A. "The Anatomy of a Superb Wine," *San Francisco* **1964**, *6*(13), 28–29.
14. Bioletti, F.T. "The Manufacture of Dry Wines in Hot Countries," *Calif., Agric. Exp. Stn. Bull.* **1905**, *167*, 1–66.
15. Bioletti, F.T. "A New Wine-Cooling Machine," *Calif., Agric. Exp. Stn. Bull.* **1906**, *174*, 1–27.
16. Bioletti, F.T. "A New Method of Making Dry Red Wine," *Calif., Agric. Exp. Stn. Bull.* **1906**, *177*, 1–36.
17. Bioletti, F.T. "Sulfurous Acid in Wine Making," *Eighth Intern. Cong. Appl. Chem.* **1912**, *14*, 31–59.
18. Bioletti, F.T. "Winery Directions," *Calif., Agric. Exp. Stn., Cir.* **1914**, *119*, 1–8.
19. Bioletti, F.T. "The Wine-Making Industry of California," *Intern. Inst. Agr., Agr. Intelligence Plant Dis. Mon. Bull.* **1915**, *6*(2), 1–13.
20. Bioletti, F.T.; Cruess, W.V. "Enological Investigations," *Calif., Agric. Exp. Stn. Bull.* **1912**, *230*, 1–118.
21. Cruess, W.V. "The Effect of Sulfurous Acid on Fermentation Organisms," *J. Ind. Eng. Chem.* **1911**, *4*, 581–585.
22. Jordan, R. "Quality in Dry Wines Through Adequate Fermentations, by Means Defecation, Aeration, Pure Yeast, Cooling and Heating;" Pernau: San Francisco, CA, 1911.
23. Amerine, M.A.; Joslyn, M.A. "Table Wines: Technology of Their Production," 2nd ed.; Univ. of California Press: Berkeley, Los Angeles, 1972.
24. Cruess, W.V. "Fermentation of Wines at Lower Temperatures," *Wines Vines* **1948**, 29(9), 19–21. (See also *Wine Technol. Conf., University of California, Co. Agr., Davis, CA, Aug. 1948, pp. 90–97.*)
25. Cruess, W.V. "The Principles and Practice of Wine Making," 2nd ed.; Avi: New York, 1947.
26. Amerine, M.A.; Berg, H.W.; Kunkee, R.E.; Ough, C.S.; Singleton, V.L.; Webb, A.D. "The Technology of Wine Making," 4th ed.; Avi: Westport, CN, 1980.

RECEIVED July 24, 1980.

# White Table Wine Production in California's North Coast Region

ZELMA R. LONG

Simi Winery, Healdsburg, CA 95448

The North Coast area of California is well known for the excellence of its white table wines. Climate factors, primarily the cooling effects of the bays and ocean, provide optimum conditions for production of grapes and wines of distinctive character and proper balance. A history of wine production in the area has provided time for development and improvement of viticultural and vinification techniques. Recent substantial increase in demand for varietal white table wines has encouraged further development of new and improved winemaking techniques and has resulted in increased plantings of white wine grapes.

## White Grape Acreage in the North Coast

The "North Coast" grape growing region is defined as Napa, Sonoma, Mendocino, Solano, Lake, and Marin Counties (1). Napa, Sonoma, and Mendocino have been, and continue to be, the major wine-grape producing counties of the North Coast (Table I). Since 1969, white grape acreage in these three counties has increased from 7500 acres to 21,700 acres in 1978. In 1969, 31 percent of the total grape acreage was planted to white grapes; in 1978, the white grapes represented 36 percent of the total acreage (Table II).

White varieties grown in the North Coast include Burger, Chardonnay, Chenin blanc, Flora, Folle Blanche, French Colombard, Gewürztraminer, Grey Riesling, Green Hungarian, Malvasia bianca, Muscat blanc (Muscat Canelli), Palomino, Pinot blanc, Sauvignon blanc, Sauvignon vert, Sémillon, Sylvaner, and White (Johannisberg) Riesling. The major increase in plantings has been in the "premium" varietals, varieties made and marketed under a varietal label, rather than blended and marketed as generic wines. Since 1969, 13,000 acres have been planted in Napa, Sonoma, and Mendocino to Chardonnay, Sauvignon blanc, White Riesling, Chenin blanc, and Gewürztraminer (Table III). Chardonnay and Gewürztraminer plantings have increased almost tenfold.

The North Coast area represents 20 percent of California's total wine-grape acreage. Its plantings of Chardonnay, Sauvignon blanc, White Riesling, and Gewürztraminer represent a substantial portion of the state crop of these white varieties (Table IV).

0097-6156/81/0145-0029$07.25/0

### Table I. Wine Grape Acreage: Napa, Sonoma, and Mendocino (2)

|  | Acreage Standing (1969) | Acreage Standing (1978) |
|---|---|---|
| Burger | 284 | 333 |
| Chardonnay | 781 | 7,001 |
| Chenin blanc | 977 | 2,613 |
| Flora | 134 | 147 |
| Folly Blanche | 26 | 154 |
| French Colombard | 2,414 | 2,697 |
| Gewürztraminer | 126 | 1,395 |
| Grey Riesling | 285 | 582 |
| Green Hungarian | 140 | 207 |
| Malvasia bianca | 14 | 14 |
| Muscat blanc | 74 | 172 |
| Palomino | 481 | 482 |
| Pinot blanc | 105 | 390 |
| Sauvignon blanc | 413 | 1,639 |
| Sauvignon vert | 366 | 377 |
| Sémillon | 200 | 229 |
| Sylvaner | 196 | 208 |
| White Riesling[a] | 546 | 3,113 |
|  | 7,562 | 21,753 |

[a] Johannisberg Riesling

**Trends in White Wine Consumption.** The 1970s have brought increasing consumer interest in white table wines. In 1979, California wineries shipped 114 million gallons of white wine to markets, up from 38 million in 1974. The 1979 shipments represented 53 percent of the total table wine shipped that year (Table V).

### Table II. White Wine Grape Acreage: Napa, Sonoma, and Mendocino (2) 1969–1978

|  | Total Wine Grape Acreage | White[a] Wine Grape Acreage | Percent White |
|---|---|---|---|
| 1969 | 24,557 | 7562 | 31 |
| 1978 | 61,025 | 21,753 | 36 |
| percent | 248 | 58 | 287 |

[a] Includes: Burger, Chardonnay, Chenin blanc, Flora, Folle Blanche, French Colombard, Gewürztraminer, Grey Riesling, Green Hungarian, Malvasia bianca, Muscat blanc, Palomino, Pinot blanc, Sauvignon blanc, Sauvignon vert, Sémillon, Sylvaner, White Riesling.

**Table III.  Selected Varietals Increase in Acreage: Napa, Sonoma, and Mendocino**

|  | *Acreage Standing* | | *Acre* | *Percent* |
|---|---|---|---|---|
|  | *1969* | *1978* | *Increase* | *Increase* |
| Chardonnay | 781 | 7001 | 6220 | 896 |
| Chenin blanc | 977 | 2613 | 1636 | 267 |
| French Colombard | 2414 | 2697 | 283 | 11 |
| Gewürztraminer | 126 | 1395 | 1269 | 1107 |
| Sauvignon blanc | 413 | 1639 | 1226 | 397 |
| White Riesling | 546 | 3113 | 2567 | 570 |

**Table IV.  1978 Wine Grape Acreage: Napa, Sonoma, and Mendocino vs. all California**

|  | *Total:* *Napa, Sonoma,* *Mendocino* | *California* | *Napa, Sonoma,* *Mendocino,* *Percent* *of all* *California* |
|---|---|---|---|
| Chardonnay | 7001 | 13,486 | 52 |
| Chenin blanc | 2613 | 22,390 | 12 |
| French Colombard | 2697 | 28,985 | 9 |
| Gewürztraminer | 1395 | 2795 | 50 |
| Sauvignon blanc | 1639 | 5301 | 31 |
| White Riesling | 3113 | 8327 | 37 |

**Table V.  Bottled California Table Wines Shipped to Market in 1000 Gallons**

|  | *1974* | | *1977* | | *1979* | |
|---|---|---|---|---|---|---|
|  | *Gallons* | *Percent* | *Gallons* | *Percent* | *Gallons* | *Percent* |
| White | 38,583 | 31.6 | 73,533 | 42.3 | 114,200 | 52.8 |
| Rosé | 33,577 | 27.5 | 48,674 | 28.0 | 52,991 | 24.5 |
| Red | 49,939 | 40.9 | 51,629 | 29.7 | 49,097 | 22.7 |
| Total | 122,099 | | 173,836 | | 216,288 | |

Source: Prepared by the Wine Institute in November 1979 and updated in February 1980. Prepared from confidential reports obtained from California wineries and reports of the California Board of Equalization and the BATF of the U.S. Treasury Department.

## Table VI. Bonded Wineries and Bonded Wine Cellars

|           | February 1960 | July 1968 | July 1977 |
|-----------|:-------------:|:---------:|:---------:|
| Napa      | 30            | 33        | 68        |
| Mendocino | 4             | 2         | 7         |
| Sonoma    | 36            | 27        | 60        |
| Total     | 70            | 62        | 198       |

Source: Prepared by the Wine Institute from BATF reports.

**Effect on White Table Wine Production.**   The increase of plantings of premium varietals has gone hand in hand with the "wine boom" of the 1970s.   Consumer demand for white varietal wines encouraged this increase in plantings and development of new wineries.   Bonded wine premises in the Napa, Sonoma, and Mendocino Counties increased from 70 in 1960 to 198 in 1978 (Table VI).   Production of generic white wines (chablis, rhine wine) gave way to emphasis on varietal production, and in the later 1970s, while white varietal production remained strong, a renewed interest developed in producing wines blended from lower cost varietals and sold under "white table wine," nonvarietal labels.   Increased vineyard planting and wine production intensified interest in, and investigation of, viticultural and vinification practices.

### Characteristics of North Coast Counties

Climate affects grape character and quality.   In the North Coast, warm summer days with night cooling from coastal influences provide excellent conditions for grape maturation.   Marked climate differences occur within North Coast counties because of topography and varied coastal influence.   In general, in comparison with the San Joaquin Valley, the North Coast has cooler summer temperatures, more annual rainfall, less irrigation, a shorter growing season, lower crop levels, and fewer fungus problems.   North Coast grapes tend to have higher titratable acidity and lower pH at maturity than San Joaquin Valley grapes.   For a summary of the viticultural characteristics of white varieties from the North Coast see Table VII.

### Viticultural Practices Affecting Wine Production and Quality

Sound grapes of intrinsic good quality for wine are vital for production of quality table wines.   Changes in viticultural practices have affected wine quantity and quality.   The change of greatest impact since 1950 has been the change in varietal composition of North Coast vineyards discussed earlier.   Other trends have been increased mechanization in vineyard work, emphasis on full production of vineyards and healthier vines, and greater pricing variations reflecting more closely grape quality and maturity.

**Table VII. Summary of Viticultural Characteristics (3) of White Varieties from the North Coast Counties**

| | Leafing | Vine Growth | Pruning Method | Harvest Period | Average Cluster Weight (1b) | Productivity (tons/acre) |
|---|---|---|---|---|---|---|
| Chardonnay | v. early | v. vigorous | cane | early | 1/8–1/4 | 2–5 |
| Chenin blanc | v. early | v. vigorous | spur | midseason | 1/3 | 5–8 |
| Flora | early | moderate | spur | early–mid | 1/5–1/3 | 4–6 |
| French Colombard | mid | v. vigorous | spur | midseason | 1/3 | 6–9 |
| Gewürztraminer | early | moderate | cane | early | 1/5–1/6 | 2–4 |
| Grey Riesling | early | v. vigorous | spur | early | 1/5–1/3 | 5–7 |
| Pinot blanc | early–mid | moderate | spur | midseason | 1/6–1/4 | 3–5 |
| Muscat blanc | early–mid | moderate | spur | midseason | 1/3–1/2 | 2–4 |
| Sauvignon blanc | early–mid | v. vigorous | cane | early–mid | 1/6–1/5 | 4–6 |
| Sémillon | late–mid | moderate | spur | early–mid | 1/3 | 5–8 |
| Sylvaner | late–mid | moderate | spur | midseason | 1/5–1/4 | 3–5 |
| White Riesling | early–mid | moderate | cane | midseason | 1/5–1/6 | 4–6 |

**Clonal Selection.** A good example of improvement in vine quality and productivity is the clonal improvement work done with Chardonnay. Fifteen to twenty years ago, growers were reluctant to plant Chardonnay, not only because of lack of winery interest but because of problems with shot berries, poor set, low crop, and disease susceptibility. Professor Olmo of the University of California at Davis began selections of Chardonnay, grown first in the Carneros area in Napa County and then in Oakville. The best of these selections went into the University certification program for virus-free stock. The clones were selected for better set, fuller clusters, and higher yield.

**Certification Program.** The virus-free certification program for rootstock and budwood began slowly at the University of California at Davis in the 1950s. By the early 1970s, nearly all major varieties had virus-free certified stock available. Certification stock came from two sources: heat-treated vines or indexed vines. The former undergo a heat program to kill virus present; the latter are grafted onto other virus-sensitive plants to test their freedom from virus. Clones for the certification program were based on visual selection of healthy plants with good crop loads. No studies were made relating selections to wine quality, and no studies have been done since comparing the effect of heat treatment on wine quality.

**Mildew and Botrytis Control.** Control of mildew is the major fungicide problem in North Coast vineyards. Occurrence of mildew and botrytis affects the grape quality, and mildew has been shown to have a negative effect on wine quality (4). Mildew is controlled by sulfur applications, and nearly all North Coast vineyards receive four to six sulfur applications each year. The North Coast has less mildew and insect problems than does the San Joaquin Valley, attributable to a cooler climate and shorter insect seasons.

Benlate (benomyl [methyl 1-(butylcarbamdyl)-2-benzimidazole carbamate]), applied in the spring at first bloom, is used for control of botrytis where control is desired. Varieties most sensitive to botrytis are those with later ripening habits, thin skin, tighter clusters, and dense foliage. White Riesling and Chenin blanc often are affected. Sauvignon blanc is more resistant because of its thicker skinned berries. Chardonnay rarely is affected because of its early harvest. It may be that current viticultural practices create more favorable conditions for botrytis than in the past: more plantings on heavier valley soils, heavier crops, later ripening patterns, and denser foliage.

**Pruning and Trellising.** Pruning systems most often used are the head trained, with spur pruning, cane pruned, and the cordon trained, with spur pruning. More varieties are being cordon pruned to simplify pruning, to aid mechanical harvesting, to "open up" or spread vine growth evenly, and to improve mildew control. Changes in trellising include crossarm or "T" trellising, providing more leaf exposure to the sun, fruit protection from sun, and better access for sulfur applications (5). These changes result in healthier, better quality fruit being delivered to the wineries.

**Maturity.**    The trend in harvesting has been toward grapes of higher maturity (Table VIII).    This has been largely through substantial economic incentives provided by some wineries for more mature grapes.    Factors hindering proper maturation, such as overcropping, late irrigation, and poor site selection, have been eliminated by vineyardists wishing to maximize returns from grape crops.    However, with the demand for white wine grapes, and high grape prices, some still profit by overcropping.

*Harvest*

Harvest in the North Coast begins in late August or early September and continues into October.    The majority of the white grapes are harvested in September.    The first varieties to be harvested are Grey Riesling, Flora, Gewürztraminer, and Chardonnay, followed by Chenin blanc and Sauvignon blanc.    French Colombard and White Riesling are usually the last grapes to be harvested.

Decision to harvest is based most commonly on grape maturity.    Individual wineries set standards for maturity needed in their grapes to produce wine meeting their quality and style standards.    These standards take into account the need for the balance of ethanol, acids, and varietal flavors in a premium wine.    As the grapes ripen, sugar increases, color changes, malic acid is metabolized, phenolic synthesis continues, and the grapes soften.    The most commonly used indicator of maturity is °Brix, a measure of soluble solids, mostly sugar, of the grape juice.    For the best quality wine, grapes must be harvested at "optimum" maturity, usually 21°–23° Brix.    In general, the trend of the 1970s has been to harvest grapes riper, i.e., at higher °Brix levels (*see* Table VIII).

However, °Brix is not the only indicator of optimum harvest time.    Field sampling, using a representative sampling technique, is used to procure grape samples for measurement of °Brix, titratable acidity, and pH.    Winemakers consider these factors, combined with tasting of the grapes for flavor and observation of their condition, to select a harvest date.    Climatic conditions, such as the drought of 1976–1977, the heavy botrytis infections of 1978, and fall rains, also affect timing of harvest.

Trends in grape payment have been to reward growers producing better quality, more mature grapes.    Payment for quality has taken two directions: a higher base payment for vineyards thought to produce superior grapes, and °Brix or the °Brix–titratable acid ratio.    These are related to bonus payments.    Wineries set minimum and maximum acceptable °Brix levels and structure bonuses to provide highest payment per ton for grapes coming closest to their "ideal" °Brix, within the acceptable range.    The California Department of Food and Agriculture listed 371 °Brix adjustment factors used for °Brix-based grape payments in 1979 (9).

Factors affecting grape quality at harvest time are not only the composition of the fruit but the resistance of the fruit to change during harvest and transportation.    Crushing of the grapes during the picking process acceler-

**Table VIII. °Brix at Harvest of Grapes Delivered to Wineries**

|  | 1969 (6) | 1971 (7) | 1974 (8) | 1978 (1) | | 1979 (9) | |
|---|---|---|---|---|---|---|---|
|  | Coastal Region | Coastal Region | North Coastal Region | Napa | Sonoma, Marin | Sonoma, Marin | Napa |
| Chardonnay | 21.8 | 21.9 | 22.4 | 23.4 | 23.1 | 22.6 | 22.8 |
| Chenin blanc | 21.1 | 20.4 | 21.0 | 22.4 | 21.9 | 20.8 | 21.5 |
| French Colombard | 20.2 | 19.3 | 20.5 | 20.8 | 20.9 | 20.5 | 20.3 |
| Gewürztraminer | 20.1 | 20.8 | 22.0 | 21.9 | 22.4 | 22.3 | 22.0 |
| Sauvignon blanc | 22.1 | 21.0 | 22.4 | 23.8 | 23.0 | 22.1 | 23.1 |
| White Riesling | 20.7 | 20.3 | 21.6 | 23.6 | 23.0 | 21.1 | 21.5 |

ates enzymatic oxidation and phenolic extraction, and can cause pH and color changes.   Noble et al. *(10)* reported increased color in white wines made from damaged or machine-harvested grapes, or grapes to which leaves had been added.   Factors affecting juice quality after harvest are the timing of sulfur dioxide ($SO_2$) addition, the holding time until pressing, and the must temperature.   Warmer temperatures accelerate phenolic extraction and color increase.

*Mechanical Harvesting*

   Machine harvesting has become increasingly widespread in the 1970s, although harvesters are used more commonly in the San Joaquin Valley than in the North Coast.   Introduction of the proper grape trellising systems for mechanical harvest by the University of California, private development of several types of harvesters, increased grape acreage, increasing labor costs, and vineyard labor problems have encouraged the movement from hand to machine harvesting.   In 1973, less than 10 percent of the California grape acreage was mechanical harvested *(11)*.   Current estimates of volume of grapes mechanical harvested in California are 20–25 percent *(12)* and in Napa County are 5–10 percent *(13)*.

   Two basic types of mechanical harvesters are operating in the vineyards.   One type uses a set of "fingers" to beat the grape directly off the vine onto moving conveyor belts.   The other hits the trunk of the vine, shaking the grapes off the vine indirectly.   The machines normally pick about one acre per hour.   Since North Coast pickers harvest 0.5–2 tons per day, the machine can pick the equivalent of 12 to 15 men in an eight-hour day.

   Mechanical harvesting has several advantages over hand harvesting: night harvest is possible, enabling delivery of grapes at cool night temperatures (10°–18° C) rather than warm daytime temperatures (18°–35° C).   Because machines can pick more quickly than most picking crews, grapes can be allowed to reach optimum maturity; then the entire crop is brought to the winery in a few days, very close to optimum maturity, rather than spreading the harvest out, bringing the grapes in over a longer period of time, with fewer tons per day, at more variable maturity.   Under normal conditions, grapes that are nearly ripe can change 0.5°–1° Brix per week, or even faster.   Also, mechanical harvesters can bring grapes to the winery quickly in event of poor grape conditions, such as developing mold infections after harvest rains.   Machine harvesting also permits field crushing, field $SO_2$ additions, and must transport to the winery.

   Disadvantages of machine harvest include increased juice loss, particularly with certain varieties, tendency of leaves to get into harvested fruit (which varies with the type of harvester), potential for inclusion of second crop fruit with ripe grapes, and, because of crushing of berries during harvest, more potential oxidation and phenolic extraction from skins.   Much work has been done to reduce these side effects, e.g. improving blowers that remove leaves and additions of $SO_2$ in the field to reduce enzymatic oxidation.

Grape suitability for mechanical harvest depends on density or abundance of foliage, tendency of berries to adhere to the cluster framework, and firmness of berries. White varieties best suited for machine harvest are Flora, Gewürztraminer, and Grey Riesling. Most difficult varieties are Burger, Malvasia bianca, Muscat blanc, and Sémillon (11). Sauvignon blanc can be difficult because of its dense growth.

## Crushing

Crushing of the grapes traditionally has been done at the winery with equipment that crushes the grapes using rollers or paddles and removes the stems. Immediately after crushing, $SO_2$ is added to control enzymatic oxidation. With the advent of machine harvesting, some wineries began field crushing; crushing, destemming, and adding $SO_2$ in the field, then transporting the must to the winery.

**Use of $SO_2$.** $SO_2$ is used in the winemaking process as an atioxidant, an enzyme inhibitor, and an inhibitor of yeast and bacteria. The $SO_2$ protects juice and wines from the harmful effects of excess oxygen: loss of fruitiness, development of aldehydes, increase in total color, and change of color from green, straw, or yellow to tan or brown.

At the crusher, its primary function is to inhibit or inactivate polyphenoloxidase, an oxidative enzyme. The amount to be added varies with the variety and condition of grapes. Traverso–Rueda and Singleton (14) showed varying oxidase activity in musts of different varieties and reported that grapes that are bruised or broken have a much higher level of oxidase activity. Grapes that are moldy, excessively warm, high in pH, and low in titratable acidity will need more $SO_2$. Levels commonly used for North Coast white grapes have been 70–100 mg/L, though trends recently have been to reduce $SO_2$ use if the grapes are sound. Singleton et al. (15) found that wines made with some $SO_2$ addition were consistently better than those made with none; those made with 50 mg/L were generally, though not invariably, better than those made with higher amounts.

## Crusher to Press

After crushing, the enologist has a choice of three variations of techniques for juice removal from the grapes: crushing directly to the press, going to the press through a dejuicer, or providing a period of skin contact prior to pressing. These methods affect the juice composition, the amount of free-run yield, and percentage of solids in the juice.

**Skin Contact.** "Skin contact" (also called "pomace contact" or "maceration") is a system of holding the crushed must for a period of two to thirty-six hours prior to dejuicing and pressing. The grapes are crushed into a holding tank and, after one to two hours, juice and skins begin to separate, and the cap (skins) rises. At the end of the contact period, free-run juice is drawn off through a screen, and the balance of the juice, skins, and seeds is conveyed to a press by gravity, screw conveyor, or pump. Yields of this "free-run" juice vary from 70 to 120 gallons per ton, depending on length of contact, design and type of screen, and design of dejuicing tank. Suspended solids in juice range from 0.5 to 3 percent.

Skin contact is a widely used technique in the North Coast, especially with wines to be of richer or heavier styles. It strongly alters juice composition, and the degree of extraction depends on condition of grapes, length of contact, and must temperature. As length of contact increases, acid decreases, pH increases, and phenolic and potassium extraction increases (*15, 16*). Arnold and Noble reported an increase in total aroma and fruity aroma of Chardonnay with skin contact up to sixteen hours, with no significant increase in bitterness or astringency (*17*). Singleton et al. (*15*) reported changes in general quality and fruitiness of wine through skin contact, varying both with variety and length of contact. °Brix also may increase during skin contact if grapes are raisined, botrytized, or shriveled. Higher temperatures seem to accelerate the extraction effects. This skin-contact technique is in contrast to European methods of white winemaking, where grapes are crushed directly to the press or held for only very short periods prior to pressing.

**Dejuicing.** Crushing the grapes, moving them across a dejuicing screen and into the press, is a second method of juice removal. The grapes are conveyed by pump or conveyor across a stationary or moving screen. Juice yield varies from 80 to 140 gallons per ton. This juice often has higher percentage of solids than juice from a static drainer (skin-contact tank). This system is excellent if the enologist wishes to avoid the compositional changes of skin contact but wants to increase the efficiency of press operation by removing some juice prior to the press.

**Direct to Press.** Crushing the grapes directly from the crusher to the press, a third method, is slower because a greater volume of must (crushed grapes) must go through the press since there has been no prior juice removal. It has the advantage of simplicity and need for less equipment. This system is used more often in smaller wineries where speed and efficiency of pressing are not such critical factors. Reasons to crush directly to the press could also be those of style—to achieve different composition effects than those from skin contact. Also, when handling grapes in poor condition (i.e., moldy), skin contact may be detrimental, and immediate crushing and pressing may reduce potential off aromas and oxidative effects associated with moldy grapes.

### Pressing

In the North Coast, four basic types of presses are used: horizontal basket presses, vertical basket presses, bladder presses, and continuous presses. They vary in their throughput (tons per hour); ability to screen out solids; effect on the type of solids, effect on juice composition, and total yield. Vertical basket presses, the traditional small winery hand- or hydraulic-operated presses, are used rarely. These labor-intensive presses often are not efficient in extracting juice but yield excellent quality juice very low in suspended solids. Horizontal basket presses are the "workhorses" of small wineries, giving better yields and faster pressing than the vertical basket presses. Bladder presses, using a pressurized air bag instead of a screw to create the needed pressure for juice extraction, have been popular for their gentle pressing action and ease of operation. Continuous presses, using a forward-turning screw that forces grapes against a door, creating back pressure, have the best throughput of the four types. They also operate under the highest pressures and so not only can extract more juice from the pomace but, if not operated carefully, can extract too many phenolics during the press cycle, yielding a bitter, astringent press wine.

The variety and condition of grapes affect rate of pressing, measured in tons per hour. Grapes that tend to retain juice more easily in their cellular structure are more difficult to press efficiently and are called "slippery" grapes. White Riesling, Sylvaner, and Muscat blanc cultivars are among the slowest and most difficult North Coast whites to press.

Composition of the juice coming from the press changes as pressure increases through the pressing cycle. The first fraction of juice that drains from the press, under minimum pressure, is called free-run. If no prior juice removal has taken place, it will constitute 50–60 percent of the total juice. Depending on the type of press, it could range from 1 to 4 percent solids. As pressure increases, juice composition changes: extract increases, phenolics increase, pH increases, and acidity decreases. Total juice yield is 160–180 gallons per ton, depending on type and conditions of grapes, and type and duration of press. Enologists have different systems of separating free-run and press-wine fractions at the press, depending on press-juice quality and desired wine style. Often, free-run and press fractions initially are kept separate and may be reblended before, during, or after fermentation.

*Treatment of Juice Prior to Clarification*

In warmer vintages in the North Coast, grapes, especially riper grapes at 23°–24° Brix, may be low in titratable acidity. Desirable levels of acidity in white juice prior to fermentation range from 0.7 to 1.0 g/100 mL, depending on final wine composition and wine style desired. Tartaric acid is used most commonly for acidulation and often is added to juice prior to fermentation. Malic acid and citric acid also are used for acidulation.

If $SO_2$ addition at crusher has been inadequate, $SO_2$ may be added again to the juice. It is important that $SO_2$ be added before, not during, fermentation, for if added during fermentation, it will result in a higher acetaldehyde content in the wine.

Fining also may be done to juice prior to fermentation.   Protein fining agents may be used to reduce phenolics in press juice, or bentonite used for protein reduction or reduction of potential for hydrogen sulfide ($H_2S$) production (*18*).

## Juice Clarification

Juice clarification is an important technique in North Coast quality wine production.   Removal of suspended solids from the juice prior to fermentation results in a wine described as "fruity, clean tasting, fresh, delicate" (*19*, *20*).   Level of solids in clarified juice ranges from 0.5 to 2.5 percent.   Juice clarification also reduces the level of elemental sulfur, reducing potential for later $H_2S$ production.

Several methods are used to clarify juice: settling, centrifugation, and vacuum filtration.   Settling is a common and simple method.   After pressing, the juice is put into a tank and held at 7°–15° C to prevent onset of fermentation.   Twelve to forty-eight hours later most of the solids will have settled out of the juice, leaving the juice with 0.25–1.0 percent solids.   The initial amount and type of solids (often related to type of press) will affect the rate of settling.   Juice "lees" (settled solids) in the bottom of the tank entrain some juice and represent 5–10 percent (by volume) of the original juice.

Pectic enzymes sometimes are used in conjunction with settling to aid in juice clarification, and may assist in clarifying varieties slow to clarify naturally.   Ough and Crowell (*21*) report pectic enzyme treatment to increase juice yield from the press and juice clarity after racking or centrifuging.   They found wine quality either enhanced or unchanged by the treatment, although Ough and Berg (*22*) reported slightly less sensory quality in pectic-enzyme-treated white and rosé wines.

Centrifugation as a means of solids removal was started in the North Coast area in 1970.   It is now a widespread technique of solids removal all over California.   It has two advantages over settling—speed of solids removal, and ability to better separate solids from entrained juice, reducing lees loss.   The centrifuge will clarify successfully musts with solids up to 8 percent, or musts that, because of the nature of the suspended solids, are hard to settle.   Centrifuging also gives the enologist the ability to "fine tune" the percentage of solids left in the juice, depending on the wine style desired.   Williams et al. (*20*) reported wines made from centrifuged juice to be light bodied, fruity, and clean tasting, as opposed to wines with more solids, or longer solids contact, described as full flavored, harsh, and complex.   Singleton et al. (*19*) reported clarified juice as fresh, clean, and delicate, contrasted with juice or high solids described as harsher, lacking in fruitiness, and more susceptible to development of off odors, including $H_2S$.

Vacuum filtration is used less often for juice clarification.   It is very efficient for juice solids removal on a high throughput basis but introduces a high level of oxygen into the juice during filtration.     The energy efficiency of various processes and equipment varies greatly.     In this cost-conscious period, enologists will want to consider this in selection of equipment and processes.

### Fermentation

Variables in alcoholic fermentation, the yeast-enzyme conversion of grape sugar to ethanol and carbon dioxide, have a major impact on the character, composition, and quality of North Coast white table wines.     Type of yeast, juice solids content, juice $SO_2$ content, juice protein content, fermentation temperature, and fermentation rate are factors the enologist may consider and control.

**Effect of Yeast on Fermentation.**     North Coast enologists recognize the important effects yeast strains have on the management of the fermentation, its evenness and completion, and the wine composition.     Rankine (23) reviewed the different effects of yeast strain on wine composition and noted especially the relationship of yeast strain to sulfur dioxide, hydrogen sulfide, and acetaldehyde production.

Different yeast strains have varying rates of fermentation: certain yeasts will ferment the same juice faster than others.     Yeasts are temperature sensitive; some ferment more slowly at cool temperatures.     Some yeasts produce more foam during fermentation, an important factor since efficient use (fullness) of fermentors is difficult with a strong foaming yeast.     Yeasts are also sensitive to alcohol in different degrees; alcohol-tolerant yeasts are best suited for fermenting high-sugar juice.     Champagne yeast strains usually settle and clarify better after fermentation.     The enologist considers conditions under which he intends to ferment his wines, weighs the end result desired, and chooses yeast best suited for these conditions.

### Yeast Cultures

Yeasts are available in dry or liquid cultures.     Dry yeast has the advantage of ease of use and storage—a certain amount of the dry yeast can be added directly to the fermentor.     Liquid cultures usually are propagated to larger volumes in clean or sterilized grape juice to provide volume sufficient for use.

Montrachet (University of California, # 522), champagne (University of California, # 505), Steinberg, and French White yeast are used most commonly in the North Coast, though other strains are available.     The first two are widely available in dried form and the second two have come from Geisenheim Institute, Germany, and Pasteur Institute, Paris, respectively.     The latter no longer supplies yeast cultures.     Some wineries maintain their own cultures from year to year, and occasionally fermentations will be allowed to proceed with the grapes' natural yeast population.

*Inoculation*

Yeast usually is added one to five percent by volume if a liquid culture is used, or one to three pounds per 1000 gallons if a dry culture is used. Once fermentations are started initially, many enologists will start new batches using wine from current fermentors, rather than from new, pure, dry or liquid cultures. Optimum yeast transfer would occur during the most active stage of fermentation, usually at 15°–19° Brix.

*Juice Solids*

Juice solids have a critical effect not only on wine quality (discussed under juice clarification) but also on yeast activity. A juice that is too clean, from excessive pectic enzyme treatment, filtration, or centrifuging, may have difficulty completing fermentation. Groat and Ough (24) and others have reported that juice solids levels below 0.1 to 0.5 percent resulted in slower fermentations. Levels of 0.5–2.5 percent solids are used commonly in the North Coast.

*Juice SO₂*

High levels of $SO_2$ (200 mg/L) may affect initiation and length of fermentation and result in higher aldehyde content after fermentation (25). Desirable juice levels of $SO_2$ are 50–100 mg/L $SO_2$, depending on grape condition.

*Juice Protein Content*

It is not uncommon among North Coast winemakers to add bentonite, one to three pounds per 1000 gallons, to the fermenting juice. This has been done to reduce fermentation foam and promote protein stability in the finished wine. Ough and Amerine confirmed the action of bentonite in helping stabilize the wine for protein (26). More recently, Vos and Gray (18) observed that bentonite treatment of must, prior to fermentation, reduced protein concentration and $H_2S$ development while fermentation conducted in contact with bentonite increased $H_2S$ production.

*Hydrogen Sulfide Production*

Another factor the enologist watches for during fermentation is production of $H_2S$. Occurrences of $H_2S$ during fermentation have been attributed to yeast strain (23), the kind and amount of elemental sulfur in the juice (27), and free amino nitrogen in the juice (18).

Enologists' techniques for prevention of $H_2S$ include monitoring sulfur applications in the vineyard to be sure they are timely and not excessive, proper selection of yeast strain, proper juice clarification for elemental sulfur removal, and, more recently, addition of diammonium phosphate to must, according to recommendations of Vos and Gray (18).

**Botrytis Effect on Fermentation.** Peynaud et al. (28) suggest that *Botrytis cinerea* ("noble rot") produces a substance that inhibits yeast activity. While this substance has not been isolated in the United States, it has been the author's observation that botrytis-infected grapes ferment at a slower rate and have more difficulty completing fermentation. This fermentation inhibition also may be attributable to the higher initial °Brix and, later, to the ethanol and higher residual sugar content of the botrytized wines.

*Fermentation Temperature*

White juice fermentations are controlled at temperatures ranging from 7° C to 15° C. Most enologists feel that cooler, longer, slower fermentations give wines of greater fruitiness. Killian and Ough (29) have shown that fermentation temperatures affect both formation and retention of wine esters.

Fermentations in this temperature range will take two to eight weeks to complete, depending on yeast strain, juice composition, and temperature management.

Methods of temperature management most commonly used are double-jacketed, stainless steel tanks with glycol or ammonia used as refrigerant. Although probably the most expensive method of temperature control, this system gives close, constant temperature control with no external movement of the wine required. It is also an extremely effective method for close control of large volumes of fermenting juice. Other methods less widely used are water cooling over the outside of the tank (popular in other parts of the world), pumping wine through an external heat exchange, cooling coils inside of the fermentors, and use of small vessels (such as barrels) in a cool room.

Barrel fermentation has become a popular method of fermenting Chardonnay and other dry whites such as Sauvignon blanc and occasionally Chenin blanc. Juice is clarified and yeasted, then moved to oak barrels. Barrels usually are kept in a room at 15°–21° C and fermentation temperatures are in this range. Fermentations usually will be complete in ten to fourteen days, although enologists report more instances of extended or "stuck" fermentations with barrel fermentation than with tank fermentation. The author feels that barrel fermentation changes the character of the wine from a fruitier, crisper, lighter style to a richer, less fruity, heavier-bodied, smoother style.

**Wines with Residual Sugar.** Many North Coast white table wines, particularly White Riesling and Chenin blanc, are bottled with a residual sugar of 0.5–5 percent. Residual sugar is retained in the wines in several ways: stopping fermentation before all sugar has been changed to ethanol, fermenting "dry" and later adding back a mute or "sweet reserve" or a juice concentrate. The majority of winemakers are retaining sugar by stopping fermentation at the desired sugar level.   When this level is reached, the wine is cooled to 0°–5° C to shock and stop yeast activity.   The wine is clarified by bentonite fining and racking and filtering or centrifuging.   Centrifuging is a popular clarification technique for "stopped fermentation" because of its effectiveness in removing yeast and ease of handling the level of solids found in fermenting juice.

If a "sweet reserve" is to be made, the juice usually is fermented to 1–2 percent ethanol, then chilled, clarified, stabilized, and held at 0°–2° C.   Sweet reserve also can be made from unfermented grape juice, clarified and stabilized.   The sweet reserve technique, which originated in Germany, is used less often than "stopped fermentation," because of difficulty in keeping the sweet reserve from refermenting.   Also, although unsubstantiated by research, enologists feel that wines made with "stopped fermentation" technique give fresher, fruitier wines of more distinct varietal character than those made with sweet reserve.

Use of juice concentrate, 40°–60° Brix, is the least common method of sweetening the wines.   The quality of the concentrate, and its effect on the wine, is improved if production methods minimize heat damage and the concentrate is stored subsequently at cool temperatures until use.

### Clarification After Fermentation

When fermentation is complete, the yeast and remaining grape solids must be removed from the wines.   Three basic clarification methods may be employed: settling and racking, centrifugation, or filtration.   The choice of method depends on the turbidity of the wine, desired clarity, and desired speed of clarification.

Racking is the removal of the clear wine off its settled solids (lees) after a period of natural settling.   Because racking is always the slowest method of clarification, wine may require several settlings and rackings over a period of months to clarify well.   Generally, natural settling and clarification will occur more quickly in smaller containers; wine in barrels usually clarifies well.

Centrifuging is used quite commonly in the North Coast to clarify white wines after fermentation.   While it will not clarify as well as diatomaceous earth filtration, the centrifuge will handle and clarify wines of higher turbidity than the diatomaceous earth filter and, therefore, can be used immediately after fermentation.

Filtration requires a medium to screen out solids—diatomaceous earth, cellulose pads, or cellulose asbestos pads—and a support structure, the filter, to hold the media.   After fermentation, wines usually require a short period of natural settling before they are clear enough to be filtered.   Diatomaceous earth is the filtration medium most often used after fermentation because its porosity allows filtration of wine moderately high in suspended solids without quick plugging of the filter.   Pads will give a more effective, cleaner filtration but need cleaner wine going into the filter to avoid plugging.

Other factors affecting choice of clarifying methods are equipment available, if wines are sweet or dry, desire to combine clarification and stabilization operations to reduce movement and handling of the wine, condition of yeast lees, and initial clarity of wine.   Sweet wines likely will referment if left in contact with yeast, so quick chilling and efficient clarification are essential.   With dry wines, enologists sometimes choose to leave the wine in contact with yeast lees, allowing it to clarify naturally with settling and racking.   However, prolonged contact with yeast lees occasionally causes $H_2S$ production, making quick, effective yeast lees removal mandatory.

### Stabilization

Unfavorable bottled wine storage conditions may cause the appearance of haze or deposits in white wines.   Excessive heating of a bottle of white wine may precipitate protein, causing a haze or cloud; excess cold may crystallize potassium bitartrate, creating a layer of small crystals in the bottle.   Such haze and precipitates in wines may or may not have negative sensory effects but often affect adversely consumer reaction to the wine.

White wines are considered "stable" if they do not show haze or deposits under most shelf storage conditions.   Enologists have tests to show which wines are sensitive to excess heat or cold, and reducing this sensitivity, or potential for forming haze or precipitate is called "stabilization." Most North Coast winemakers stabilize their wines, if needed, to prevent these haze and precipitates from occurring under normal handling and storage conditions. Many also feel that excess stabilizing treatments reduce the wine quality and will only stabilize a wine to the minimum level of stability they judge is needed.

**Protein Stabilization.**   All grapes have a certain natural protein content of proteins both sensitive and insensitive to heat.   The quantity of heat-sensitive protein varies with the vintage, cultivar, grape maturity, and pH.   In the North Coast, Sauvignon blanc and Muscat cultivars have consistently high levels of heat-sensitive proteins.

Protein stabilization of wines is the removal of excess heat-sensitive protein.   The process has two stages: laboratory determination of degree of heat sensitivity and use of bentonite for removal of excess protein.

Laboratory tests for protein instability are either heat treatments or the addition of protein coagulants to detect potential instability.   Several protein precipitants are used, including trichloroacetic acid and phosphormolybidic acid in hydrochloric acid (Bentotest).   Protein coagulants are easy and effective testing agents but may indicate an excessive requirement for protein stabilization.   Laboratory heat treatments subject the wine to a selected time–temperature.   Cooke and Berg (30) reported a variety of tests being used by wineries, including 60° C for twenty-four hours and 60° C for forty-eight hours plus twenty-four hours at −4° C.   Berg and Akyoshi (31) used a "heat–cold" test, four days at 49° C, room temperature for one day, and –5° C for two days.   Wine haze or precipitate after the test indicates excess heat-sensitive protein and the need for its removal.   The tests attempt to simulate the "worst conditions" a wine may meet in the marketplace.   But the tests rarely can duplicate exactly market conditions, so correlations of laboratory tests and actual stability of the wine "on the shelf" are difficult to make and remain a matter of judgment by the enologist.

If, after the laboratory tests, a wine is judged to be protein-unstable, a laboratory fining series is run, adding different levels of bentonite to the wine.   The series is tested for protein instability with one of the tests previously mentioned, and the level of bentonite needed to prevent haze occurring under the test conditions is selected for use in the cellar.

In the North Coast, bentonite is used most commonly for protein removal.   Bentonite is a montmorillonite clay with an expanding crystal lattice structure that has two modes of protein removal: electrostatic attraction of positively charged protein by negatively charged bentonite and hydrogen bonding.   Proper preparation of bentonite is critical to its effective protein removal.   When mixed with water it swells, producing a surface area approaching 750 square meters per gram of sodium bentonite.   Berg (32) recommends mixing bentonite into 46° C water, 96g/L, then agitating with steam and reheating to 60° C once daily for three days prior to use.   Once bentonite is prepared, it is mixed into the tank of wine, allowed to settle, and the wine retested.   If stable, the wine may be removed from bentonite lees by racking, centrifugation, or filtration.

Juice pasteurization (holding at 82° C for 30–60 seconds) can also remove protein and is used in some parts of the world for oxidase inactivation and protein removal.   It has been tried experimentally in the North Coast but its use is not widespread.

**Bitartrate Stabilization.**   Potassium and tartaric acid are natural constituents of the grape.   Wine content of these constituents depends on a number of variables, not all well understood: variety, vintage, and weather pattern; degree of skin contact; alcohol level; bitartrate holding capacity of phenolic compounds; and potassium binding capacity of the wine (30, 35).   Most wines after fermentation are supersaturated solutions of potassium bitartrate. This compound is less soluble at lower temperatures, and, thus, lower temperatures will cause precipitation of bitartrate crystals.   This lowering of temperature and subsequent removal of crystals by filtration is called "cold" stabilization.

First, laboratory testing is conducted to ascertain the stability of the wine.   Like tests for protein stability, tests for determining stability and method for correcting instability vary from winery to winery.   Berg (34) suggested that a wine stored at −4° C for four days, without a bitartrate crystalline deposit, may be considered "stable."  The wines usually are allowed to warm to room temperature before test results are read.   Absence of crystals indicates stability.   A quantitative method, the concentration product (36), also can be used to evaluate tartrate stability.

The method most commonly used to stabilize a wine, once instability is determined, is to chill the wine to −5° C and hold it until stability is achieved, usually seven to fourteen days.   Addition of fine potassium bitartrate crystals during chilling (30 mg/L) helps "seed" the formation of potassium bitartrate crystals.   When laboratory tests have shown the wine to be stable, the wine goes through a tight diatomaceous earth or pad filtration to remove the crystals.

Rhein and Neradt (37) reported an accelerated method for bitartrate removal by chilling wine, adding 4 g/L powdered potassium bitartrate, and filtering the wine ninety minutes later.   Conductivity measurements were used to monitor potassium bitartrate precipitation.   To the author's knowledge, this method has not yet been used in the North Coast.

Other methods to achieve bitartrate stability, rarely used in the North Coast, are addition of metatartaric acid, electrodialysis, reverse osmosis, and ion exchange.   Concern with potential bitartrate instability varies from winery to winery.   Some enologists prefer to keep the processing of wine to a minimum.   They rely solely on cool fermentation and winter storage temperatures to precipitate excess bitartrates.   They trust their customers will overlook any additional bitartrate crystals that precipitate out in bottled wines.

**Metallic Instability.**   Instability resulting from excess iron or copper is rare in North Coast white table wines.   Sources of these metals are brass or iron valves and fittings used in older wineries.   Post-1966 construction of new wineries has involved extensive use of stainless steel, reducing the need for concern about metal instability.

**Microbiological Stabilization.**   Dry North Coast white wines, because of normal (11–14 percent) levels of ethanol, relatively high acids, and low pH, have few potential yeast problems. Total removal of yeast after fermentation is usually not an objective of the handling of these wines.

Sweet white wines, however, are subject to refermentation in contact with yeast.   Protection from refermentation includes a combination of three factors: chilling (2°–10° C), $SO_2$ (25–35 mg/L free), and reduction of yeast population to a minimum level by pad or tight diatomaceous earth filtration.   At bottling, yeasts are 100 percent removed from the wine to prevent refermentation in the bottle.

**Malo-Lactic Fermentation.**   The bacterial conversion of malic acid to lactic acid usually does not occur in North Coast white wines because of low pH, high $SO_2$, and cool storage temperatures, factors that inhibit lactic acid bacteria activity.   Some work has been done in the North Coast with malolactic fermentation in Chardonnay, following the traditional practices in Burgundy.   Factors used to encourage experimental malo-lactic fermentation in white wines have been bacterial inoculation, warmer (18°–21° C) fermentation temperatures, prolonged lees contact, and low free-$SO_2$ levels until fermentation is complete.

**Clarification and Stabilization Combinations.**  Wine clarification may be combined with a stabilization step to minimize handling of the wine.  This type of clarification, timing, and sequence vary from winery to winery.  Some options used are, after fermentation, rack the wine off yeast lees, bentonite fine for heat stability and chill for cold stability, then diatomaceous earth filter to remove remaining yeast, bentonite, and tartrate crystals; after fermentation, centrifuge the wine to remove yeast solids, then chill and add bentonite, and filter to remove yeast; and add bentonite, chill, then pad filter to remove bitartrates and protein.

## Aging

Aging provides a period of time for a wine to soften, balance, mellow, and develop its flavors and bouquet.  Aging can take place in cooperage prior to bottling and after bottling.  The amount of aging given a wine depends on the wine's ability to react positively and beneficially to aging, on the winemaker's idea of the style he wishes to make, and on economic considerations.  Many North Coast wines, especially Chenin blanc and White Riesling, are produced to be a fresh, lively, fruity wine and, therefore, are given short aging periods in stainless steel or oak tanks or casks, prior to bottling.  These wines usually are released for sale the spring or summer after fermentation.  Sauvignon blanc is made in two styles, a fresh, fruity, short-aged wine, and a richer wine, usually barrel aged two to six months.  Chardonnay is most commonly barrel aged and is often aged six to twelve months after bottling.  The barrel aging is needed to achieve the rich, intense, complex style of Chardonnay.

**Barrel Aging.**  Oak barrel aging is a common and important winemaking practice in the North Coast.  Singleton (33) cites three reactions that occur in wood cooperage aging and are not found in impermeable (stainless) containers: ethanol and water evaporate through the sides of the container, oxygen is admitted into the wine as a result of the permeable container, and wood substances, such as wood tannins, vanillin, and syringaldehyde, are extracted into the wine.  Physical and chemical changes, over a period of time, modify and enhance wine bouquet and flavor.

White wines, primarily Chardonnay but also Sauvignon blanc, Chenin blanc, and Pinot blanc, are aged in barrels from two to twelve months.  Many factors affect the aging period; style considerations have been mentioned previously.  Age of oak is critical—new oak barrels contribute more oak extract to a wine than older barrels, and care must be taken not to leave the wine in the new oak so long that it becomes excessively oaky and astringent.  The composition and structure of the base wine are important—a thinner, more delicate flavored wine can be more easily over-oaked than a heavy, intensely varietal wine.  Type of oak plays a role in length of aging—European oak contributes more extract and tannin to a wine, yet less flavor per unit of tannin than American oak (33). Temperature also has its effects—wines will mature faster in barrels stored at higher temperatures. Barrel aging cellars are usually kept at 15°–20° C for optimum aging.

Winemakers in the North Coast have been testing European and American oaks to determine their optimum use with wine. European coopers usually divide oaks into two types: lighter, less dense, wider-grain oak (Limousin) and denser, tighter-grained oak (Never, Allier, Tronçais). Singleton (33) defines European oaks as two species: *Quercus rober* (also called *Q. pedunculata*), growing better in deeper, heavier soils, and *Q. sessilis*, generally preferred for replanting and forest management. North Coast winemakers have obtained oak from different sources through European coopers and experimentally aged the wines in the different oaks to see if wine differences exist. Reports of results vary, but the author's experience would tend to substantiate Singleton's opinion (33) that the two oak species, grown in the same habitat, are essentially equal in properties, and when differences occur, they are as likely to result from different growing conditions of the oak as from the difference between the species.

*Q. alba* (American oak) is used less frequently with white wines than red wines, and it is widely acknowledged that American oak has a distinctively different effect on wines' chemical and sensory properties than does European oak. The strong and distinctive oakiness of *Q. alba* can overwhelm the varietal character of a white wine, if not used with care. Some winemakers combine use of both European and American oak in their oak-aging practices.

Barrels from different European and American coopers have been evaluated for their effects on the wine. It is the author's observation that variations in coopering techniques, wood selection, aging, drying, splitting, heating, and firing, have a substantial impact on the wine, but research remains to be done to precisely define these effects.

Small (50–60 gal) barrel aging is a far more expensive technique of wine aging than use of larger containers. The barrels themselves cost more than larger cooperage ($4–$5/gal for French oak barrels vs. $1–$3/gal for stainless steel tanks). Also, if a winemaker wishes to maintain oak extract from the barrels, he must replace a portion of his barrels every year. In the author's experience, the barrel's contribution of oak extract is reduced greatly after two years and completely disappears in seven to ten years. More cellar labor is required to clean, fill, empty, and top (replenish evaporated wine) wine in barrels than in tanks. Finally, a greater evaporative loss is experienced with barrel aging, 4–7 percent loss in evaporation per year is common, and depends on cellar temperatures, humidity, and barrel stave thickness.

## Fining

Fining is a winemaking technique used to enhance sensory or clarity properties of the wines. Common fining agents used with North Coast white wines are bentonite (a clay), casein (milk protein), gelatin (animal protein), isinglass (fish protein), and PVPP (polyvinylpolypyrrolidone). Bentonite, previously discussed, is used for protein removal. All the other fining agents have two major effects, clarification of the wine and phenolic removal. PVP and PVPP are quite specific for removal of catechins, and monomeric phenolic compounds sensitive to browning.

Fining can be done at several points in the winemaking cycle: in the juice, usually for phenolic removal in press juice; after fermentation, to clarify the wine or to reduce protein (bentonite); and prior to bottling, for sensory reasons, to reduce astringency of young wines.

*Bottling*

A number of steps are taken to prepare a wine for bottling. First, by sensory evaluation, the enologist determines that the wine has developed the desired bouquet, flavor, and balance for its particular style, and is indeed ready to prepare for bottling. If the wine is to be blended, sensory evaluations of blends are conducted and blends selected and made in the cellar. Examples of types of blends made would be blends of the same varietal from different vineyards; blends of wines aged in different containers (wood vs. stainless) or for different lengths of time; for sweet wines, blends of the "sweet reserve" to a dry base wine; or varietal blends. Although current law requires a wine to be only 51 percent to be given a varietal designation, most North Coast white varietals are over 75 percent varietal and many are 100 percent varietal. (The percentage will be at least 75 percent in 1983.)

Next, further need for sensory modification is determined in tasting, and acid adjustment or fining is done if needed to balance or soften the wine. The wine is checked to be sure its bitartrate and protein stability meet the winery's requirements. The amount of $SO_2$ is adjusted, usually to 30–35 mg/L free $SO_2$ for bottling.

When the wine is ready for bottling, it is given a final clarification: occasionally a racking or centrifuging, but most frequently, filtration. Factors affecting clarification decisions are: (1) Presence of residual sugar—most North Coast sweet white wines go through a membrane filtration prior to bottling and must have a tight pad filtration first. (2) Potential for microbiological instability— presence of malo-lactic bacteria, and therefore potential for malo-lactic fermentation in the bottle, may cause a winemaker to do a tight pad or membrane filtration. (3) Current clarity of wine—an extremely clear, dry wine may not need further clarification. (4) Market considerations—expensive wines going to a knowledgeable, wine-educated market need not have the same degree of clarity and stability as mass-marketed wines. Consumers unfamiliar with bitartrate crystals may interpret them as a severe wine problem or chips of broken glass. (5) Sensory effects— there has been much discussion among North Coast winemakers about the comparative sensory effects of fining, filtration, and centrifuging. It is generally felt that the less processing a wine has, the better its aroma and balance will be, but controlled experiments with statistical analysis would be welcome.   Therefore, prebottling clarification is usually only the minimum needed to achieve the winery standard of clarity and microbiological stability.

Sweet wines, with potential for yeast refermentation, or wines with potential for malo-lactic fermentation, go through a membrane filtration prior to bottling.   The membrane filters come in different porosities: 0.65-μ pore size is used most commonly when 100 percent yeast removal is desired, and 0.45-μ pore size is used for malo-lactic bacteria removal.   Proper sterilization of bottling equipment downstream of the membrane filter is essential to maintain the yeast- or bacteria-free nature of the wine after filtration.

Sorbic acid, a yeast inhibitor, is used sometimes in conjunction with membrane filtration as an extra "safety" factor.   However, excessive amounts of sorbic acid may affect the wine's aroma, and most North Coast winemakers avoid its use.

### Oxidation

Excess oxygen and undesirable oxidative reactions in white wine can cause pinking or browning of wines, loss of varietal aroma, and acquisition of an oxidized aldehydic aroma.   Most browning reactions observed in North Coast wines result from enzymatic oxidation of phenolic compounds in the juice.   Polyphenoloxidase (orthodiphenol oxidoreductase [E.C. 1.10.3.1]), a natural grape enzyme, accelerates oxidation of grape phenolic compounds sensitive to browning.   Laccase (paradiphenol oxidoreductase [E.C. 1.10.3.2]), an enzyme associated with botrytis grapes, also promotes oxidative reactions.

A variety of practices are used in North Coast white winemaking to protect wines from the undesirable effects of oxidation.   Proper use of $SO_2$ is an essential part of North Coast winemaking because it is an effective antioxidant and results in less polyphenoloxidase activity.   $SO_2$ is added as soon as the grapes are crushed, at levels of 50–100 mg/L, and maintained at 25–30 mg/L free $SO_2$ after fermentation, until bottling.   At bottling, most white wines have 30–35 mg/L free $SO_2$.

Attention is given to proper cellar techniques and proper maintenance of equipment to minimize oxygen pickup during the winemaking process. Quality control personnel use oxygen meters to monitor cellar movements of wine to ensure no more than normal oxygen pickup.   Inert gas ($N_2$ or $CO_2$) blanketing of partially full tanks of wine protects them from oxygen pickup.   Proper selection of bottle fillers reduces oxygen pickup at bottling, and many wineries use corkers with a vacuum attachment to reduce oxygen in the bottle headspace prior to corking.

### Quality Control

Techniques for monitoring the status of wines, whether done in a small winery by a winemaker or in a larger winery by a quality control staff, are essential for the production of consistently fine wines.    North Coast quality control techniques have become increasingly intensive and complex over the last twenty years.    Common monitoring procedures include (1) field sampling grapes prior to harvest to check °Brix, titratable acidity, pH, and grape condition; (2) sampling of loads of grapes delivered for crushing for °Brix, titratable acidity, pH, condition, and material other than grapes (MOG); (3) phenolic monitoring of press-juice fractions; (4) $SO_2$, pH, titratable acidity, percentage solids, and temperature checks of settling juice; (5) daily or twice daily tasting, °Brix, and temperature check of fermenting juice; (6) total analysis of finished wines—ethanol, titratable acidity, volatile acidity, reducing sugar, pH, free and total $SO_2$, and phenolics.

Other procedures done less frequently would be enzymatic malic acid and fructose–glucose determination, aldehydes, and extract; sensory and clarity evaluations of finished wines, and stability determinations; oxygen pickup in wines in cellar operations; $SO_2$ plus sensory checks during aging; analytical, clarity, sensory, and stability checks prior to bottling; microbiological monitoring of bottled wines for yeast and bacteria; and monitoring $SO_2$ depletion, clarity, and stability after bottling.    Less common monitoring would be yeast count of juice inoculum and volatile acidity of fermenting botrytis wines.

Promising new analytical tools are further enzymatic analysis, coated wire electrodes, high-pressure liquid chromotography, sulfide electrode use, and use of computers for data storage and retrieval and for monitoring laboratory instrumentation.

Good laboratory chemical and microbiological analysis is important for consistent production of quality white wines, but North Coast enologists consider sensory evaluation the most important tool to monitor and guide the winemaking process.    Generally, frequency of sensory evaluation parallels speed of change of the wine.    During fermentation, when wines are changing rapidly, they are tested once or twice a day.    As the wine finishes fermentation and begins its aging, testings vary from weekly to monthly. Sensory evaluation may range from informal testings of cellar wine samples to fairly sophisticated triangle, pair, or duo–trio testings of experimental wines.    Most enologists frequently compare their wines in blind testings with those of other California and European wineries.    Sensory evaluation is done through all phases of the winemaking process but is often not subjected to statistical analysis.

*New Directions*

It is well known that a malo-lactic fermentation generally does not occur in North Coast white wines because of high $SO_2$ levels, low pH, high acidity, and cool storage temperatures, all conditions inhibiting the activity of *Leuconostoc oenos*, the common lactic acid bacteria used in the North Coast region.    Some work has been done promoting malo-lactic fermentation in

Chardonnay to soften the wine and gain complexity. To accomplish this, wines are inoculated during fermentation, fermented at 18° C, and left unsulfured and unclarified (except for racking) until malo-lactic fermentation is completed. Juice pasteurization for inhibition of oxidative enzymes and protein removal has been tried experimentally and pectic enzyme used for juice clarification and as a pressing aid is more common. Winemakers have been experimenting with different acids, malic for acid adjustment and fumaric for inhibiting malo-lactic fermentation. Centrifuges have gained widespread acceptance and new high speed centrifuges, capable of 100 percent yeast and bacteria removal, are being tested. Methods of juice–skins separation, from specially designed juice draining tanks to decanters and Centri-De-Juicers, are being tested. Must heat exchangers for quick must cooling, common in Australia, are being introduced to the North Coast. More sophisticated fermentation temperature control systems are being used, with controllers or computers. Fermentation rate control parameters are being investigated at the University of California, Davis. Decanters and flotation units are being tested for juice–solids separation. A new low pressure bladder press has been in use for two years, while continuous presses find widespread use in larger wineries. New cold stabilization systems, including those using high dosages of potassium bitartrates with subsequent removal, may find future use in larger North Coast wineries. pH adjustment with acid or ion exchange, while uncommon, may be used where high pH problems occur. More specialized selection of yeast is likely to occur as winemakers become more familiar with the different yeasts available, behavior characteristics and their sensory effects. Changes in regulations have allowed production of low alcohol white wines, 7–10 percent ethanol.

Production of more wines from botrytis-infected grapes has occurred in the last five years. Special considerations facing winemakers making these wines are (1) harvest decision—how much botrytis infection is desired (initial °Brix has ranged from 26–52), (2) amount of skin contact—related to grape condition, (3) inhibition of laccase, (4) clarification of the high density juice, (5) monitoring of volatile acidity changes during fermentation, (6) maintaining fermentation to the desired balance of alcohol, acid, and sugar, and (7) protection after fermentation from oxidation. Yields are low from botrytis grapes; yield per acre is drastically reduced to 0.5–1 ton/acre, and juice yield from the grapes is only 80–120 gal/ton. However, several North Coast wineries have successfully made botrytized wines that have been received widely as luscious and appealing dessert wines.

North Coast winemaking techniques are being developed and modified by a progressive, aggressive, dynamic industry, interested in consistent improvement of white wine quality, and aimed at world-wide recognition and enjoyment of that quality.

For a review of the sequence of operations on white table wine production see Figure 1.

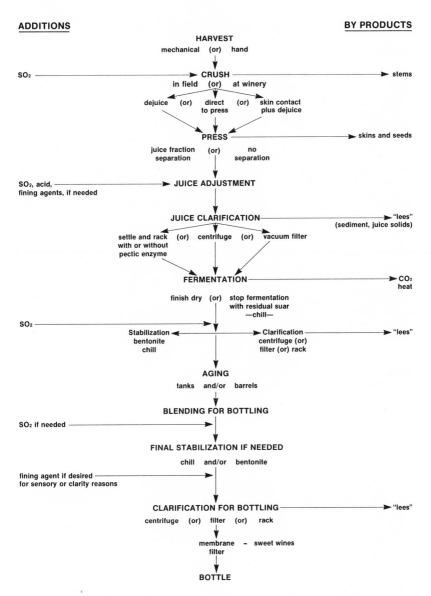

*Figure 1. Diagram of operations in white table wine production*

### Literature Cited

1. McGregor, R.A.; Cain, M.; Seibert, J.C. "California Grape Acreage, **1979**," California Crop and Livestock Reporting Service, Sacramento, CA, 1980.
2. McGregor, R.A.; Lockhart, D. "California Grapes, Raisins, and Wine, 1978," California Crop and Livestock Reporting Service, Sacramento, CA, 1978, pp. 15–32.

3. Kasimatis, A.N.; Bearden, B.E.; Bowers, K. "Wine Grape Varieties in the North Coast Counties of California," *Univ. Calif. Coop. Ext. Serv. Sale Publ.* **1977**, *4069*, 1–30.
4. Ough, C.S.; Berg, H.W. "Powdert Mildew Sensory Effect on Wine," *Am. J. Enol. Vitic.* **1979**, *30*, 321.
5. Singleton, V.L.; Trousdale, E.; Zaya, J. "Oxidation of Wines. 1. Young Wines Periodically Exposed to Air," *Am. J. Enol. Vitic.* **1979**, *30*. 49–54.
6. McDowell, A.M.; Heltzel, G. "Marketing California Wine and Wine Grapes, 1969 Season," Federal–State Market News Service, San Francisco, CA, 1970, p. 19.
7. McDowell, A.M.; Heltzel, G. "Marketing California Wine and Wine Grapes, 1971," Federal–State Market News Service, San Francisco, CA, 1972, p. 27.
8. Henderson, W.W.; Johnson, M.K. "Production and Marketing California Grapes, Raisins and Wine, 1974," California Crop and Livestock Reporting Service, Sacramento, CA, 1975, p. 49.
9. Anonymous. "Final Grape Crush Report, 1979 Crop," *Calif. Dep. Food and Agric.*, Sacramento, CA, 1980, p. 35.
10. Noble, A.C.; Ough, C.S.; Kasimatis, A.N. "Effect of Leaf Content and Mechanical Harvest on Wine "Quality"," *Am. J. Enol. Vitic.* **1975**, *26*, 158–163.
11. Christensen, L.P.; Kasimatis, A.N.; Kissler, J.; Jensen, F.; Luvisi, D. "Mechanical Harvesting of Grapes for the Winery," *Univ. Calif. Agric. Ext. Serv. Publ.* **1973**, *AXT-403*, 1–22.
12. Kasimatis, A.N., personal communication.
13. Bowers, K., personal communication.
14. Traverson-Rueda, S.; Singleton, V.L. "Catecholase Activity in Grape Juice and Its Implications in Winemaking," *Am. J. Enol. Vitic.* **1973**, *24*, 103–109.
15. Singleton, V.L.; Zaya, J.; Trousdale, E. "Table Wine Quality and Polyphenol Composition as Affected by Must $SO_2$ Content and Pomace Contact Time," *Am. J. Enol. Vitic.* **1980**, *31*, 14–20.
16. Ough, C.S.; Berg, H.W.; Coffelt, R.J.; Cooke, G.M. "Effect on Wine Quality of Simulated Mechanical Harvest and Gondola Transport of Grapes," *Am. J. Enol. Vitic.* **1971**, *22*, 65–70.
17. Arnold, R.A.; Noble, A.C. "Effect of Pomace Contact on the Flavor of Chardonnay Wine," *Am. J. Enol. Vitic.* **1979**, *30*, 179–181.
18. Vos. P.J.A.; Gray, R.S. "The Origin and Control of Hydrogen Sulfide During Fermentation of Grape Must," *Am. J. Enol. Vitic.* **1979**, *30*, 187–197.
19. Singleton, V.L.; Sieberhagen, H.A.; de Wet, R.; Van Wyk, C.J. "Composition and Sensory Qualities of Wines Prepared from White Grapes by Fermentation with and without Solids," *Am. J. Enol. Vitic.* **1975**, *26*, 62–69.
20. Williams, J.T.; Ough, C.S.; Berg, H.W. "White Wine Composition and Quality as Influenced by Method of Must Clarification," *Am. J. Enol. Vitic.* **1978**, *29*, 92–96.
21. Ough, C.S.; Crowell, E.A. "Pectic Enzyme Treatment of White Grapes: Temperature, Variety and Skin Contact Time Factors," *Am. J. Enol. Vitic.* **1979**, *30*, 22–27.
22. Ough, C.S.; Berg, H.W. "The Effect of Two Commercial Pectic Enzymes on Grape Musts and Wines," *Am. J. Enol. Vitic.* **1974**, *25*, 208–211.
23. Rankine, B.C. "The Importance of Yeasts in Determining the Composition and Quality of Wines," *Vitis* **1968**, *7*, 22–49.
24. Groat, M.; Ough, C.S. "Effects of Insoluble Solids Added to Clarified Musts on Fermentation Rate, Wine Composition and Wine Quality," *Am. J. Enol. Vitic.* **1978**, *29*, 112–119.
25. Amerine, M.A.; Ough, C.S. "Studies with Controlled Fermentation. VIII. Factors Affecting Aldehyde Accumulation," *Am. J. Enol. Vitic.* **1964**, *15*, 23–33.
26. Williams, J.T.; Ough, C.S.; Berg, H.W. "White Wine Composition and Quality as Influenced by Method of Must Clarification," *Am. J. Enol. Vitic.* **1978**, *29*, 92–96.

27. Schütz, M.; Kunkee, R.E. "Formation of Hydrogen Sulfide from Elemental Sulfur During Fermentation by Wine Yeast," *Am. J. Enol. Vitic.* **1977**, *28*, 137–144.
28. Peynaud, E.; Ribéreau-Gayon, J.; Sudraud, P.; Ribéreau-Gayon, P. "Sciences et Techniques du Vin;" Dunod: Paris, 1975; Vol. 2, p. 367.
29. Killian, E.; Ough, C.S. "Fermentation Esters—Formation and Retention as Affected by Fermentation Temperature," *Am. J. Enol. Vitic.* **1979**, *30*, 301–305.
30. Cooke, G.M.; Berg, H.W. "Varietal Table Wine Practices in California. II. Clarification, Stabilization, Bottling and Aging," *Am. J. Enol. Vitic.* **1971**, *22*, 178–183.
31. Berg, H.W.; Akiyoshi, M. "Determination of Protein Stability in Wine," *Am. J. Enol. Vitic.* **1961**, *12*, 107–110.
32. Berg, H.W., personal communication.
33. Singleton, V.L. In "Chemistry of Winemaking," *Adv. Chem. Ser.* **1974**, *137*, 184–211.
34. Berg., H.W. "Stabilization Studies in Spanish Sherry and on Factors Influencing KHT Precipitation," *Am. J. Enol. Vitic.* **1958**, *9*, 180–193.
35. Bertrand, G.L.; Carroll, W.R.; Foltyn, E.M. "Tartrate Stability of Wines. I. Potassium Complexes with Pigment, Sulfate and Tartrate Ions," *Am. J. Enol. Vitic.* **1978**, *29*, 25–29.
36. Berg, H.W.; Keefer, R.M. "Analytical Determination of Tartrate Stability in Wine. I Potassium Bitartrate," *Am. J. Enol. Vitic.* **1958**, *9*, 180–183.
37. Rhein, O.; Neradt, F. "Tartrate Stabilization by the Contact Process," *Am. J. Enol. Vitic.* **1979**, *30*, 265–271.

RECEIVED July 17, 1980.

# Red Wine Production in the Coastal Counties of California 1960–1980

LOUIS P. MARTINI

Louis M. Martini Winery, St. Helena, CA 94574

Most of the best California red table wines come from the coastal counties of California. The counties north of San Francisco Bay generally are considered to be the premier areas for the production of quality red wines. To help understand the reasons for this, a short review of the growing characteristics and history of these areas would be helpful.

The padres first introduced the grape into California and planted it at their Mission sites as they progressed northward from San Diego.

As indicated earlier (p. 8), a number of importations of vines from the wine growing areas of Europe were made into California. Those of Agoston Haraszthy were planted near the town of Sonoma, about fifty miles north of San Francisco. His and other importations helped lay the foundation for the wine industry of the coastal counties. Most of these varieties flourished in the soil and climate of Sonoma and soon spread throughout northern California. However, it was in the counties of Napa and Sonoma that the red table wine grapes were particularly well suited to the climate and soil of the area.

## The Climate

The state of California has been divided into five climatic regions by Amerine and Winkler (1) according to the temperature accumulation above 10° C during the growing season of the grapevine. The coastal counties of California contain the three coolest regions. Grapes for red table wines generally do best in one of these three regions, depending upon the characteristics of the individual variety.

Rainfall in the North Coast counties is sufficient (about 60–90 cm per year) to farm grapes on deep soils without irrigation. However, if water is available, it is desirable to have some irrigation to supplement natural rainfall, particularly in dry seasons. When properly applied, irrigation does not affect grape quality. Water sources are existing aquifers, mountain reservoirs, and reclaimed winery wastewater. Studies are being conducted now into the feasibility of using reclaimed municipal wastewater. Application in vineyards is generally either by permanent set or portable sprinklers or by

0097-6156/81/0145-0059$06.50/0
© 1981 American Chemical Society

drip.   Fertilizers and pesticides also have been distributed successfully through irrigation systems.   Water quality is generally good, except for a few localized problems with high boron and salt contents.

In contrast to the North Coast counties, the Central Coast counties, south of San Francisco, generally do not receive enough rainfall to grow grapes economically without irrigation.   In this latter area, high salt contents of well water and high winds during the daytime have presented problems that have been mitigated by specialized irrigation practices.

### The Soils

Soil types in the coastal counties vary from deep rich loams to shallow clay–loams with underlying impervious clay or rocks.   Well-drained, gravelly soils with good depth and moderate fertility are considered ideal for high quality red table wine grapes.   They generally produce a moderate crop of very high quality grapes when the proper variety is planted to match the climate and exposure of the area.   While climate is the dominant factor in producing quality grapes, soil type should not be ignored.

Fertilization generally is used very sparingly in coastal vineyards.   No real correlation between fertilization and crop response has been determined. Cook (2) indicated that vine requirements were determined best by leaf petiole analyses.   Excessive fertilization resulting in vigorous vine growth must be avoided, however, as this may affect berry set and thus reduce crop.   Mountain vineyards often are fertilized to assure a good covercrop for erosion control.

### The Grapes

Kasimatis et al. (3) described the principal grape varieties grown in the North Coast counties of California.   They are the Pinot noir, Petite Sirah, Zinfandel, Merlot, Carignane, Cabernet Sauvignon, and Gamay.   These are listed in the approximate order of ripening from early September through late October.   Each generally is planted in the climatic region most suitable to it; however, since lines between regions are not identified clearly, considerable overlapping of maturity dates can be found among the varieties.   Fairly large differences in the quality of wines made from the same variety grown on different soils and microclimates have been observed by the author.   Areas such as the north or south side of a mountain or near the mouth of a canyon have been observed to make considerable differences in the time of maturity and the balance of sugar and acid in the grapes.   Work such as that reported by Kliewer (4), and still under way, may explain the reasons for some of these differences in the future.   The importance of crop level should not be overlooked.

Differences in microclimates, soil types, and general climatic conditions are difficult to measure and relate to grape quality.   Most of the advancements in adapting the right grape to the right location have come about by trial and error. As knowledge has accumulated, each generation has done a better job of fine tuning its planting practices. With the normal cycle of a grapevine being about thirty years, progress is very slow, but it is positive and very encouraging.

Spring frosts are a problem in most of the wine growing areas of the North and Central Coast counties. This is especially true of the lower lying areas. Lider (5) found no satisfactory way to treat frosted vines so that they could recover and produce an economic crop. Hence, it is essential that all vineyards in the areas subject to frost have some protection. Water from overhead sprinklers delivered at approximately fifty gallons per acre per minute has proved to be the best method. However, if enough water is not available, wind machines or a combination of wind machines and orchard heaters have proved effective for most areas. Recent advances in oil prices may well make the heater–wind machine combination too expensive to operate in the future.

Practically all vineyards in the North Coast are planted on rootstocks resistant to the plant louse phylloxera, which is endemic to the area. This is not yet a problem to the new growing areas of the Central Coast and most of their vineyards are planted on their own roots. Eventually, these areas also will have to revert to rootstocks unless science finds an acceptable way of destroying or preventing the spread of phylloxera in the interim.

Powdery mildew (oïdium) is the most serious fungus disease of grapes and must be controlled in all areas of California with properly timed application of sulfur dust or sprays. There are a number of other diseases and pests that attack grapevines and fruit but these usually are localized to given areas or occur intermittently only. Various sprays, dusts, or biological control methods are used to control them. Viruses that diminish vine vigor and fruit maturity are prevalent in older vineyards but have been practically eliminated from newer vineyards by a grape certification program started about twenty years ago. Most vineyards developed in the past decade are practically disease-free. This has been a major factor in raising the productivity of all varieties as well as opening up areas for planting that would have been marginal with diseased vines.

It is accepted generally that crop level has an effect on grape quality. It has been the author's experience that the best quality years for red table wines have been associated with lower crops, although high quality wines have been made in years when a full crop could be brought to proper maturity. A bumper crop usually results in wines of lesser quality. Within limits, crop levels can be controlled by pruning practices. These usually are based upon the growth the vine made in the previous year. The more growth the vine made, the more buds are left to produce fruit and, hence, the larger the crop. If the vine is allowed to produce more fruit than it can bring successfully to maturity, it is overcropped. This produces inferior fruit and tends to weaken the vine. Undercropping is also undesirable as it may produce excessive vegetative growth and an uneconomical crop. Therefore, the balancing of the crop and vegetative growth by judicious pruning is essential to producing quality wines.   In recent years, some growers have been experimenting with improved trellising techniques to expand the vine surface and leaf exposure to allow the vine to bring a larger crop into full maturity.   A fair degree of success has been observed in some varieties for certain areas.

### Production Trends

In the late sixties and early seventies, the apparent demand for premium red table wine grape varieties was so great that many varieties were planted indiscriminately, with little regard to location or actual consumer demand. Experience has shown that actual demand is always lower than apparent demand because of the tendency of wholesalers, retailers, and consumers to hoard a product they think will be in short supply.

The problems of overproduction came about in the late seventies simply because too many red grapes were planted in the early seventies.   Table I shows the bearing and nonbearing acreage of the principal red table wine varieties for the major grape growing counties of the North Coast and Central Coast for 1971 and 1978.   Figure 1 illustrates the comparative trends of red and white wine sales for the state of California and the total acreage of red table and white table wine grapes in California.   It is clear that in the

### Table I. Bearing and Nonbearing Acreage of Red Wine Grapes in the North Coast[a] and Central Coast[b] Regions

| | | Bearing | | Nonbearing | | Total | |
|---|---|---|---|---|---|---|---|
| | | 1971 | 1978 | 1971 | 1978 | 1971 | 1977 |
| North Coast | Cabernet Sauvignon | 2932 | 12,083 | 1971 | 725 | 4894 | 12,808 |
| Central Coast | Cabernet Sauvignon | 808 | 9263 | 1390 | 0 | 2198 | 9263 |
| North Coast | Carignane | 4733 | 3866 | 70 | 10 | 4803 | 3876 |
| Central Coast | Carignane | 332 | 279 | 0 | 0 | 332 | 279 |
| North Coast | Gamay (Napa) Gamay Beaujolais | 1344 | 3904 | 794 | 117 | 2138 | 4021 |
| Central Coast | Gamay (Napa) Gamay (Beaujolais) | 410 | 3444 | 847 | 0 | 1257 | 3444 |
| North Coast | Pinot noir | 1149 | 6064 | 699 | 98 | 1848 | 6162 |
| Central Coast | Pinot noir | 1053 | 4002 | 263 | 2 | 1316 | 4004 |
| North Coast | Petite Sirah | 2940 | 2528 | 52 | 155 | 2992 | 2683 |
| Central Coast | Petite Sirah | 170 | 2628 | 324 | 31 | 494 | 2659 |
| North Coast | Zinfandel | 5234 | 7749 | 255 | 700 | 5489 | 8449 |
| Central Coast | Zinfandel | 868 | 5017 | 475 | 71 | 1343 | 5088 |
| North Coast | Merlot | 119 | 1555 | 112 | 97 | 231 | 1652 |
| Central Coast | Merlot | 120 | 1559 | 286 | 58 | 406 | 1617 |
| | Total | 22,203 | 63,941 | 7538 | 2064 | 29,801 | 66,005 |

[a]Counties of: Alameda, Lake, Marin, Napa, Sonoma, Mendocino, Contra Costa
[b]Counties of: Monterey, San Benito, San Luis Obispo, Santa Barbara, Santa Clara, Santa Cruz

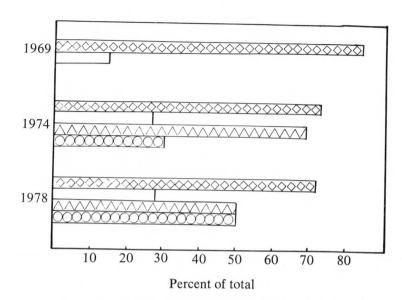

*Figure 1. Grape acreage: (⬙) red, (□) white; and wine sales; (◬) red and rosé, (◲) white. Source: California Grape Acreage (1978) and Wine Institute (1980).*

past decade, the acreage of red table wine varieties and white table wine varieties has maintained almost the same ratio while the sales of white table wines have risen sharply.

Data on the ratio of sales of red table wines to white table wines have been available only since 1974. For this analysis, rosé wines are considered to be red wines since they require red grapes for their production. Figure 1 also shows that in 1974, red and white grape acreage and red and white wine sales were quite well balanced. However, by 1978 the accelerated growth of white wine sales had completely thrown the relationship out of balance, resulting in a surplus of red grapes and a shortage of white grapes.

Some conversion of red varieties to whites has taken place and most new plantings are white varieties, which should mitigate the white grape shortage fairly soon. Because of the slow increase in red wine sales, the industry may experience a red grape surplus in some varieties for some time to come.

## *The Harvest*

Grape harvest in the North Coast counties usually starts early in September and lasts into the first week in November. Some of the Central Coast counties (e.g., Monterey) have a more extended period of harvest, often not finishing until well into December.

When to harvest grapes may be one of the most quality-oriented decisions a winemaker has to make.   To obtain the full flavor, body, and color,
the grape must be mature when harvested.   Both immature and overripe
fruit produce inferior red wines.

    There are four criteria that can be used to determine the proper maturi-
ty at which the fruit should be picked.   These are sugar, expressed as total
soluble solids (°Brix), total acidity, pH, and the sugar/acid ratio.   Although
more attention has been paid to some of the other criteria in the past twenty
years, the sugar content commonly is used.   In 1979, out of 321 different
purchasing formulas reported in the Grape Crush Report by the California
Department of Food and Agriculture (6), only six mentioned acidity; none
mentioned either pH or sugar/acid ratios.   Individual enologists have indicated that they do use pH as a quality factor in determining future desirability of a grower's grapes but do not assess penalties or bonuses to it.   Yet as
early as 1944, Winkler and Amerine (1) and, as late as 1977, Berg and Ough (7)
reported on the value of these other measurements in determining maturity.

    Proper determination of maturity is, of course, dependent upon proper
sampling in the field.   Roessler and Amerine (8) compared several sampling
methods and the single berry method has been accepted generally as the
simplest and most accurate for field sampling and is used widely.   Grapes
that are to be purchased on a sugar basis are sampled when they reach the
winery (by a county or state agent) and the °Brix determined at that time.   For
red table grapes 22° Brix usually is considered minimum for a sound wine
and bonuses and penalties generally are applied to grapes over or under that
point.   Cooke and Berg (9) surveyed the production practices of the premium wine industry and found the desired °Brix at which red table wine grapes
were harvested was between 22.5° and 23.0° Brix, with an average Brix/acid
ratio of about 30.

    In addition to physical measurements, the winemaker should not ignore
his visual observations and past experiences.   Grapes can reach their optimum maturity at somewhat different °Brix in different locations.   Sometimes
the appearance of the fruit is as good a criterion of maturity to the trained
eye as is the °Brix.   Grapes that have reached a uniform dull black color and
are beginning to soften or shatter usually are mature physiologically regard-
less of their sugar content.   The °Brix at which a winemaker wishes the
grapes picked often is determined by the style of wine he wishes to
produce.   The higher the °Brix of the grapes, the higher are the alcohol,
body, and varietal flavor in the wine.   The pitfalls of high sugar grapes are
alcoholic tasting wines, a possible raisiny character, and often lack of
acidity.   While there are some specialty wines made with these characteristics that are of interest, to make a well-balanced wine it takes well-balanced
grapes.

    A possible exception to the desirability of not allowing grapes to reach a
very high °Brix may be observed in the cooler parts of the recently developed
vineyard areas of the Central Coast counties.   The red wines from young

vines have a strong vegetative odor.    There is some evidence that letting the grapes reach a high sugar mitigates this condition.    The evidence is still incomplete.    Baldwin and Berti (*10*) and Peterson (*11*) agree that the increasing age of vines and wine tends to lessen the vegetative (asparagus) flavor in the wine.

In the past two decades, radical changes in the techniques of picking and delivering grapes have taken place.    Prior to 1960, nearly all grapes were picked by hand and delivered to the winery in the wooden picking box.    In the early 1960s, bulk handling of grapes became popular (Figure 2).    This reduced labor but more importantly reduced the length of time between picking and delivery.    This was a significant step in improving quality since the grape, like other fruits, can be no better than it is at the moment it reaches maturity and is picked from the vine.    Picked fruit is no longer left in the fields overnight, a practice that prevailed in the past.

The late sixties saw the introduction of the mechanical harvester (Figure 3) in the vineyards, and in the seventies, the first of these were starting to be used in the coastal counties.    After considerable experimentation with dif-

Wine Institute

*Figure 2. Bulk handling of grapes directly from the vineyard into the crusher*

Wine Institute
*Figure 3. Mechanical grape harvester in coastal vineyard*

ferent harvesting principles, the slapper-type picking action emerged as the most popular. This involves a series of fiberglass rods that beat the vines by horizontal pivotal action. This works well on all wine grapes except those with very heavy foliage or large juicy berries. Juice loss can be high for these varieties. A new impactor-type action recently introduced shows considerable promise for some varieties. While machine harvesting saves labor at harvest time, more labor generally is required to prepare the vines for it. This is desirable as it increases year-around employment and decreases high seasonable labor demand. Wine quality, particularly red wine, is little affected by machine harvesting, provided the time between picking and crushing is minimized. When long hauls are anticipated, it is recommended that the fruit be field crushed and about 75 mg/L of $SO_2$ be added to the crushed fruit. Transport to the winery should be done in a sanitary, stainless steel, closed container. Picking operations conducted during cool night temperatures further ensure minimum affect upon fruit quality and are one of the major advantages of mechanical over hand harvesting. The cool fruit is less subject to deterioration during transport and considerable energy can be saved at the winery by reducing the refrigeration requirements. Austin (12) has observed significantly lower pH in fruit picked during the cool night temperatures.

*Crushing*

Once the grapes reach the winery, they generally are put through a mechanical device that separates the berries from the stems, lightly ruptures the skins, and pumps the juice, skins, pulp, and seeds into a fermenting tank.   At this point, the crushed grapes are called "must." The stems are nearly always eliminated although there is some interest in retaining part or all of the stems with some of the varieties, such as the Pinot noir, to extract some of the stem tannins.   Special crushers that can do this are available although seldom used.   Part of the crushing operation may occur in the field with the winery receiving the must directly from a tank truck.

Crushing equipment has changed little over the past century although during the past twenty years the appendages have been modernized.   Wooden drag conveyors have been replaced by stainless steel screw conveyors, troughs, and hoppers.   Stainless steel also has replaced brass pumps, must lines, and fittings.   Crusher areas are now all concrete with daily cleaning and sanitation programs in most wineries.   Cleanliness, sanitation, and corrosion-resistant alloys are in greater evidence now than in 1960.   Although working with a product that resists pathological contamination, wineries rapidly are becoming as sanitary as creameries.

Fermenting rooms now are designed for ease of handling the fruit, the pomace, the stems, and the wine.   Most are designed to allow for expansion.   Ease of cleaning and maintenance is one of the major considerations in the design of any new fermenting room (Figure 4).

Sulfur dioxide, either as a gas or a salt, is added to the must shortly after crushing.   The normal dosage is about 75–100 mg/L.   This is done to both field crushed and winery crushed grapes if the $SO_2$ was not added in the field.   The purpose of the $SO_2$ at this point is to retard the growth of incoming organisms (principally yeast), thus allowing the cultured yeast to start the fermentation.   The $SO_2$ also serves as an antioxidant, although this is not as important in red wines as it is in whites.   Friedrich (13) reports removing seeds at this point to produce low tannin wines with full color as specialty wines.   Such wines he calls "soft wines," which will be described later in this chapter.

Mt. La Salle Vineyards

*Figure 4.   A modern fermenting area.   Note the sugar testing station in foreground.*

*Alcoholic Fermentation*

A number of different strains of *Saccharomyces cerevisiae* yeast are used in the coastal counties for the fermentation of red musts. The three most common ones are montrachet, burgundy, and champagne. These generally produce satisfactory fermentations, although some wineries prefer to use their own special strains. In the past, most yeast cultures were propagated by the winery from slant cultures. In recent years, commercial dried yeast of the above-mentioned strains has become available and many wineries are finding it simpler and more convenient to use these. Other yeast strains have been reported on by researchers but very little sensory evidence exists to support their use. The same applies for experiments conducted with mixed strains. The montrachet strain has lost some favor in recent years because it appears to be linked with hydrogen sulfide formation (*14*) when residual sulfur dust has remained on the grapes. However, more recently, its sulfide-forming property appears to be smaller.

With few exceptions, red table wine grapes contain their pigments and tannins in the skins. The seeds also contribute some tannin. For this reason, red wines must be fermented in contact with the skins to extract tannins and color. The chemical nature of grape tannins and coloring matter is reviewed thoroughly by Singleton and Esau (*15*). The skins float as a cap on the juice, and control of the cap is one of the major problems in the fermentation of red wines. To get the proper extraction of color and tannins and to keep the cap from overheating or becoming a source of spoilage and off flavors, the cap must be submerged frequently.

To accomplish this it is common practice for small wineries to punch the cap down at least twice daily. Larger wineries usually draw the juice from the bottom of the vat and pump it over the cap. There are a number of automatic fermentors designed that utilize the pressure of the generated carbon dioxide to force the liquid over the top of the cap. These have not become popular in northern California mostly because of their costs and difficulty of cleaning. They also produce a very rapid fermentation and generally are considered to be useful only for ordinary quality wines.

European special-purpose rotating tanks have been used successfully by at least one North Coast winery, but the cost of the equipment and space required has discouraged expansion of this facility. Continuous fermentation systems have been introduced in foreign countries but are only in very limited use in northern California. Dangers of contamination, cooling difficulties, and the need for a continuous flow of must make them unsuited for premium wine production. Heating is another way to liberate color and tannins from the skins but until recently all experiments have produced wines of inferior quality and, therefore, have not been used in the coastal counties of California.

During the past decade, the Gasquet thermovinification system has been used by one coastal winery (Paul Masson) with some success. Lowe et al. *(16)* reports that the final wine produced by this system was free of "cooked" or oxidized characteristics, at least as intense as conventional wines in color, at least equal to conventional wines in overall quality, and more economical to produce.    In subsequent years, the system proved to be very energy intensive and not as economical as originally thought.    There was some loss of fruity character and the wines matured more rapidly than with conventional methods.    It was not recommended for producing high quality wines for aging *(17)*.

The manipulation of the cap, the length of time the juice is kept in contact with the skins, and the temperature of fermentation are three important variables available to the enologist to produce a wine of the depth of color and flavor, degree of astringency and bitterness, and general texture and longevity that he wishes his wine to have.    Later in the process there are additional variables but none is more important than these three.

Fermentation generates heat, and red wines must have some type of temperature control during their fermentation.    They must not be allowed to get too hot or to become too cold.    Ough and Amerine *(18)* recommended temperatures of 18°–29° C and found that cap temperatures can exceed liquid temperatures by over 6° C.    In large stainless steel fermentors, the author has noted cap–liquid temperature differences of 11°.

Extremely high or low temperatures can cause a fermentation to "stick" and it then becomes difficult to start again.    Temperature also has an effect on the degree of extraction both from the skins and the seeds.    Singleton and Esau *(15)* reported that increasing the temperature and the ethanol content increased the extraction of seed tannins.    Although these tannins are mostly precipitated, they could become an important part of some wines.

Total phenols extracted into red wines by skins and seeds usually increase with an increase in contact time, temperature, ethanol, $SO_2$, and maceration.    These are the factors at the winemaker's disposal that have a large effect upon the style of wine he wishes to produce.

Except for rosés and specialty wines, the juice usually is drawn from the skins for one to five days after fermentation starts or between 9° and 0° Brix.    After drawing, the wines that are still fermenting are placed in a vented closed container to complete their fermentation.    Cooke and Berg (9) showed in their survey that the degrees Brix at which the juice is drawn from the skins in red wines is between four and twelve with skin-contact time between two and five days.    In more recent years, the author has observed that many wineries desiring to produce more tannic wines allow the fermentation to go to dryness on the skins.    A few have even allowed skin-contact times from two to three weeks.    This produces slow-aging wines.

In 1979, the California Department of Health lowered the minimum alcohol requirements for red table wines from 10.5 percent to the federal standard of 7 percent.    This opened the door for the production of a completely new style of red table wine.    Friedrich *(13)* calls this "soft wine" and it is made with ethanol contents of from 7 percent to 10 percent, usually with some residual sugar.   This wine style has been introduced in the past year and it is too soon to speculate on its acceptance and eventual popularity.   It is characterized by its low alcohol, low tannin, and some degree of sweetness.   It is produced by removal of seeds prior to fermentation, normal skin contact times, and arresting the fermentation at some point before all of the sugars have been fermented.   It also may be fermented dry and sweetened later with grape juice.   Experiments are contemplated on using grapes picked at a lower °Brix.   See also p. 12 for an earlier opinion.

In the past decade, some North Coast wineries have experimented with a completely anaerobic fermentation technique known as carbonic maceration.   In this system, whole grapes are placed in a vat and fermentation is allowed to start.   Since there is no pumping over or aeration, the fermentation proceeds very slowly under a blanket of carbon dioxide.   The fermentation relies upon the intercellular production of ethanol to kill the skin cells and release the color and tannins.   The results are claimed to be wines with a special bouquet, earlier maturity, slightly more alcohol, and a softer taste.   They are easily recognizable by their special bouquet.   Although popular in France, where they are drunk very young, they have not gained widespread acceptance with the North Coast wineries.

After the wine has been drained, the skins are pressed and usually the press wine is kept separate.   The press wine is generally more tannic and of lower quality than the free-run.   It often has higher flavor and frequently some or all of it may be blended into the free-run at a later date.

Equipment used in pressing has shown considerable change in the last twenty years.   Until 1960, most red pomace was pressed in vertical hydraulic basket presses.   In the 1960s and 1970s, the Willmes-type pneumatic horizontal bag press as well as horizontal screw presses became popular.   These were batch process operations.   More recently, horizontal continuous screw presses preceded by an inclined dejuicer have appeared in the North Coast and will probably increase in popularity.   They are designed to separate automatically different grades of press juice (Figure 5).

Fermentations are monitored daily by the enologist, and the fermentation process is controlled on a tank-to-tank basis.   This involves sampling each fermentor at least once, and often twice, each day to determine temperature, rate of fermentation, and general appearance of the fermenting must.   From these data the enologist determines how often the wine should be pumped over, at what level the temperature should be controlled, and when the wine should be drawn from the skins.   Some modern installations have continuous computer monitoring of their fermentations and centralized control over wine movements.

Once the fermentation is complete, it is essential to remove the wine from the lees (at this point consisting mainly of yeast cells and pulp) as soon as possible.   Prolonged contact with lees may result in the formation of

*Figure 5. A battery of modern dejuicers and continuous presses.  Note the multiple outlets for separating different qualities of press juice.*

hydrogen sulfide.   Separating the wine from the lees may be done by racking or centrifuging.   Most wineries rack but a few are now centrifuging, especially those wines showing signs of possible hydrogen sulfide formation.   If racking is employed, it is usually necessary to rack about three times with a period of time between each racking to allow additional solids to settle.   One centrifuging usually suffices.   Thereafter, the wines should be racked at least twice a year until aging is completed.   There is some evidence that centrifuging may remove some of the body that gives the wine its full "mouth feel."   The author has observed this on wines immediately after centrifuging but this difference seems to either disappear or be greatly reduced after aging.   The removal of some of the higher-molecular-weight polyphenols might be responsible for this change but much work still needs to be done to determine the effects of centrifugation on red table wines.   When centrifuging is practiced at this stage, great care is taken to not render the wine completely free of solids.   The author prefers to leave about 0.5 percent solids in the wine to ensure that the wine is not stripped of too much body and to ensure that enough yeast cells are left to support fermentation.

### The Malo-Lactic Fermentation

Most of the great red wines of the world undergo a secondary fermentation in which malic acid is converted to lactic acid with a subsequent reduction in total acidity and rise in pH.   The cool coastal counties of California are no exception.   In addition to acid reduction, many feel that a malo-lactic fermentation in red wines contributes other desirable qualities of flavor and complexity.   A tremendous amount of work has been done on the malo-lactic fermentation in the past twenty years.   It is only in the past five to ten years that much of it has been put to practical use.

Prior to 1960, few made any attempts to control the malo-lactic fermentation in red wines.   Ingraham et al. (19) showed that there were at least five types of lactic acid bacteria capable of decomposing malic acid in California wines.   Webb and Ingraham (20) showed that the malo-lactic fermentation could be induced in the winery.   Prior to that time, most malo-lactic fermentations occurred spontaneously from the inoculum normally present in the vats.

*Leuconostoc oenos* (ML-34) was isolated from California wines and it has become the most popular organism to be used in induced fermentations. Myers (21) reports successful use of a frozen culture of the strain PSU-1 introduced at the start of the alcoholic fermentation.   He finds that, in most cases, the malo-lactic fermentation parallels the alcoholic fermentation and both come to completion at about the same time.   PSU-1 is a strain of *Leuconostoc oenos* similar to the ML-34 and was first reported on by Beelman et al. (22).

Some wineries are fortunate to have a natural flora of the organism in their vats, and their wines generally need no inducement to complete the malo-lactic fermentation satisfactorily.   Others, with less desirable strains, have had problems with the malo-lactic fermentation producing off flavors and odors.

By necessity, many wineries, especially newer ones with new wood cooperage, have had to induce the fermentation.   The fermentation usually takes place near the end of, or immediately after, the alcoholic fermentation. However, it has been known to wait until warmer temperatures of the spring and summer.

Most enologists desire a malo-lactic fermentation in their premium red wines not only because of the desirable chracteristics it adds to the wine, but because it is the only way to ensure that it will not take place in the bottle.   One of the standard laboratory checks made on red wines before bottling is for the absence of malic acid.   The danger of a fermentation occurring in the bottle is that the wine becomes both cloudy and gassy and usually develops an off smell and flavor.

Those who wish to prevent the malo-lactic fermentation from occurring have had some success by maintaining a low pH, cleaning up the wine early, maintaining a high $SO_2$, and sterile filtering into the bottle.   This is not 100 percent foolproof.   Tchelistcheff et al. (23) reported on the use of fumaric acid as an inhibitor of the malo-lactic fermentation and this method is now being used with some success by a number of commercial wineries in California.

The Cooke and Berg (9, 24) survey showed that only one winery in eight induced a malo-lactic fermentation and only one in eight checked to see that the fermentation had gone to completion before bottling.    Only one of the eight wineries reported never experiencing a malo-lactic fermentation in their red wines.    Although a more recent formal survey is not available, informal talks with other enologists indicate that today most wineries induce their malo-lactic fermentations and nearly all check to make sure the malic acid has disappeared before bottling.    This usually has been done by paper chromatography but the more accurate enzymatic technique is growing in popularity.

The author is one who believes that a malo-lactic fermentation is desirable in all high quality red wine.    It adds a complexity to the flavor and a bouquet unattainable by simple aging.    There are those who would argue that the quality of wines with low acidity would not be enhanced and that is correct.    However, wines with low acidity are made from grapes with low acidity and from such grapes do not come high quality red table wines.

## Aging

Following the alcoholic fermentation and several rackings or centrifuging to clean the wine of suspended solids, the wine is ready to start its wood aging process.    With the exception of certain wines produced by carbonic maceration or sold as "Nouveau," all coastal red wines benefit from aging in wood.    The length of time red wines are aged and the type and size of wood cooperage used are choices the enlogist has to produce his style of wine.

Before starting wood aging, some enologists believe in clarifying and filtering wines; others do not.    There are no substantal data to indicate that one method is better than the other.    Wines to be aged in very small cooperage are usually allowed to complete malo-lactic fermentation before barreling down.    Such wines generally are cleaned up to a greater degree at this point than are wines to be aged in larger vats.    Ease of subsequent racking of the larger vats may have some influence on this practice.

Prior to 1960, practically all wood aging was done in larger redwood vats, although a few wineries aged also in oak casks and fifty-gallon barrels.    It is easy to see why North Coast wineries started aging in redwood vats.    The redwood was readily available, easy to work, and easy to maintain.    Figure 6 shows some of the typical aging containers used.

In the late 1960s and throughout the 1970s, wineries imported European oak barrels to try to duplicate some of the flavors and complexities found in certain European wines.    Some of these characteristics had been missing from the red wines of the North Coast.

During the wood aging process of red wines, the wine comes in contact with considerable oxygen because of frequent rackings, ullage, and topping and through the pores of the wood.    Peterson (25) reported that each barrel differs in its ability to allow entrance of oxygen through the pores of the wood and speculates that this may be the least imporant source of oxygen in the wine during its aging process.    During this time, the phenols in the wine

*Figure 6. Typical aging vats, puncheons, and barrels*

are very important.    Their reaction to oxygen and other constituents of the wine are important for increasing the complexity of flavor and color while improving or maintaining the harmony and balance of the wine.    Singleton and Esau (15) review these reactions in considerable detail.

As previously mentioned, the modern trend in the North Coast has been to style red table wines into wines with heavier bodied, higher alcohol, greater tannins, and moderate-to-heavy oak flavors, usually, but not always, of European oaks.    In many wines, harmony, balance, finesse, and delicacy seem to have been ignored.

The past decade saw much interest in European oak barrels and many experimental lots of wines were aged in American, French, Yugoslavian, and Italian oak.    Enterprising entrepeneurs started producing extracts of oak chips and started selling these extracts to wineries.    They even broke the extracts down into several fractions, claiming different flavor and aromas for the various fractions.    Some of these found considerable favor among wineries as an easy way to add oak flavoring.    It is not possible at this time to come up with any conclusions as to which oak is the best for each wine type, or for that matter, as to which size container is best for aging red wines.    However, it is accepted generally that oak is a better aging media than redwood.    Each enologist seems to have his favorite type and degree of oakiness that a wine should have.    Cooke and Berg (24) found that 75 percent of the wineries they surveyed used barrels for aging red wines, about 50 percent also used oak casks, and all used redwood tanks.

Barrels impart an oak flavor to a wine only for so many years and, as the barrels grow older, the resident time of the wine must grow longer to achieve the same degree of oakiness.    Many wineries that wish to maintain a pronounced oak flavor have adopted a policy of purchasing a certain percentage of new barrels each year and either selling the oldest barrels or delegating them to lower priced wines.    As the prices of foreign barrels soar with increased demand, this can become a very expensive practice.

In the author's opinion, the "oak craze" has been overdone by some enologists to the detriment of fruitiness, balance, harmony, finesse, and pleasurable drinkability.    Oakiness as a subtle complexing flavor is desirable but when oakiness, heavy tannins, and high alcohols become the dominant characteristics of a wine, its ultimate desirability as a pleasant mealtime beverage becomes questionable.    The author realizes that originally this style of wine was created to attempt to imitate some foreign wine styles by using the same processing and aging techniques used in Europe.    It might be questionable that the same length of time on the skins, the same fermentation temperatures, and the same oak extractants would give the same results with grapes from California that they do with grapes from Europe.    European growing areas generally produce lighter bodied wines with a lower alcohol and higher acid than do California grapes.    What we seem to need is a balance between large and small cooperage aging that will retain some of the recognizable flavor of the fruit but harmoniously blended with the complexities and subtleties of aging in oak and bottle.  Hopefully, such wines would have the smoothness and finish to be consumed relatively young, yet possess the capacity to benefit from prolonged bottle age. The general concept that red wines must have very high tannins and oak flavors to age well is questionable.  Experience has shown that wines with well-balanced tannins and little or no oakiness have aged and developed very well over a period of forty years.  While high tannins may require long aging to make a wine palatable, longevity may not necessarily require high tannins.

Aside from the extractants resulting from new wood, most of the aging process in wood is mainly oxidative.  Detailed knowledge of how each phenolic substance acts in the wine is not now available.  We do know that during aging some of the "tannins" are precipitated; color slowly changes from a red (sometimes purple) hue to a more brownish hue.  We also know that the fresh grapy flavor and aroma subside and a more complex flavor and bouquet develop.  The texture changes also from the crisper, simple feeling of individual sensations to a fuller, rounder, more harmonious feeling that fills the mouth with a single, more complex sensation.

## *Blending*

Sometime during its aging period or just before preparing the wine for bottling, the wine may be blended.  Little progress has been made in blending techniques in the past twenty years.  In fact, less blending probably is done today by North Coast wineries than was done twenty years ago.  The concept that 100 percent is best and anything under that results in an inferior product has been made popular by self-appointed consumer advocates.  This has been unfortunate.

Blending is a very valuable tool to the enologist.  It enables him to accentuate or reduce a flavor or aroma.  For nonvintage wines, it provides the means of mitigating yearly variations in wine characteristics.

There is one area of blending that has caught the fancy of the consumer in the past decade.  This has been the use of Merlot to blend with Cabernet Sauvignon.  Experiments carried on by Martini (26) since 1972 on 1968 wines have shown that a small amount of Merlot (<20 percent) is useful in producing a Cabernet Sauvignon wine that is softer, faster aging, and a more pleasant beverage at a younger age than one produced from 100 percent Cabernet Sauvignon grapes.  A number of tastings were held across the United States with wine-interested consumers and an informal poll was taken at each tasting.  The wine containing the Merlot was preferred by the majority up until about three years after the wine was bottled.  For the next two years the preferences were about even.  In recent years, the 100 percent Cabernet Sauvignon appears to have become the favorite.  The tastings are still continuing.  A few wineries are now following a similar blending pattern.   No other pattern of blending seems to exist in the industry.   Each enologist appears to have his own techniques that fit his winemaking philosophy (or that of his employer) and the wines he has to work with.

It has been the author's experience that certain varieties of grapes seem to be more compatible when blended together than others.   In addition to the Cabernet Sauvignon and Merlot blend, Pinot noir, Gamay, and Pinot St. George seem to go well together, as do Barbera and Petite Sirah.   Often a blend of these grapes is used to produce superior generic wines.   Singleton and Ough (27) reported that when two wines are blended together, a quality score greater than the mean of the individual scores can be expected a significant number of times.   In no case was the composite score lower than the lowest individual score and in a number of cases it was higher than either individual score.   They reported that the blending significantly improved quality and speculated that this may have been because of the complexity created.

It would appear that in modern day winemaking, blending can be used to good advantage to regulate the intensity of some of the acquired characteristics of red wines, such as oakiness.   This is being done to some extent but the flavor of many wines on the market suggests that the practice could be used more often and more skillfully.   Also, more basic knowledge on the reactions of blending and on the synergistic and antagonistic flavors in wine is needed.

Blending can be done at any time from the grapes to the finished wine.   The author prefers to make the final blend after the wine has had its period of wood age and before finishing the wine for bottling.

## Stabilization

Before the wine is bottled, it must be rendered stable to quality-degrading changes in the bottle.   Malic acid stability has been discussed already.   Other changes that the wine must be stabilized against are precipiation of cream of tartar, unstable color deposits, iron and copper casse, oxidation, and, of course, microbiological breakdown.

New wines contain an excess of potassium bitartrate.   Precipitation of cream of tartar during storage and aging reduces this excess.   Sometimes the length of storage given red wines ensures stability but the wine may be subject to very cold storage temperatures in many parts of the country during the winter months.   Therefore, many enologists prefer to ensure stability by chilling the wine.   This increases the degree of supersaturation of the potassium bitartrate and speeds up the precipitation of the cream of tartar. Temperatures of about $-3°$ C for a period of about ten days usually will stabilize red table wines.   Filtration to remove cream of tartar crystals before the temperature rises must follow.   Pilone and Berg (28) showed that addition of potassium bitartrate during chilling of red wines speeded up the stabilization period.    Some wineries routinely chill all red wines, others only if tests show that the operation is needed.

Cation exchange columns for cold stabilizing also are used, although less for premium red wines than for the standard wines.    Usually the potassium ion is replaced with sodium (or hydrogen if a lower pH also is desired).    In recent years, voluntary controls within the industry on the maximum concentration of sodium in the wine have discouraged ion exchanging for cold stability.    It is now used sparingly and carefully and occasionally combined with refrigeration.

*Fining*

Sound wines often become brilliantly clear by natural settling.    Fining sometime during the aging process is desirable.    Many materials are available but the two most commonly used for red wines are gelatin and the white of eggs (egg albumin).    The material to use and the quantity should be determined by laboratory trials.

When not needed to clarify the wine, fining may still be done for the purpose of altering the sensory characteristic.    The fining materials combine with the tannin complexes of the wine in different fashions.    A properly carried-out fining process should make the wine smoother and more harmonious by removing those fractions of astringency or bitterness that are most noticeable.    In recent years, the increased use of egg albumin for the higher quality red wines has been noticeable.    Gelatin is still a popular fining agent when indicated.    Bentonite, used extensively in the past for standard wines, usually is not used for premium red wines because of its tendency to reduce color.    Many other fining agents are available for special effects or to correct specific conditions but generally are not used on fine wines.

During the finishing operations, wines usually are checked for excess iron and copper, which may cause clouding after bottling.    Several proprietary compounds are available for reducing these metals to a point where future clouding will not occur.    A standard practice in many wineries is to add a small amount of citric acid to chelate the iron and prevent its forming phosphate cloudiness.

*Filtration*

Filtration usually follows clarification after allowing the wine to settle for a period of time.    Centrifuging also may be used at this point.    Larger wineries usually filter their bulk wines through diatomaceous earth while smaller wineries may use pad filters.

A number of unclarified, unfiltered wines have appeared on the market lately.    While this may be a good sales gimmick, its effect upon wine quality is debatable. Most enologists prefer the security of stabilization, clarification, and filtration. California red wines with sediment are still not acceptable to the general public.

Perhaps the greatest change in filtering techniques has come about at the final filtration into the bottle. Up to about ten years ago, most polishing filtration into bottles was done through asbestos pads. In the past decade, the industry has converted to cellulose pads. This was brought about by the asbestos scare, and although it has never been shown that ingested asbestos fibers are carcinogenic, most wineries decided to switch to cellulose. While a good filtering medium, cellulose does not give the wine the final brilliance that asbestos did. Although the difference is detectable, the level of filtration is still acceptable. Since red table wines are dry, membrane filtration usually is not used except in attempts to eliminate possible spoilage organisms known to be present.

### Bottling

A number of techniques to reduce aeration have been employed during the bottling of red wines in the past twenty years. Bottles generally are swept with either carbon dioxide or nitrogen before filling to minimize oxygen pickup. In addition, bottom fill machines were developed to prevent excessive agitation. In some cases, wines are nitrogen stripped going into the filler. If properly done, this will remove about two-thirds of the dissolved oxygen from the wine (26). At the corker, the headspace can be either evacuated or filled with nitrogen before inserting the cork. Most North Coast wineries use one or more of the above techniques when bottling red wines. See Figure 7.

Most enologists agree that after a North Coast red wine is bottled it would be desirable to give it two to three years of bottle age. Economics prevent this as a general practice. Usually, about six months' time elapses from bottling to shipping, which gives the wine a chance to recover from the shock of being bottled and minimizes the chance of bottle sickness (through excess aeration during bottling). Wine, unlike distilled spirits, does age in bottles. The length of time it is desirable to age red table wines varies considerably. Some, once past the bottle-sick stage, improve very little or not at all. Others, especially those produced from the better grape varieties grown in their proper location, may develop for ten to twenty years and may hold their quality for another twenty years. However, it is necessary to have ideal storage and temperature conditions to accomplish this.

It has been the author's experience that most high quality red wines require at least three years in the bottle to develop a significant bottle bouquet. Few wineries can afford to store all their red wines until they reach this stage. In recent years, a number of wineries have been holding back a portion of their wines for additional bottle age and releasing them

Wine Institute

*Figure 7. Automatic bottling line*

later at a higher price.   The author feels that this is a desirable practice and should be encouraged.   Principal changes in the bottle are generally anaerobic in nature.   They involve the development of a complex flavor and bottle bouquet, a color change toward a brick-red hue, sometimes a small deposit of tannin and coloring matter, and the development of a smoother, mellower quality.   Ideal conditions for developing these characteristics are cool, even, storage temperatures (12°–18° C) and a good cork.   To maintain the integrity of the cork, the bottles should be stored on their sides.

Red wine production in the coastal counties generally is associated with premium varietal wines, that is, wines named after the grape variety from which they are produced.   However, the area also produces a substantial amount of standard wines or "vin ordinaire," which are used as carafe or everyday drinking wines.   These wines are generally blends of several varieties of grapes, often from several of the winegrowing areas of the state.   In recent years, the popularity of these wines has grown mainly for sale in the larger containers from 1.5 to 3 liters.

A very recent development for the marketing of these wines is showing some promise in the United States.   It is the "Bag in the Box" package.   These are containers, originally developed in Australia, made of flexible, laminated, vapor-proof plastic ranging in size from 1.5 to 12 liters.   They are enclosed in sturdy cardboard boxes that serve as the structural support for the bags.   The bags collapse as the wine is withdrawn, thereby allowing the wine to be used over a period of time without exposing the remaining wine to air and deteriorating its quality.   These packages are very popular in Australia, where a large portion of their standard wines are sold in this manner.   The larger containers are generally used by restaurants and the smaller ones by home consumers.   So far they have not been popular in California.

For a generalized flow diagram of current red table wine production in California, see Figure 8.

## Regulations

During the past five years, the federal government has made the first major changes in the wine production regulations initially adopted more than thirty years ago.

These changes have incorporated into the regulations a dual appellation of origin concept with different requirements for each.   There also has been an increase of the percentage of a grape variety needed to qualify a wine for a varietal appellation.

Effective in 1983, subject to possible appeals and subsequent changes in the regulations, two appellations of origin will be recognized.   One, defined by a political subdivision such as a state or county, will require that at least 75 percent of the grapes from which the wine is produced must come from the designated area.   If such a wine is a varietal, the wine must contain at least 75 percent of the grape variety named.   If the origin is defined by an area other than a political subdivision, such area will be known as a "Viticultural Area" and must be delineated and accepted by the federal government after suitable hearings.   When labeled as coming from a "Viticultural Area," the wine must contain at least 85 percent of the grapes from that area.   If it is a varietal wine, it must be produced from at least 85 percent of the stated variety of grape.

Although current regulations require only 51 percent of a varietal wine be produced from the stated variety, most premium varietals already have a considerably higher percentage of the stated variety.   The new requirements probably will have little effect on either the quality of the wine or the availability of grapes.

California regulations differ only slightly from the Federal.   With the removal of the previously mentioned minimum alcohol requirements, the major difference now is that chaptalisation (the addition of sugar) is not permitted in California.

January 1, 1979, saw the end of the gallon as a standard of measurement for wines.   Since that date all wines must be packaged in metric containers.

## Personnel

No report on the advancements made on the production of red table wines in the coastal counties of California would be complete without mentioning the contribution made by young enologists and viticulturalists entering the industry during the past two decades.

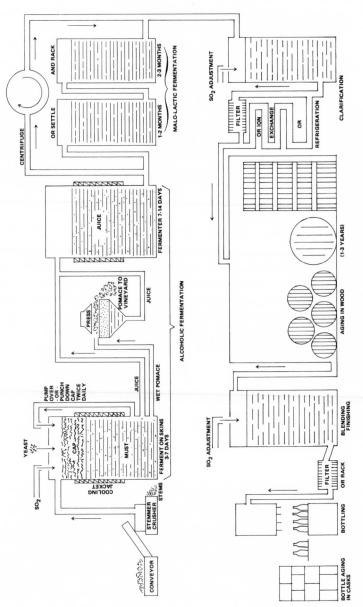

*Figure 8. Flow diagram of red wine production*

Until about 1965, nearly all the graduate enologists on the North Coast were concentrated in a handful of the larger wineries. With increased enrollment in the Enology and Viticulture Departments of the University of California at Davis and Fresno State University, many highly trained young men and women became available to the industry. Many were hired by the rapidly increasing number of new small wineries. These often were built and owned by persons in other professions. The young graduates immediately found themselves in the position of being cellarman, winemaker, vineyard manager, and enologist. With their newly acquired technical knowledge, a head full of ideas, and a free hand, they set about creating new wine types, changing old wine styles, introducing new production techniques, planting grapes where there were none before, and turning out good, clean, sound wines that have caught the fancy of the consumer. To this new generation should go much of the credit for the diversity and excellence of the current red wines from the coastal counties.

### Acknowledgments

The author is indebted to Professors Maynard Amerine and Harold Berg for reviewing this chapter and making many helpful suggestions. Thanks are also due to Tony Austin, Guy Baldwin, Leo Berti, Ed Friedrich, Ralph Kunkee, and Richard Peterson for helpful information involving modern production practices.

### Literature Cited

1. Amerine, M.A.; Winkler, A.J. "Composition and Quality of Musts and Wine of California Grapes," *Hilgardia* **1944**, *15*, 493–675.
2. Cook, J.A. In "Fruit Nutrition," 2nd ed.; Childers, N.F., Ed.; Rutgers: New Brunswick, NJ, 1966; pp. 777–812.
3. Kasimatis, A.N.; Berden, B.E.; Bowers, K. "Wine Grape Varieties in the North Coast Counties of Calif," *Univ. Calif. Agric. Ext. Serv.* **1977**, *4069*, 1–30.
4. Kliewer, W.M. "Effect of Root Temperature on Bud Break, Shoot Growth, and Fruit Set on Cabernet Sauvignon Grapevines," *Am. J. Enol. Vitic.* **1975**, *26*, 82–89.
5. Lider, J.V. "Some Responses of Grapevines to Treatment for Frost in Napa Valley," *Am. J. Enol. Vitic.* **1965**, *16*, 231–236.
6. Anonymous, "Final Grape Crush Report 1979 Crop," *Calif. Dep. Food and Agric.* Sacramento, CA, 1980.
7. Berg, H.W.; Ough, C.S. "The Relation of Degrees Balling to Wine Quality," *Am. J. Enol. Vitic.* **1963**, *14*, 144–147.
8. Roessler, E.B.; Amerine, M.A. "Further Studies on Field Sampling of Wine Grapes," *Am. J. Enol. Vitic.* **1963**, *14*, 144–147.
9. Cooke, G.M.; Berg, H.W. "Varietal Table Wine Processing Practices. I. Varieties, Grape Juice Handling and Fermentation," *Am. J. Enol. Vitic.* **1969**, *20*, 1–6.
10. Baldwin, G.; Berti, L., personal communication, (1980).
11. Peterson, R.G., personal communication, (1980).
12. Austin, A., personal communication, (1980).
13. Friedrich, E., personal communication, (1980).

14. Kunkee, R.E., personal communication, (1980).
15. Singleton, V.L.; Esau, P. "Phenolic Substances in Grapes and Wine and their Significance," *Adv. Food Res.* **1969**, *1*, 1–282.
16. Lowe, E.J.; Oey, A.; Turney, T.M. "Gasquet Thermovinification Systems, Perspective After Two years Operation," *Am. J. Enol. Vitic.* **1976**, *27*, 130–133.
17. Berti, L., personal communication, (1980).
18. Ough, C.S.; Amerine, M.A. "The Effects of Temperature on Wine-Making," *Calif. Agric. Exp. Stat. Bull.* **1966**, *827*, 1–36.
19. Ingraham, J.L.; Vaughn, R.H.; Cooke, G.M. "Studies on Malo-lactic Organisms Isolated from California Wines," *Am. J. Enol. Vitic.* **1960**, *11*, 1–4.
20. Webb, R.B.; Ingraham, J.L. "Induced Malo-Lactic Fermentations," *Am. J. Enol. Vitic.* **1960**, *11*, 59–63.
21. Myers, T., personal communication, (1980).
22. Beelman, R.B.; Gavin III, A.; Keen, R.J. "A New Strain of *Leuconostoc oenos* for Induced Malo-Lactic Fermentation in Eastern Wines," *Am. J. Enol. Vitic.* **1977**, *28*, 159–165.
23. Tchelistcheff, A.; Peterson, R.G.; Van Gelderen, J. "Control of Malo-Lactic Fermentation in Wine," *Am. J. Enol. Vitic.* **1971**, *22*, 1–5.
24. Cooke, G.M.; Berg, H.W. "Varietal Table Wine Processing Practices. II. Clarification, Stabilization, Bottling and Aging," *Am. J. Enol. Vitic.* **1971**, *22*, 178–183.
25. Peterson, R.G. "Formation of Reduced Pressure in Barrels During Wine Aging," *Am. J. Enol. Vitic.* **1976**, *16*, 224–230.
26. Martini, L.P., unpublished data.
27. Singleton, V.L.; Ough, C.S. "Complexity of Flavor and Blending of Wines," *Food Sci.* **1962**, *27*, 189–196.
28. Pilone, B.F.; Berg, H.W. "Some Factors Affecting Tartrate Stability in Wines," *Am. J. Enol. Vitic.* **1965**, *16*, 195–211.

RECEIVED July 22, 1980.

# Sparkling Wine Production in California

LEO A. BERTI

18560 Montevina Road, Los Gatos, CA 95030

Naturally fermented sparkling wines have been produced in Europe since the early eighteenth century. The first commercial production in California was in the late 1850s. The growth of the California sparkling wine industry was slow and cyclic. As late as 1960, only 1,984,000 gallons of sparkling wine were produced in California. By 1965, the volume had increased to 10,202,000 gallons. In 1979, California shipped to U.S. markets 19,100,000 gallons; this quantity was about 70 percent of all sparkling wine consumed in the United States that year; 17 percent was imported and 13 percent produced in other states.

In 1979, there were thirty wineries in California producing sparkling wine. The annual sales of sparkling wine from these wineries ranges from less than 2000 to over 4,000,000 cases per year. A few of the wineries make only sparkling wine but most produce still wines as well.

*Definitions*

In the United States, there are two classes of wine, depending on the carbon dioxide content (*1*). Still (i.e., nonsparkling) wines have less than 0.392 g $CO_2$/100 mL of wine. A wine containing this amount of $CO_2$ will exert about 15 psi pressure at 15.56° C in a bottle and will show a few bubbles when poured into a glass. Effervescent wines are those containing over 0.392 g/100 mL of $CO_2$. Effervescent wines are termed sparkling wines if the $CO_2$ is the result of natural fermentation. If $CO_2$ from outside sources has been added to the wine, the wine is termed artificially carbonated. These are important distinctions from excise tax and labeling viewpoints. The federal excise tax on still wines containing less than 14 percent ethanol by volume is 17¢ per gallon. On still wines with 14 to 21 percent ethanol, the tax is 67¢. Artificially carbonated wine, less than 14 percent ethanol, must be labeled "Artificially Carbonated" and the tax is $2.40. Sparkling wines under 14 percent ethanol have a federal tax of $3.40. In addition to the federal tax on sparkling wine, each state has its own tax, up to $3.50 in one of the less-enlightened states.

White sparkling wines produced in the United States may be labeled "Champagne" but the area of origin must also be prominently stated, such as "California Champagne," "New York State Champagne," "Napa Valley Cham-

0097-6156/81/0145-0085$09.25/0

pagne," "American Champagne." Our French cousins do not approve of this use of the word "champagne." While the author has his own opinions on the subject, no further comment will be made in this chapter. There are many laws in the United States, both federal and state, covering the production of wine, and they are enforced vigorously.

Most of the sparkling wine made in California is light straw in color and is often, but not always, labeled "champagne." Frequently, a second term is added to denote degree of sweetness—Natural, Brut, Extra Dry, Sec. Other terms may be used implying grape varieties, i.e., Johannisberg (White) Riesling, Blanc de Pinot, Moscato, Sparkling Green Hungarian, Cuvée de Gamay. The word "Crackling" means the same as sparkling. Terms of origin are used on sparkling wines, i.e., "California Champagne," "American Cold Duck," or "Napa Valley Sparkling Wine." Wines made in California that are labeled "American" usually have grapes, juice, or wine from other states blended in.

Pink-colored sparkling wines are termed "Pink Champagne," "Pink Sparkling Wine," "Crackling Rosé," etc. The red sparkling burgundy is made from red wine blends and represents less than 5 percent of all sparkling wine produced. Cold Duck, a blend of sparkling burgundy and white sparkling wine, became phenomenally popular in the early and mid 1970s, but sales of Cold Duck are small today. Sparkling wines fermented in containers over one gallon in size, if labeled "Champagne," must state on the label "Bulk Process," "Bulk Charmat Process," or some phrase including those words.

*Processes*

There are several processes for producing effervescent wine, but only three are of importance in California. These are the classic or traditional "méthode champenoise," the transfer system, and the bulk or Charmat process. These are all batch methods for making sparkling wine. The continuous fermentation method, used extensively in the Soviet Union, is not employed in California. Little artificially carbonated wine is made in California.

In 1979, about sixteen wineries produced by the traditional method about 8 percent of the 8,300,000 cases of sparkling wine made in the state. Two major wineries using the transfer system produced about 9 percent, and the balance of the production (83 percent) was made by ten or eleven bulk process producers.

Briefly, the traditional process consists of secondary fermentation of a sweetened still wine in a bottle, removal of the yeast sediment from the bottle, sweetening, recorking, and sale in the same bottle. Sparkling wine made in this manner is often labeled "Fermented in This Bottle." In the transfer system, secondary fermentation is in the bottle, the fermented sparkling wine is transferred under pressure to a tank, filtered into a second tank, sweetened, and rebottled under counterpressure. These wines may

TRADITIONAL METHOD

TRANSFER SYSTEM

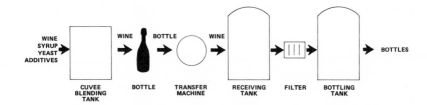

BULK PROCESS

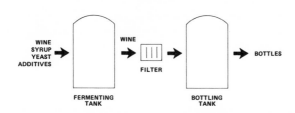

*Figure 1. Flow diagrams for three methods of sparkling wine production*

state on the label "Fermented in the Bottle."    Bulk process wines are those fermented in a closed tank, filtered into a second tank, and bottled under counterpressure.    These processes will be discussed in more detail later in this chapter.    See Figure 1.

### Carbon Dioxide

**Fermentation.**    The effervescent gas in sparkling wine is $CO_2$ produced by the fermentation of sugar.    The Gay–Lussac equation for alcoholic fermentation of glucose is:

$$
\begin{array}{llll}
C_6H_{12}O_6 & \rightarrow & 2C_2H_5OH & + & 2CO_2 \\
180.1\ g & \rightarrow & 92.1\ g & + & 88.0\ g \\
1.000\ g & \rightarrow & 0.511\ g & + & 0.489\ g
\end{array}
$$

Thus, 0.538 g ethanol and 0.575g $CO_2$ are formed, theoretically, from 1.000 g sucrose.

In fermentation practice, the yields of ethanol and $CO_2$ have been reported to vary from 92 to 98 percent of theory.   This is attributable to the formation of small amounts of aldehydes, volatile and fixed acids, glycerol, and other substances, to use of sugar in the yeasts' metabolism, and to small losses of ethanol during the fermentation.

The quantity of $CO_2$ in beverages is often expressed as a standard $CO_2$ volume to liquid volume ratio, i.e., the liters of $CO_2$ gas at 760 mm Hg pressure and 0° C dissolved in 1 L of liquid.   One liter of $CO_2$ at 760 mm and 0° C weighs 1.977 g.   Theoretically, 4.04 g glucose or 3.84 g sucrose, upon fermentation, will yield 1.000 L $CO_2$ (760 mm and 0° C) weighing 1.977 g.   In actual practice, sparkling wine producers estimate that 4.1–4.3 g glucose are needed.   Traditional and transfer method wines are refermented completely in the bottle to dryness, i.e., leaving no residual fermentable sugar.   If the cuvée is without fermentable sugar to start, then only that needed for the formation of $CO_2$ is added.   For example, if 6.0 gas volumes of $CO_2$, 1.186 g/100 mL, are desired, and a 4.2 g sugar/L $CO_2$ factor is used, $6.0 \times 4.2 = 25.2$ g sugar is added per liter.   If the wine contains fermentable sugar, this must be accounted for.   For example, if the wine contains 5.0 g/L sugar, only $25.2 - 5.0 = 20.2$ g/L glucose need be added.   The sugar content of wine is determined by chemical analysis and is expressed as reducing sugar.   From 1.0 to about 1.5 g/L of the reducing sugar is not fermentable, and a refinement of the above equation becomes:

$$(6 \times 4.2) - (5 - 1) = 21.2 \text{ g/L glucose}$$

While most wineries make these adjustments for the sugar in the wine, to the author's knowledge none adjust the quantity of sugar to be added by the quantity of $CO_2$ that may be in the cuvée.   Young wines that have been stored cold may have a considerable quantity of $CO_2$ resulting from the primary fermentation, even as much as one gas volume.

Bulk producers normally arrest the secondary fermentation to leave sufficient sugar in the wine so that it has the desired sweetness.   For example, to produce a sparkling wine with 5 gas volumes $CO_2$, 0.989 g/100 mL, and a residual sugar of 30 g/L from a wine of 10 g/L reducing sugar, the glucose to be added is determined as follows:

$$(5 \times 4.2) + 30 - (10 - 1) = 42 \text{ g/L glucose}$$

The above also neglects any $CO_2$ that may be present in the cuvée.

**Solubility.**   The quantity of $CO_2$ in beverages also is expressed in other terms than gas volumes.   For still wines, the Federal government states the maximum quantity of $CO_2$ gas that may be present in g/100 mL (0.392).   Several wineries determine the $CO_2$ content of sparkling wine by chemical analysis and express the results as g (or mg)/100 mL. Expressions such as atmospheres, pounds per square inch, or kilograms per square centimeter, at some determined temperature, also are employed. The term "atmosphere" is used ambiguously, both to indicate the quantity of gas dissolved and as a pressure measurement. Water at atmospheric pressure, 760 mm Hg and 15.56° C, dissolves one gas volume of $CO_2$; thus, one "atmosphere" is one gas volume. Unfortunately, the term "atmosphere" is used by some to mean pressure above 1 atmosphere absolute. Pressures expressed in pounds per square inch (psi) usually mean above 1 absolute atmosphere, as few pressure gauges are set to read 14.7 psi at atmospheric pressure (760 mm). When the pressure is expressed as atmospheres above absolute, the value should be so indicated.

The solubility of $CO_2$ in water at atmospheric pressure (760 mm Hg) is shown in Table I.

Following Henry's gas law relationship, as the pressure of the gas increases, the solubility increases in direct ratio. Doubling the pressure of $CO_2$ doubles the solubility. Charts such as the ABCB "Gas Volume Test Charts" indicate the gas volumes of $CO_2$ dissolved in water at different pressures and temperatures. The charts are based on the solubility of $CO_2$ in water and the absence of other gases. Using these charts for sparkling wine and not correcting for the presence of other gases can lead to substantial error.

The pressure in a closed tank or bottle containing sparkling wine is that of $CO_2$ and other gases combined. As the solubility of oxygen and nitrogen is much less than that of $CO_2$, small quantities of these gases in the vessel can result in considerable error if $CO_2$ content is determined by pressure-temperature relationships not corrected for other gases. To correct this error, pressure-testing devices for bottles consist of a hollow piercing needle, pressure gauge, and a gas release valve. The bottle is pierced with the needle with "snifting" valve closed. The valve is then opened until pres-

### Table I. Solubility of $CO_2$ in Water at 760 mm Hg Absolute (2)

| °C | Volume $CO_2{}^a$ (L) | $CO_2{}^b$ (ng/L) |
|----|----|----|
| 0 | 1.713 | 3.386 |
| 5 | 1.424 | 2.815 |
| 10 | 1.194 | 2.360 |
| 15.56 | 1.000 | 1.977 |
| 20 | 0.878 | 1.735 |
| 25 | 0.750 | 1.483 |
| 30 | 0.665 | 1.315 |

$a$ Volume $CO_2$ reduced to 760 mm and 0°C
$b$ Volume $CO_2$/Liter × 1.977 = g $CO_2$/L

sure drops to atmospheric, the valve is closed, and the bottle shaken until the maximum pressure is obtained.   The purpose of the sniffing is to release "air" so that it does not influence the pressure reading.   Another method is to measure the "air" contained in the bottle and correct the pressure by the ratio of the "air" to headspace volume.   The greater the volume of "air" and the smaller the headspace, the greater is the pressure in the bottle.

Many researchers, including Agabal'iants (3) and Jaulmes (4), have studied the solubility of $CO_2$ in wine.   Lonvaud–Funel and Matsumoto (5), based on their experiments, developed formulas and a nomogram showing the relationship between solubility of $CO_2$ in wines at different alcohol and sugar content over a wide range of temperatures, as Table II illustrates.

It requires less $CO_2$ gas in a sweetened sparkling wine in a closed vessel to have the same pressure as water at the same temperature.   For example, from the table it may be calculated that at a $CO_2$ pressure of 73 psig (absolute atmospheres) and 15° C, water will contain about 6.1 volumes $CO_2$/L, while a 12 percent alcohol wine with 40 g/L sugar will have only 5.1 volumes $CO_2$.

In Europe, the minimum pressure for sparkling wines recommended by the l'Office International de la Vigne et du Vin is 4.4551 absolute atmospheres (51 psig) at 20° C in bottles over 250 mL capacity.   Accurate determination of the $CO_2$ content of sparkling wine is, therefore, important.   In the United States, there is no minimum limit and accurate measurements of $CO_2$ are less important.   However, sparkling wine producers should understand the relationships between $CO_2$, other gases, alcohol, and sugar in sparkling wine.   Measuring $CO_2$ by chemical analysis and expressing the result as g/100 mL is the most accurate method.

The length of time sparkling wine bubbles when poured into a glass depends on the $CO_2$ content and temperature of the wine, manner of pouring, cleanliness and temperature of the glass, irregularity in the glass, and the natural $CO_2$ retention properties of the wine.   Naturally fermented sparkling wine bubbles longer and has smaller bubbles than does artificially carbonated wine.   The researchers who have studied this phenomenon,

**Table II.  Solubility of $CO_2$ in Wine at 760 mm Hg (5) (Volume $CO_2$ per Volume Wine)**

| Alcohol Percent | Water (2) | | | Dry Wine | | | Wine + 40 g/L Sugar | | |
|---|---|---|---|---|---|---|---|---|---|
| Volume | 10°C | 15°C | 20°C | 10°C | 15°C | 20°C | 10°C | 15°C | 20°C |
| 0 | 1.19 | 1.02 | 0.88 | | | | | | |
| 10 | | | | 1.04 | 0.92 | 0.80 | 1.00 | 0.88 | 0.77 |
| 11 | | | | 1.02 | 0.90 | 0.78 | 0.97 | 0.87 | 0.75 |
| 12 | | | | 1.01 | 0.88 | 0.77 | 0.96 | 0.85 | 0.74 |
| 13 | | | | 1.00 | 0.87 | 0.76 | 0.95 | 0.84 | 0.73 |
| 14 | | | | 0.98 | 0.85 | 0.74 | 0.94 | 0.82 | 0.72 |

including Brusilovskij et al. (*6*) and Klyatchk et al. (*7*), believe that in sparkling wine, $CO_2$ is not only in the free dissolved state but is also in an unstable bound form that exists only under pressure.   The bound forms are possibly $CO_2$ esterification products and/or physically linked $CO_2$—proteins and peptide materials.   It is agreed generally that a slow secondary fermentation at temperatures below 15° C is necessary to obtain fine bubbles.   Other factors reported to influence $CO_2$ retention and bubble size include the length of time under pressure in contact with yeast, yeast strain, and nature of the still wine.

## Grapes

The nature of the still wine from which sparkling wine is made is an important, perhaps the most important, element in the quality of the final product.   The character of the wine is based on the quality and degree of ripeness of the grapes selected and on the winemaking procedure.

In the last twenty years, the quality of California sparkling wines has increased greatly because better varieties of grapes are now more abundant and winemaking procedures have improved.   Many varieties of *Vitis vinifera* (European) grapes are grown in California and most have been used for sparkling wine at one time or another.   Today, California wineries are selective in the type of grapes they use.   Wineries producing competitively priced sparkling wine use the more prolific grapes grown in the warm San Joaquin Valley.   Generally, these grapes are less flavorsome, sweeter, and less acidic than those raised in the cool coastal regions.   Predominate grape flavors are not considered desirable.   French Colombard, Chenin blanc, and Thompson Seedless are the most common grapes for these wines. Sémillon, Emerald Riesling, Burger, and Ugni blanc (Trebbiano, St. Emilion) are also important varieties.   Ten years ago, Thompson Seedless was the widest used variety.   Although still an important grape, proportionately it is used less today and only in competitively priced sparkling wines.   Many of the quality faults formerly associated with Thompson Seedless have been eliminated by better control of the picking date and superior winemaking techniques.

Medium-priced sparkling wine producers commonly use French Colombard, Chenin blanc, and Sémillon grown both in the Valley and in the coastal counties in their blends.   Sylvaner, Folle Blanche, Emerald Riesling, and White Riesling also are employed frequently.   The grape of choice for the most expensive sparkling wine is coastal-grown Chardonnay, one of the true champagne varieties.   Within the last five years, Pinot noir as a sparkling wine grape has become popular, because of its abundance and different techniques for making white wine from this black grape.   Pinot blanc and Chenin blanc also are used in premium sparkling wines.

A sweet white sparkling wine termed "Sparkling Muscat" or "Moscato" is prepared from Muscat of Alexandria grapes. Muscat also is used sometimes in small quantities to add flavor to other white sparkling wines.

Pink or rosé sparkling wines are made either from cuvées of pink wines or white sparkling wine to which red wine is added for color. Those wineries that ferment cuvées of rosé-colored wines generally use Napa Gamay, Zinfandel, Pinot noir, Ruby Cabernet, or Carignane wines prepared by early withdrawal of the juice during primary fermentation. Some wineries prepare pink sparkling wine by adding small quantities of dark-colored wines. These wines usually are made from Zinfandel, Carignane, Ruby Cabernet, or dark-colored Rubired or Petite Sirah if used in small amounts. The advantages of adding red wine for coloring are brighter colors of desired hue in the product and fewer types of wines undergoing secondary fermentation.

Sparkling burgundy is made mostly from Zinfandel, Grenache, Barbera, Carignane, and Ruby Cabernet, but some Petite Sirah and Rubired are used also.

"Cold Duck" is a blend of white and red sparkling wines. It probably originated in the Middle States, and the flavor of Concord grapes is predominate, or at least recognizable. For this reason, some California producers import Concord grape juice or concentrate from other states for use in this product.

In California, grapes of different varieties are not mixed before crushing, and the wines are kept separate until the winemaker makes blends. There is an optimum range of "ripeness" for grapes for sparkling wine. This depends not only on the variety but also on the season, microclimatic area, and soil where grown. The measure of "ripeness" commonly used is that of soluble solids, expressed in degrees Brix. Of equal importance is the acidity of the grapes, both total fixed acids and pH.

In the San Joaquin Valley, grapes intended specifically for sparkling wines are picked early, before sugar and pH become too high and the fixed acids too low. The preferred range, depending on variety, etc., is from 16°–19° Brix, with fixed acids over 7 g/L (as tartaric) and pH 3.6 or less. In the cool coastal region, the grapes often are allowed to reach a fuller degree of ripeness, 17°–22° Brix with acids 1.0 g/100 mL or more and pH 3.0–3.3. The above figures are illustrative and are not to be considered inclusive.

Table III illustrates the increase in the quantity of better wine variety grapes that are now available.

### Wine Processing

The production of wine for sparkling wine is similar to that for table wines. In fact, most wineries do not make wine specifically for sparkling wine but select the most appropriate wines from their still wine inventories.

Table III. Bearing Acreage in California (acres)

| Variety | 1969 | 1978 |
|---------|------|------|
| Chardonnay | 1545 | 11,338 |
| Pinot noir | 1912 | 10,211 |
| White Riesling | 915 | 7963 |
| French Colombard | 5595 | 26,773 |
| Chenin blanc | 1941 | 19,671 |

Some producers purchase wines in bulk from others. Those wineries that crush grapes specifically for sparkling wine cuvée employ gentle methods of juice separation from skins and seeds, using the free-run and the first pressing for sparkling wines and the firmer pressed juices for other wines. Depending on variety, etc., the first 110 to 160 gallons of the 170 to 190 gallons of juice per ton (2000 lbs.) is best suited for sparkling wine. These juices are lighter in color, fresher in aroma, lower in pH, less subject to oxidation, and less astringent than are the harder pressings. Cold settling, centrifuges, and filters are used to reduce suspended solids in the juices before primary fermentation, and these operations also result in cleaner-tasting wines. White wines universally are fermented cool and stored at temperatures ranging from 12° to 20° C.

Base wines are tartrate–stabilized by refrigeration at -3°–5° C for eight to fourteen days, and then filtered cold to remove potassium acid tartrate crystals that have formed. These wines may be tartrate-unstable after secondary fermentation when the ethanol content of the sparkling wine has increased 1–1.5 percent. Bottle-fermented wines, aged one or more years in cool cellars, usually become tartrate-stable. Formerly, bulk process producers chilled the sparkling wine after secondary fermentation to -2° C or less for a week or more to stabilize the wine. Most bulk and transfer producers now ion exchange (as well as refrigerate) the wine before refermentation. By replacing a portion of the potassium ion with sodium (less than 300 mg/L) by means of a cation resin, the wine can be tartrate-stabilized. Preferably, this is done after the potassium level already has been reduced by refrigeration. Tartrate stability also can be obtained by replacing potassium with hydrogen in a cation exchanger and neutralizing excess hydrogen with hydroxide ion, using a weak base phenolic anion resin. This double ion exchange method also is used to lower the pH and increase total acidity. Ion exchange resins sometimes remove oxidized chromospheres and cold-labile proteins in wines. Ion exchange usage has increased production capacity of bulk sparkling wine plants by eliminating the holding time needed for tartrate stabilization.

Red wines foam easily during handling and for that reason low tannin wines are preferred for sparkling wine. Low tannin wines may be obtained by selection of grape variety, early withdrawal of fermenting juice off skins and seeds during primary fermentation, treatment with gelatin and other clarifying agents, blending with white wine, etc.

In California, winemakers do not want white wine to undergo the bacterial malo-lactic fermentation that changes malic acid to lactic acid. The loss of acidity, increased pH, and freshness is considered to be detrimental. On the other hand, malo-lactic fermentation of red wines before secondary fermentation is common. This is because red wines undergo malo-lactic fermentation more easily than do whites and they generally are aged longer before use. The producers do not want a malo-lactic fermentation in the bottle.

### The Cuvée

**Wine Blending.** The most important tool of the champagne master is that of blending. Blends of wines of different varieties are made to obtain the desired flavor and aroma characteristics, chemical balance, distinctiveness of product, and continuity of product. Blending is a highly skilled art that requires years of devoted practice to perfect. The result of a good blend always is better than the sum of its parts. There are only a few California sparkling wines that are made from only one variety of grape, and those are small lots of varietal wines such as White Riesling and Chardonnay. Although most sparkling wines are blends of one vintage, there is some blending of different vintages, particularly at the beginning of the new year. One winery carries on the French practice of blending up to 25 percent of one-year-old wine with fresh juice during primary fermentation. This practice results in a cool fermentation with less need for refrigeration and contributes to continuity of product. The presence of ethanol at the start of fermentation also inhibits growth of unwanted microflora.

The cuvées are filtered after they have been blended and before sugar and yeast are added. Diatomaceous earth filters commonly are used for this purpose, but some producers also use pad filters and one or more use membrane filters, 0.6 μ pore size.

Final blends, i.e., cuvées, as prepared by different wineries before sweetening and secondary fermentation, vary in their composition. The ranges found by the author during recent visits to wineries are ethanol, 9.5–12.0%; pH, 2.9–3.5; titratable acidity (as tartaric), 0.6–1.0 g/10 mL; total $SO_2$, 60–150 mg/L; free $SO_2$, 0–40 mg/L; copper, 0–0.5 mg/L; and iron, 1–10 mg/L.

**Yeast.** The desirable characteristics of yeast for secondary fermentation include the capability to ferment sugar in wines containing 11–14 percent ethanol and 150 mg/L or more $SO_2$ at low temperatures, 10°–15° C, without producing off flavors or odors and withstanding high pressure. For bottle-fermented sparkling wine, the yeast also should agglutinate well and form a compact sediment that does not cling to the glass.   Certain so-called champagne strains of *Saccharomyces cerevisiae* and *S. bayanus* yeasts have these properties.

A few California wineries import yeast strains from French champagne companies, but most yeast cultures are purchased from local suppliers.   The strains most commonly used for sparkling wine are "Pasteur" (U.C. Davis Enology, #595) and California Champagne (U.C. Davis Enology, #505), which are *Saccharomyces bayanus* (*S. cerevisiae* in 1981).   Other strains used include "Ay Champagne" (U.C. Davis Enology, #503) and BYL (Berkeley Yeast Laboratory).   Yeast cultures are obtained as fresh colonies of yeast on agar slants or as active dried yeast.   Those wineries using yeast slants increase the volume of the culture step by step.   To the bottle, usually of one-half-pint size, sterile diluted grape juice, diluted grape concentrate, or sweetened wine is added.   After two or three days storage in a warm place, about 25° C, fermentation should be active.   The volume is then increased to 1 gallon, and successively to 5, 50, 500 gallons, etc.   Many wineries have special yeast culture tanks.   Bottle-fermented sparkling wine producers usually use sweetened wine base as the culture media.   Yeast food, such as urea, and $SO_2$ (for acclimization) sometimes are added to the media.   When built up to full volume, cultures are used only partly for blending with the cuvée and then are replenished with medium or cuvée.   In this manner, yeast cultures may be used for weeks or months without starting over.   Yeast cultures will contain in the magnitude of $10^8$ yeast cells/mL when most active.   A rule of thumb is to use the culture when about half the original sugar has fermented.   Fring aerobic fermentors have been experimental within California.   With proper operation, the Fring apparatus can produce $10^9$ yeast cells/mL in a short time.

Active dried yeast is preferred to fresh culture by many wineries as it is consistent in quality and is convenient to store and use.   Active dried yeast contains $20–30 \times 10^9$ live yeast cells/g.   The yeast culture may be started by adding one pound to 0.5 gallon of media, and when actively fermenting, increasing the volume to 5 or 10 gallons, etc.   Some suppliers recommend that active dried yeast be rehydrated before use by immersion in sweetened (5%) water or wine base in proportions of one pound active dried yeast per one gallon, at 30°–35° C for five to ten minutes.   When active dried yeast is mixed directly with the wine to be fermented, the recommended dose is two to three pounds active dried yeast per 1000 gallons wine.   As previously stated, the quantity of yeast culture varies widely between wineries.   Bottle-fermented sparkling wine producers add 2–5 percent culture, resulting in a starting level of about $1–4 \times 10^6$ cells/mL.   During secondary fermentation, the yeast population may be expected to grow five- to tenfold (8).   At least one producer carefully controls the number of cells in the cuvée by varying the volume of culture added, depending on the cell count of the culture.   Most wineries empirically add a given percentage of culture.   Bulk sparkling wine producers usually add 5–10 percent culture as they want faster fermentations.

**Sugar.**   Different wineries use several sugar substances for the secondary fermentation (tirage) and for the final sweetening (dosage).   It formerly was the general practice for wineries to prepare their own syrups from sucrose, water, and a little citric acid to invert the sucrose.   Only one winery in California now practices the old custom of adding brandy to syrups to be used for dosage.   It imports French Cognac for this purpose.   Syrups prepared with water must be at least 60° Brix by Federal regulation.   Many wineries purchase liquid sugars in fifty-gallon drums or tank carloads.   These heavy 77° Brix syrups are mixtures of sucrose and invert sugar.   Several bulk sparkling wine producers use grape concentrate for fermentation and sweetening.   These concentrates are carefully produced and stored in order that off flavors will not be added to the wine.   Two or more wineries are using high fructose corn syrup, which is 20–25 percent less expensive than the equivalent sucrose syrup.   A disadvantage of high fructose corn syrup is that it must be kept at about 27° C during storage to prevent crystallization.

**Additives.**   Materials other than those used during primary fermentation or wine processing often are added to the cuvée before secondary fermentation.   Only materials that have been approved by the government may be used (1).   Yeast foods such as urea or Yeastex sometimes are added.   A good strain of champagne yeast should settle well after fermentation in bottles, but many bottle-fermented sparkling wine producers add a clarifying (fining) agent to the cuvée.   Gelatin, isinglass (with or without tannin), and bentonite are the most popular fining agents.   Tannins are USP tannic acid or special tannins imported from France.   Most bulk and transfer process wineries do not add fining agents; the few that do use bentonite.   Hydrogen peroxide, 30 percent strength, in amounts less than 3 mg/L, occasionally is added to the cuvée to reduce the free $SO_2$ content before fermentation. Copper salts are sometimes added in quantities up to 0.5 mg/L copper to prevent formation of $H_2S$ and other sulfide odoriferous compounds during fermentation.   By government regulation, the copper level must be less than 0.2 mg/L and usually is less than 0.1 mg/L after clarification.

After secondary fermentation in tanks, some producers centrifuge or filter the sparkling wine to remove yeast cells immediately.   Other wineries allow the yeast to settle before clarifying and add bentonite or Sparkoloid to assist the settling.   Activated carbon or polyvinylpolypyrrolidone (PVPP) occasionally is added at this stage to lighten the color of the wine.   Some bulk producers also add the dosage syrup, $SO_2$, citric acid, and/or erythorbic acid to the tank before bottling.   Other wineries make their additions to the filtered wine in the bottling tank.

**Bottling of the Cuvée.**   Cuvées for both traditional method and the transfer system generally are fermented in 750-mL bottles of 32- or 34-oz weight. Small quantities are also fermented in 375-mL and 1.5-L bottles. The bottling operation may be on a simple semiautomatic line consisting of a gravity or vacuum bottle filler and a crown capper. The capacity of these lines ranges from about 6000 to 10,000 bottles per day. Fully automatic lines have capacities of 40,000 or more bottles per day.

*Fermenting and Aging*

Bottles of cuvée are stored in the fermenting–aging cellars in three ways.

**Bottle Storage.** These are stacks of individual bottles, Figure 2, bottles in wooden pallet bins, and bottles in cartons. Stacks of individual bottles are the classic method of storage, but only a few California wineries use it now. The bottles are brought from the bottling room and are hand stacked, bottle by bottle. There are two types of stacks, on slats or between bulkheads. These stacks are up to 36 or more bottles wide, 20–45 bottles high, and many tiers deep. Tens of thousands of bottles are often in one stack. It is remarkable how steady these stacks are, even in our famous California earthquakes. This is a labor-intensive method, as one person can stack only about 2000 bottles in a day.

About fifteen years ago, some wineries replaced the stacking method with a movement and storage of bottles in wooden pallet bins holding 380–500

Wine Institute

*Figure 2. Sparkling wine bottles stacked for fermentation*

bottles laid on their sides.    The bins are moved and stacked one above the other, as high as seven.    At present, most wineries store the bottles necks up in 12- or 20-bottle cases on wooden pallets.    The pallets of 45 or 60 cartons are moved and stacked by forklifts.    One person with a forklift can move and stack 40,000 or more bottles per day.    More bottles per given space can be stored by bin or carton methods than by individual bottle stacks.

**Secondary Fermentation.**    In addition to $CO_2$, ethanol is formed during fermentation. Theoretically, 15.56 g/L glucose will yield 1.0 percent ethanol by volume.    In practice, 16–17 g of glucose are needed.    A sparkling wine in which 25 g/L sugar has been fermented will have an increase of ethanol content of 1.4–1.6 percent.    The cuvée wine usually contains 11.5 percent or less ethanol before secondary fermentation to ensure complete fermentation.

The solubility of potassium acid tartrate (KHT) decreases with increased ethanol, and the increase in ethanol during secondary fermentation may cause KHT crystals to form.    Young base wines, which have been tartrate stabilized by refrigeration only, often form crystals after secondary fermentation.    Wines that have been refrigerated and ion exchanged are more resistant.

The other products of fermentation have been studied by many investigators and are not the subject of this chapter.    Amerine and Joslyn (9), Amerine et al. (10), and Bidan (11) reviewed the literature on this subject and others pertaining to sparkling wine.    The secondary fermentation at 20–30 g/L sugar is considerably less than that of the 160–220 g/L during the primary fermentation.    It would appear that the by-products of secondary fermentation would have less influence on the flavor and aroma of the product than those of the primary fermentation.    This statement is not completely true as evidenced by good or bad odors and flavors formed during and after secondary fermentation.

In California, temperatures of the secondary fermentation range from 10° to over 25° C in different wineries.    Cool, slow fermentations are preferred by some, and warm, quick fermentations by other wineries.    Bottle-fermented processors commonly chill the cuvée to 10°–15° C before bottling.    One cellar is temperature controlled to 10°–13°C and another at 18° C.    Other cellars are naturally cool summer and winter.    Unfortunately, a few cellars are not temperature-controlled or well-insulated, and the temperaures can vary from 10° C in winter to as high as 22° C in summer.    Bulk wine processors may or may not chill the cuvée before fermenting in insulated tanks.    Most do not chill during fermentation and report temperaure increases of 3°–8° C (theoretical is about 3° C).

The rate of fermentation is also a function of the number of live yeast cells present.    Generally, bottle-fermented sparkling wine producers add 2–5 percent yeast culture to the cuvée resulting in 1–4 × $10^6$ yeast cells/mL.   Fermentations in the bottles are usually 90 percent complete in ten to fifteen days and 100 percent in four to six weeks.   Bulk fermentation wineries generally add a greater quantity of the yeast culture, 5 to 10 percent.   The bulk fermentations are much faster—4 to 14 days to completion.   Fermentation rate also is influenced by other factors.   The rate is increased by higher pH, higher yeast nutrients, lower tannin, lower ethanol, lower $SO_2$, lower $CO_2$ pressure, and younger wines (*12*).   California wineries control most of these factors by winemaking techniques.

   **Aging.**   The particular bouquet associated with bottle-fermented sparkling wine is attributable to aging on yeast.   During aging, the yeast cells die and autolyze, releasing aromatic and flavorsome compounds.   These compounds include esters, amino acids, and amides.   The products of lysed yeast improve not only flavor and aroma but also $CO_2$ retention and bubble size.   It is believed generally that all yeast cells will be dead when aged for twelve months at temperatures of 15° C and below.   This is considered to be the shortest time the wine should be aged on yeast at low temperature for development of the desired bouquet.   Complete autolysis and release of all amino acids may require three or four years.   Aging in the bottle at higher temperatures is believed to accelerate the process but the sensory results are less desirable (*13*).   An increase in the number of yeast cells in the cuvée will give a fuller flavored wine, which is preferred by some.   Too many cells may result in unwanted compounds such as sulfides.   One California winery formerly prepared an autolyzed yeast–wine mixture and added it in small quantities to the cuvée.   The quality results were not the same as from bottle aging.

   In California, bulk process sparkling wines are removed from yeast soon after fermentation ends, and they do not have the character of aged, bottle-fermented sparkling wines.   In West Germany, a sparkling wine (*Sekt*) must be kept under pressure on the yeast for nine months to qualify as a *Qualitätswein*.   It is common practice to hold the wine in pressure tanks most of this time and to stir the wine and yeast daily for an hour or so.   Stang (*14*) reports that, in a recent experiment in a German winery, using the same cuvée, qualified tasters could not differentiate between tank-fermented wine treated in this manner and bottle-fermented wine.   In the Soviet Union, the ten-tank continuous system has a nine-day throughput.   In two of the last tanks, the sparkling wine passes through a bed of polyethylene rings that are coated with autolyzed yeast.   Brusilovskij (*15*) describes this system in detail and claims that the wine has the bottle-fermented character.   In Italy, many sparkling wine producers pasteurize bottles of bulk fermented sparkling wine to improve quality and ensure sterility.   However, this is in the absence of yeast cells.   In a process developed by Paronetto and Berton (*16*), sparkling wine and yeast, after secondary fermentation, are heated in the tank for three days at 40° C.   The product is claimed to have a better sensory character than the wine that is not treated.

Changes during aging of sparkling wine are not only caused by yeast autolysis, but also by normal aging of the wine itself. This is a complicated subject and will not be further discussed in this chapter. However, there is no doubt that a new and highly desirable bouquet, sometimes called the "champagne" bouquet, does develop during aging in the bottle. After disgorging, there are other changes in bouquet, some desirable and some undesirable.

### Yeast Removal and Other Procedures

**Riddling.** The procedure of settling the yeast onto the cork in the bottle is termed "riddling" in this country. The object is to collect the sediment into a compact mass on the cap or in the plastic cup, called a bidule. First the bottle must be shaken or stirred to loosen the settlings from the glass. This formerly was done by shaking the bottles by hand. Now, most wineries spin the bottles for fifteen to thirty seconds on a simple lathe-like machine. The bottles are placed into and removed from the machine by hand. Another method is to tumble a whole pallet load of cartons for a few minutes. The third method, used by a winery that riddles mechanically, is to invert the cartons so that the bottles are neck down. This is done several months after completion of fermentation and many months before riddling.

Both hand and mechanical riddling are practiced in California. Hand riddling is the time-honored method and most wineries use it. Bottles after being spun are placed on wooden A frames (Figure 3) or horizontal racks. Each

Wine Institute

*Figure 3. A-frame riddling rack*

side of an A frame has holes for sixty bottles, six high and ten wide.   The bottles are placed neck down into the holes at an angle of about 30° from the horizontal.   For a period of up to two weeks, the bottles are not touched, so that the lees settle on the lower side of the bottle.

Riddling is an art and the procedure varies from one riddler to another.   A typical method is one in which the riddler faces the riddling rack and grasps a bottle in each hand.   The bottles are lifted one-fourth inch from the racks and twisted rapidly one-eighth turn right and left a few times, then they are dropped back into the rack in a position one-fourth turn to the right from the original position and at a slightly steeper angle.   Two days later the action is repeated and the bottles returned to the original position.   On the fourth day, the bottles are again twisted and replaced, one-fourth turn to the left.   This continues for a week or two and then the bottle positions are changed only one-eighth turn after each twisting.   The angle of the bottle steepens, and when riddling is completed it is 10°–15° from vertical.   The riddling process takes from one week up to three months, depending on many factors, including the strain and quantity of yeast, character of wine, fining agents, temperature and barometric pressure changes, the riddling method used, and the skill of the riddler.   The usual period for hand riddling is from three to six weeks, and one week to ten days for mechanical riddling.   Some wineries assist the settling of lees by use of electric or hydraulic vibrators.   The vibrators are automatically turned on four or more times a day for five to ten minutes.

The largest producer of traditional method sparkling wine has been the innovator of many new procedures.   It was amongst the first to use riddling rack vibrators and has developed two means of mechanical riddling; both methods are patented.   The first mechanical racks (Figure 4) developed are seven layers of double horizontal racks.   The upper rack of each double is stationary and the lower rack is movable (Figure 5).   The bottles are placed neck down in the racks at an angle of about 20° from vertical.   The bottle rests on its shoulder in the upper stationary rack, and the neck protrudes down into the lower movable rack.   The lower rack periodically moves so that the bottles flip-flop from one position to another, i.e., eleven o'clock to one o'clock.   This movement takes place four times a day and is followed by vibrating the racks and bottles about two minutes.   The time, duration, and frequency of the vibrating can be preset by the operator.   When first used, it was found that the bottles could be riddled completely in four weeks.   The winery now stores bottles of sparkling wine in cartons for several months before riddling, and the riddling time has been reduced to one week.

The second method developed by this winery is that of riddling the bottles while still in cartons.   Again, the bottles are stored neck down in cartons prior to riddling.   Ten pallet loads of forty-five cartons, twelve bottles each, are placed one pallet high on long roller conveyors.   These conveyors are mounted permanently on a steel frame, which is supported on springs.   Air bags under the frame are positioned so that the longitudinal

Figure 4. Mechnically operated riddling rack

Figure 5. Close-up view of mechanically operated riddling rack

sides of the frame can be raised one at a time to tilt the cartons 10°.    The equipment also has vibrators.    The cycle is to vibrate for seven minutes each 1½ hours.    After vibration, the frame is tilted to one side for one minute, to the opposite side for another minute, and finally returned to horizontal.    One week, and no labor other than forklifting pallets, is all that is required for complete riddling.    The author has seen mechanical riddling devices in Europe but none as ingenious as this.

At least two wineries in California use bidules.    These are polyethylene cups, 17 mm diameter and 14 mm high, which are inserted inside the mouth of the bottle before the crown caps are applied.    During riddling, the yeast lees settle into the cups, which are ejected during disgorging.    The use of these cups is said to result in more complete removal of the sediment and to provide added seal.

**Disgorging.**    After the bottles have been riddled and the yeast lees settled on the caps or in the bidules, they are kept neck down until disgorged.    Disgorging is the removal of the sediment from the bottle and may be done by hand (Figure 6) or by machine (Figure 7).    Before disgorging, the bottles are moved gently to chill rooms for chilling.    The bottles are chilled for periods from overnight to several days.    The temperature of the bottles ranges from 4° to 10° C at time of disgorging.    The lower the temperature, the less gas is lost during disgorging.    The necks of the bottles are immersed five to ten minutes in a freezing brine or glycol liquid to form a plug of ice, about one inch long inside the mouth of the bottle.    The yeast sediment is entrapped in the ice plug.    The freezing

Wine Institute

*Figure 6. Hand disgorging*

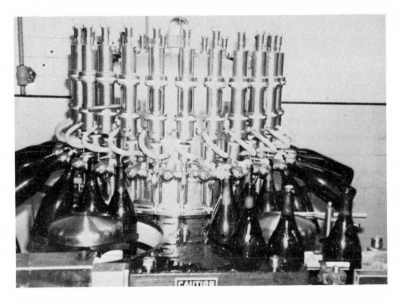

*Figure 7. Mechanical disgorging apparatus*

bath in most wineries is a simple one in which the bottles are in a stationary position. The most advanced bath is one in which rows of bottles move through the bath at a predetermined rate and are placed automatically on a bottle conveyor enroute to a disgorging machine.

Small producers disgorge the bottles by hand. The disgorger removes the bottle from the freezing bath in his left hand and points the neck away from himself at an angle of about 45°. The bottle is pointed towards the inside of a small barrel or similar shield. With a crown cap remover in his right hand, he removes the cap. The pressure within the bottle vigorously ejects the ice plug with the bidule and entrapped solids. The disgorger quickly places his right thumb over the mouth of the bottle to prevent loss of gas. He examines the wine for clarity by means of a nearby light. The bottle is next placed on a device (tourniquet) that holds the mouth of the bottle against a rubber seal while the bottle rests before the dosage operation. One person can disgorge 1200 to 2400 bottles a day. Three large California wineries use fully automatic disgorging machines. These machines have a capacity of up to 2500 bottles per hour but in some cases are limited by the capacity of the freezing bath.

**Dosage and Corking.** Dosage syrup is added to the bottle of wine after disgorging. In the hand operation, the disgorger gives the bottle a shake if excess wine is observed. A simple hand-operated dosage machine piston pumps a given amount (0–45 mL) of dosage syrup into the bottle. The same machine adds sparkling wine from another bottle to bring the volume up to the proper fill level. This machine is operated by one person who, when this procedure is completed, passes the bottle to the corker. Fully automatic machines are available for each of these steps, and at least one winery has an automatic dosage machine.

Bottles are corked on semiautomatic or fully automatic corking machines that drive a cork 31 + mm diameter by 48 mm long about 21 + mm into the bottle, which has a mouth diameter of 16.3–16.7 mm.  Before use, the corks are soaked in warm water, forty to forty-five minutes to soften them.  The corks have a paraffin band and are sometimes silicone-treated to make them easy to insert and more easily removed.  One machine maunfacturer states that the force in inserting the cork may be as much as 60 kg/cm$^2$.  All California traditional sparkling wine producers use natural corks for their products.  After corking, wire hoods to hold the corks in place are applied by machine, semi- or fully automatic.  The bottles are hand shaken, spun, or tumbled in machines to mix the syrup and the wine.  Various methods of rinsing the outside of the bottles are used, including hand wiping, rotating brushes, and water sprays.  After these operations, the bottles are ready for application of decorative capsules and labels.

A four- or five-person crew, using semiautomatic equipment, manually handling the bottles, can produce about 125–200 cartons of twelve bottles each per day.  Production can be increased by adding a second disgorger.  A fully automatic disgorging–corking line in California produces over 1500 cases per day with about four people.  The capacity of this line is to be increased in the near future.

Some wineries apply capsules and labels to the bottles on an extension of the disgorging–corking line.  Before labeling, bottles sometimes are warmed to 10° C or more surface temperature by passing through an infrared ray heating tunnel.  Moisture condenses on cold bottles and makes labeling more difficult.  Some operators use "ice proof" glue for the labels and do not warm the bottles.  Capsules are placed on the bottles either by hand or by means of automatic capsule-dispensing machines.  The capsules are crimped in another machine.  The bottles are finally labeled, inspected, and packed into shipping cartons.

Wineries that use natural corks store the corked bottles for three or more months to "set" the corks.  Corks are difficult to remove until they have set.

### Traditional Method

The traditional method stages of preparation of cuvée, fermentation and aging, riddling and disgorging, already have been explained.  The specific processes as used by two wineries will be given to illustrate differences in operation.

**Winery A.**  This winery is a small producer with an annual production of approximately 25,000 cases.  The still wine for the cuvée is made from about 25 percent grapes grown in their own vineyards, with the balance purchased from nearby growers.   Special care is taken in the selection of the grapes and in every step of processing to ensure that the grapes have the desired characteristics.   After blending, fining, and cold stabilization, the cuvée wine is pad filtered.   The average analysis of the cuvée is 11.5 percent alcohol, 8 g/L total acid, pH 3.0+, and 75 mg/L total $SO_2$.   Yeast cultures are prepared from active dried yeast.   The reducing sugar of the cuvée is increased to 25 g/L by the addition of invert sucrose syrup.   Isinglass and tannin and/or other fining agents are used.   The yeasted and sweetened cuvée is bottled on a line with an automatic vacuum filler and a crown capper.   Corrosion-resistant stainless steel crown caps are used.   The bottles are transported to underground caves where they are stacked individually in piles.   The caves have an even temperature of 15° C throughout the year.   The bottles remain untouched in the caves two to four years before riddling.   Immediately before riddling, the bottles are spun about twenty seconds to stir the yeast.   Riddling is by hand on A frames and takes an average of eight weeks.   The bottles are chilled to 8° C and a plug of ice frozen in the neck before they are disgorged.   Disgorging is by hand, and the subsequent operations are with semiautomatic machines.   Corks are treated with $SO_2$ gas and are soaked in warm water.   The sparkling wine is aged in the bottle a minimum of three months before shipping.   This winery uses both clear-colored (flint) and champagne-green-colored 750-mL bottles.   It produces only four or five different types of sparkling wine.   It enjoys an excellent reputation for its sparkling wines.   See Figure 8.

**Winery B.**   The second winery is the largest traditional method sparkling wine producer in California, with an annual production of over 360,000 cases.   It produces about ten different sparkling wines in sizes 375 mL, 750 mL, and 1.5 L.   It has a special shaped bottle (private mold) in the 750-mL size.   This winery grows many of its grapes and also purchases grapes and wine from others.   Still wines and brandy also are marketed by this company.

The equipment available and processes used for preparation of base wines are excellent.   Care is taken to use only free-run juice and light pressings (150 gal/ton for white and 120 gal/ton for Pinot noir).   The primary fermentation of the juice is conducted at cold temperatures, 10°–13° C.   Cuvée blends are made at the first part of the calendar year, although they are bottled throughout the year.   The cuvées have an analysis of 8.5–10 g/L titratable acid, pH 2.9–3.00 for whites and 3.2–3.3 for Pinot noir, and 115–130 mg/L total $SO_2$.   To the cuvée is added invert syrup, 25 g/L reducing sugar, 4 percent actively growing yeast culture, and bentonite as the fining agent.   Bottles are received from the manufacturer in specially designed cartons that also are used for storage and final shipment of the bottles.   The bottles are removed from the cartons, filled with cuvée, plastic cups inserted, crown capped, and packed necks up in cartons on a high-speed, fully automatic bottling line.   The cartons are stacked five high on wooden pallets.   The pallets are forklifted to the fermenting–aging rooms and stacked

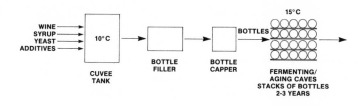

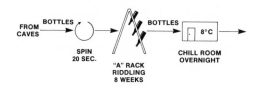

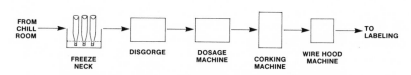

*Figure 8. Flow diagram for traditional method—Winery A*

three pallets high.   The temperature of the rooms is controlled at 19°
C.   After six to eight months, the pallets of cartons are inverted mechanically
so that the bottles become neck down.   The sparkling wine is aged another
1–1½ years, during which time most of the yeast settles in the neck of the
bottles.

After aging, the bottles are hand placed into mechanical horizontal
riddling racks (Figures 5 and 6).   In one week of periodical flip-flopping and
vibrating, the yeast completely settles into the plastic cups.   The bottles are
chilled overnight in a chill room before being brought to the automatic
disgorging–corking–labeling line.   This line, previously described, has a
capacity of 1500 cartons of twelve bottles each per day and is to be speeded
up in the near future.   The horizontal riddling racks are to be replaced with
bottle-in-cartons riddling machines.   This winery also has an excellent
reputation for its sparkling wine products.   See Figure 9.

### Transfer System

The transfer system was first developed in Germany.   Early experiments with this method were made in California in 1950 and it was first used
commercially in 1953 (*16*).   The method is used extensively by most eastern

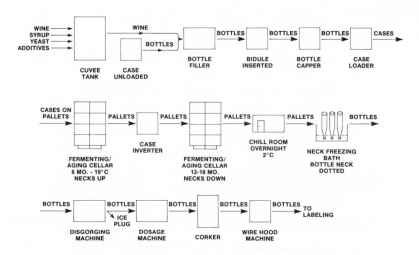

*Figure 9. Flow diagram for traditional method—Winery B*

state sparkling wine producers, but only two important wineries use it in California. The attraction of this method at the time of the California installations was that it promised the quality of traditional method sparkling wine but eliminated the labor- and space-intensive riddling stage. It probably is of less interest to future producers as the traditional method is less capital-intensive, and the product commands more prestige and price in the marketplace.

The method as used by the two larger transfer-system producers is basically the same, with only minor differences. In the transfer system, the mixing of the cuvée and bottling are the same as for the traditional method, except that fining agents are not added. After bottling the cuvée, the bottles are stored necks down in cartons on pallets in the fermentating–aging cellars. The temperature of the cellars fluctuates with ambient air temperature. As both these wineries sell their products in three price classes, the sparkling wine is aged for periods of time ranging from four months for the least expensive, twelve and fifteen months for the medium-priced, and up to three years for the most expensive. The low-priced sparkling wines compete in price with the better bulk process wines, and there is no need or incentive to age longer than necessary to ensure complete fermentation.

The operations of one transfer system winery, Winery C, will be described:

**Winery C.** After the aging period, the cartons are transported from the fermenting–aging cellars to the transfer area by forklift trucks. The bottles are removed from the cartons by an uncasing machine and are conveyed to and through a chill tunnel. They are sprayed with a chilled (-8° C) glycol solution for twenty-five minutes and emerge with a wine temperature of -3° C. The bottles are sprayed with water to remove the glycol, and the crown caps are removed by a decrowning machine. The opened bottles are conveyed within three seconds to the transfer machine (Transvasa).   This is a thirty-valve machine similar to a filler but operated in reverse.   In the machine, the bottles are lifted up to a rubber seal and pressurized to 100 psig with $CO_2$.   The pressure forces the wine up through a flexible tube into a pressurized, 55-psig holding tank within the machine.   The wine is forced by pressure out of the holding tank through a float control valve to 4800- or 9600-gallon receiving tanks that have been pressurized at 40 psig with $CO_2$.   This operation is at a rate of 120 bottles per minute.   The sparkling wine in the receiving tank is kept at -2° C.

The receiving tanks are vertical stainless pressure vessels equipped with pressure, temperature, and level gauges, pressure relief valve, inlet and outlet valves and fittings for liquid and $CO_2$ gas, a slow-moving propeller agitator, and a glycol jacket for cooling.

The transfer machine does not empty completely the bottles; 20–30 mL of liquid remains in the bottle.   This liquid is recovered by inverting the bottles in a twist conveyor, collecting the liquid, and pumping it into the receiving tank.

The sparkling wine in the receiving tank is cloudy, contains no sugar, and requires clarification, sweetening, and treatment before final bottling. After analysis, the $SO_2$ level of the wine is adjusted by adding potassium metabisulfite.   Erythorbic acid is added also.   These are for antimicrobial and antioxidation purposes.

To clarify the wine, it is filtered by pumping through a two-stage plate-and-frame filter to the bottling tank.   Most of the yeast cells and other solids are removed in the first stage of filtration.   The first stage uses both diatomaceous earth and cellulose filter pads.   The second stage has only sterilizing pads for polish filtration.   The diatomaceous earth is added to the wine as a slurry before the wine enters the filter.   If the wine is too dark in color, activated carbon is added along with the diatomaceous earth.   During this operation, the receiving and bottling tanks are equalized in pressure with a connecting gas line.

Sparkling wine in the bottling tank after filtration is brilliantly clear and sugarless.   No sweetening is added for brut champagne.   Only invert syrup is added for sparkling burgundy and extra dry champagne.   Special blends of still wine and syrup are added for color and/or flavor and sweetness for Cold Duck, pink champagne, and crackling wines.   Sparkling wine in the bottling tanks is held at  2° C and 45 psig pressure and is usually bottled within one to three days.

The addition of preblends, up to 30 percent of volume, dilutes the $CO_2$ content of the sparkling wine, and for that reason cuvées destined to be so blended are fermented to a high $CO_2$ level by adding tirage sugar in amounts up to 30 g/L.

The empty bottles from the transfer machine are inverted to drain the residual liquid, water-spray rinsed in a twist-rinser, and immediately refilled with unfermented cuvée.   Formerly, the bottles were washed in a large beverage bottle washer, using hot caustic solution, and either conveyed to the isobarometric filler for filling with final product or packed empty into cartons for reuse later.   Now, the bottles are filled with cuvée, crown capped, and automatically placed into cartons.   This operation is coordinated with transferring.   About 40,000 bottles are transferred and refilled in one day using nine persons.   See Figure 10.

The bottling of transfer system sparkling wine is the same as that of bulk process sparkling wine and will be described later.   It is reported that the loss of $CO_2$ during the entire transfer system, from tirage bottle to the final product, is ½ to 1 gas volume $CO_2$ (100–200 g/100 mL).   Most of the loss is in the transfer operation itself.   This degree of loss compares favorably with that of the traditional method, 1 to 1½ gas volumes $CO_2$.

During the last twenty years, there have been many improvements in the transfer system as practiced in California.   As in the traditional method, the handling of bottles in the fermenting–aging cellars has progressed from that of individual bottles to bottles in bins to bottles in cartons.   Hand operations of decapping and transferring at rates of 20–25 bottles per minute have been replaced by fully automatic machines capable of 120 bottles per

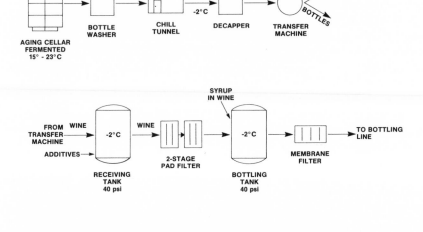

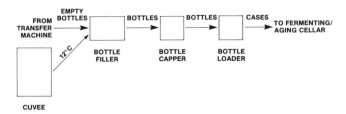

*Figure 10. Flow diagram for transfer system—Winery C*

minute.   Filters, tanks, pumps, and auxiliary equipment have been upgraded.   In one winery, the expensive bottle washer has been eliminated and
the bottles immediately refilled.   These improvements have reduced
equipment and labor costs.   On the final sparkling wine bottling wine, the
bottles are now labeled immediately after filling and corking, rather than
being stored and labeled at a later date.   Better base wines, yeast cultures,
and quality control procedures have upgraded the quality of the product.

The transfer system is capital- and power-intensive compared with both
the traditional and bulk methods.   It also requires more space and labor
than does the bulk method and less than the traditional method that employs
hand riddling.   Mechanical riddling reduces space and labor requirements.

*Bulk Process*

The bulk or Charmat process (17) was developed in France about 1907
by Eugene Charmat.   It was introduced into California in the mid 1930s.   The
original Charmat process was a three-tank batch system consisting of a tank
in which the wine was first heated and the cooled for "maturation"; a second
tank for fermentation; and the third tank for wine ready for bottling.   Charmat
later changed this process to a continuous one using ten tanks in series.   The
method used in California is a two-tank system, fermentation and bottling, as
the maturation step is not used.

Bulk produced California sparkling wines are made for mass market
customers.   They are not connoisseurs and do not require the aromas and
tastes associated with sparkling wines aged on the yeast.   For this reason,
bulk processors in California are not at present interested in aging on yeast
in tanks for a period of months as do the Germans, or in the yeast-cell-and-
wine contact method used in the Soviet Union (6) in their continuous system.

The tanks used in California for bulk process are pressure vessels and
have a maximum working pressure of 125 psig.   These are vertical cylinders
with dome ends constructed of stainless steel.   They vary in capacity from
1000 to 23,000 gallons, with diameters up to ten feet and total height over
forty feet including legs.   They are equipped with inlet and outlet fittings,
valves, gauges, and safety valves, and some have slow-motion propeller
agitators.   All the tanks are insulated and some of the small tanks are double-
wall jacketed for circulation of chilled glycol.   Many of the small tanks are
inside buildings, but the larger ones are usually outdoors.   See Figure 11.

There are as many variations of the bulk process in California as there
are producers.   The systems used in two different wineries will be described.

**Winery D.**   This winery produces about 150,000 cartons of sparkling
wine per year that sell at a higher price than do most bulk process wines.   The
winery receives grapes from its own extensive vineyards and from other
growers.   Grapes and still wines are not specially processed for use in sparkling wine.   Wines for the cuvée are selected from the large inventory of

*Figure 11. Sparkling wine fermentation tanks, 12,000 and 6000 gallons*

still wines.    Wines are processed by the usual cellar practices, including refrigeration to reduce tartrates.    White wines do not undergo malo-lactic fermentation but red wines do.    Cuvées average 11.5 percent ethanol by volume, 6.5–6.8 g/L titratable acidity, and less than 100 mg/L total $SO_2$.    Five percent yeast culture, prepared from active dried yeast, is added to the cuvée.    As the fermentation is stopped at the desired degree of sweetness, the total quantity of syrup added (30–60 gal/1000 gal) is based on the residual sugar desired in the final product plus that needed for fermentation.    Fermentation is in 1000- and 2000-gallon tanks and takes twelve to fourteen days at temperatures controlled to 15°–18° C.    When the pressure reaches a definite amount, 90 psig maximum at 15° C, the wine is refrigerated to stop the fermentation.

The wine is said to increase around 1.3 percent ethanol during fermentation. The wine is held at -6° C and about 40 psig for ten to fourteen days to settle yeast and further decrease the tartrate content. After the holding period, the wine is filtered in a two-stage plate and frame filter to the bottling tank. Cellulose pads are used in the filter, coarse pads (No. 40) in the first stage and fine pads (No. 90) in the second. A solution of $SO_2$ is added to the sparkling wine as it is being filtered, in a quantity to result in 175 mg/L total $SO_2$ in white and red sparkling wines, and 160 mg/L in rosé. The sparkling wine in the 1000-gallon bottling tank is held at about -3° C.

Heavy, thirty-four-ounce punted (push-up) bottles are used for the sparkling wine. These are rinsed with water and filled on an isobarometric (pressure) filler. Wine from the bottling tank is passed through a membrane filter to the filler. This company is the only bulk producer in California that uses natural corks. The corks are warmed in 43°–46° C water for one hour before use. The sparkling wine in the bottles is about -3° C at the time of corking. After corks and wire hoods have been applied, the bottles are warmed slightly in an infrared tunnel. Decorative capsules are placed on the bottles, which are then labeled and packed into cartons. These operations are all on one line and are automatic except for hand feeding empty bottles, applying capsules, and packing of the cartons. The wines are aged three months before shipping to allow the corks to set. The daily production is approximately 1350 cases of twelve bottles per day with eight persons. Five sparkling wine products, Brut, Extra Dry, Rosé, Sparkling Burgundy, and Cold Duck, are bottled in three sizes: 375 mL, 750 mL, and 1.5 L. See Figure 12.

**Winery E.** The second bulk wine producer sells over 1,000,000 cases annually. Base wines for sparkling wine are selected from a huge inventory of new table wines stored in tanks of up to 300,000-gallon capacity at temperatures held below 8° C year round. White wines do not undergo malo-lactic fermentation. The malo-lactic fermentation is complete in red wines, which are aged for at least one year. Base wines are processed to be heat and cold stable. The pH and total acidity are adjusted by ion exchange and/or addi-

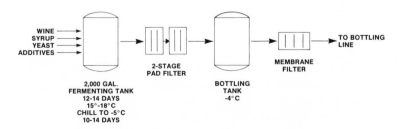

*Figure 12. Flow diagram, bulk process—Winery D*

tion of citric acid.    The analysis of the blended cuvée is 11.8–11.9 percent volume ethanol, 3.1–3.3 pH for white wines and 3.3–3.4 pH for red wines, 150 mg/L total $SO_2$, and free $SO_2$ less than 15 mg/L.    Cuvées are stored at 5°–8° C until ready to be sweetened and fermented.    The $SO_2$ and oxygen levels of the wine are monitored closely, and if oxygen is over 1 mg/L, the wine is sparged with nitrogen.    After blending, the cuvée is warmed to 12° C and pumped to the fermenting tank.    Yeast cultures are propagated from active dried yeast, pasteurized, diluted grape concentrate, and 150 mg/L total $SO_2$.    Seven percent yeast culture is added to the cuvée, resulting in a cell count of 20–30 × $10^6$ cells/mL.    Invert syrup is used for the tirage syrup, and is mixed with the cuvée in an amount to produce 0.850–0.950 g/100 mL $CO_2$ and the desired level of sweetness after fermentation.    The fermentation takes place in temperature-controlled 6000- and 12,000-gallon tanks.    Agitators slowly stir the wine during fermentation.    The fermentation is stopped by refrigerating the sparkling wine to 5° C in an external interchanger when the pressure– temperature relationship indicates 5.5 gas volumes $CO_2$ (using a water–$CO_2$ chart).    The fermentation takes five to six days.    The wines, except Cold Duck, are centrifuged immediately to remove yeast.    Cold Duck, which is in part made from Concord grape wine, tends to foam and gush.    For this reason, it is treated with bentonite and held one week at -5° C to reduce foam-producing constituents (tannins, etc.) before centrifuging.

This company centrifuges wine with a hermetically sealed centrifuge (7000 × g) to remove yeast cells.    After chilling the wine to -5° C, final adjustments of sugar (30–50 g/L) and $SO_2$ (180 mg/L) are made.    The wine is filtered first with diatomaceous earth in a pressure leaf filter, then polish filtered in a plate and frame filter, using "sterilizing" cellulose pads.    From the bottling tank, sparkling wine passes through a 0.5 μ prefilter and a 0.45 μ membrane filter to the filler at temperatures of -2° to -3° C. In this winery, nitrogen is used as the counterpressure gas.    The winery has two high-speed bottling lines for sparkling wine with a daily capacity of 6500 cases.

Two brands of sparkling wine are marketed, and the types include white, pink, burgundy, and Cold Duck.    Bottle sizes are 187 mL, 375 mL, 750 mL, and 1.5 L and are made at an adjoining glass factory.    The 750-mL bottles weigh 0.26 oz.    Plastic stoppers are used as closures for the 375-mL and 750-mL size bottles.    See Figure 13.

**Yeast Removal.**    The yeast removal techniques used by different bulk process wineries are interesting.    One winery, Winery F, centrifuges the newly fermented sparkling wine, uses a diatomaceous earth pressure leaf filter for polishing, and uses a membrane filter before bottling.    Another, Winery G, holds the fermented wine to settle the solids, and filters with a diatomaceous earth filter and finally with a membrane filter.    A large winery, Winery H, ferments in two 23,000-gallon tanks to pressures of 90 psi, chills the wine, and filters two fermenting tanks of wine with diatomaceous earth to a 46,000-gallon bottling tank.    The large, 46,000-gallon tank is constructed for only 60-psig working pressure, which is not exceeded by the

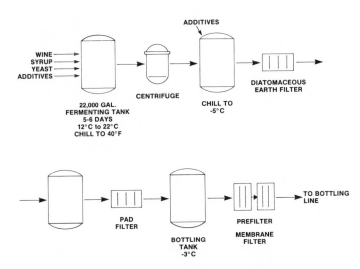

*Figure 13. Flow diagram, bulk process—Winery E*

chilled wine. Experiments have been conducted using two centrifuges, to remove yeast and polish sparkling wine, and no filters. The first centrifuge is a standard centrifuge with 7000 units of gravity force. The second centrifuge, $15,000 \times g$ force, "polished" the wine. This system shows promise. See Figure 14.

*Bottling Sparkling Wine*

Sparkling wines in the bottling tank after final adjustments of $SO_2$, sugar, acid, double-salt precipitation, etc. are held under $CO_2$ or nitrogen gas counterpressure and at a low temperature, -2° to -4° C. Wines in the tank, which are pushed through membrane filters to the filler by pressure differential, are held at high pressure, up to 100 psig. For wine pumped through the membrane to the filler, the pressure in the tank is low, 40 psig or so.

An example of one bottling operation is described as follows: The bottling tank, at -2° C, is $CO_2$-pressure regulated to 40 psi and the filler bowl to 75 psig by separate gas lines. These pressures are held constant through the filling operation. The wine is pumped through a 0.6-μ membrane cartridge to remove any yeast cells or tartrate crystals that may be present. An empty bottle is rinsed with 12° C water to clean and wet the inside surface. Cleaning, wetting, and chilling the bottle reduces the loss of $CO_2$ through foaming during filling. In a thirty-four-valve pressure filler, the empty bottle is raised and the opening sealed against a rubber cup; gas flows from the filler bowl into the bottle, equalizing pressures; the filter valve

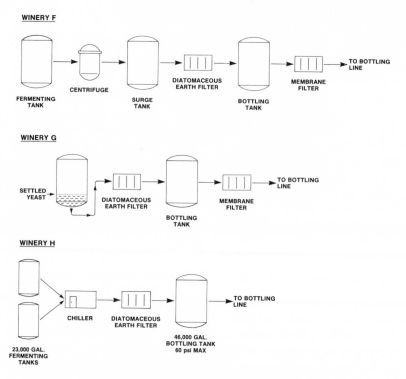

*Figure 14. Flow diagram of yeast removal—Wineries F, G, and H*

opens and the wine flows into the bottle and gases into the bowl. At a predetermined level, liquid in the bottle closes gas vent holes and flow is stopped. A "snifter" valve opens and gases in the bottle headspace are vented to the atmosphere. The rate of this filler is seventy-five bottles per minute. Some red and sweet white sparkling wines foam excessively and the rate of bottling must be lowered.

A more sophisticated pressure filler also is used in the industry. This filler vacuumizes the empty bottle before pressurizing with gas. There is less air enclosed in the bottle with this type than with the other.

After being filled, a cork or plastic stopper is placed in the bottle by specially-designed corking or plastic stopper machines. The bottle to be corked is firmly gripped and raised up to five-part closing jaws, which squeeze the cork from a diameter of 31 mm to less than 18 mm; a powerful plunger lowers and drives the cork into the bottle with a force estimated to be 20–60 kg/cm$^2$. Plastic stopper machines push the stopper into the bottle. The cork or plastic stopper is held in place in the bottle with a wire hood. A machine places the wire hood over the cork or stopper, with the lower wire loop under the lifting ring of the bottle. The loop is twisted, tightening the wire hood firmly against the closure and the bottle.

*Bottles and Closures*

**Bottles.**   Bottles for sparkling wines, as they must withstand high pressures up to 120 psig or more, are heavier than those used for still wines.   The weights of the "stock" 750-mL bottles available for sparkling wine vary from twenty-six to thirty-two to thirty-five ounces.   The similar size and shape "burgundy" bottle for still wine weighs only seventeen ounces.   In addition to the stock bottles, many wineries have specially designed bottles, private mold, for their exclusive use.   These are usually thirty-two to thirty-five ounces in weight.   The twenty-six-ounce stock bottle is not recommended for use as a secondary fermentation vessel as high pressures may develop during fermentation.   The thirty-two- and thirty-four-ounce bottles are designed to withstand pressures of seven gas volumes at 50° C, about 220 psig.   Sparkling wines are sold also in 187-mL, 375-mL, 1.5-L, and 3.0-L capacities.   All these except the 3.0-L size are made by glass companies in California; two of these companies are owned or partially owned by wineries.   The 3.0-L jeroboam size is imported from France.

The colors of sparkling wine bottles are champagne green (dark green), emerald green, and flint (clear).   Only a few wineries use flint glass for sparkling wine.

The most common upper-neck shape (finish) for sparkling wine bottles is one that accommodates a crown cap, a natural cork, and/or a plastic stopper.   The internal diameter (i.d.) of the neck is extremely important, as the tightness of the fit between the bottle wall and the cork or plastic stopper is critical.   Glass manufacturers, therefore, have tight specifications for the internal diameter of the neck.   The designed headspace is approximately 4 percent of the total volume of the bottle below the bottom of the cork.   This allows for liquid expansion without excessive increase in pressure.

Bottles have a special surface coating that helps to protect them during handling.   For this reason, and because there is better control of secondary fermentation and less manual handling, bottle breakage in a winery is less now (below 0.1 percent) than formerly.

**Caps, Corks, and Wire Hoods.**   Crown caps are used for closures on bottles before secondary fermentation.   The caps are 26 mm in diameter (one company uses 29 mm) and are coated tinplate or stainless steel.   Two companies use stainless steel to prevent corrosion and leakage during storage under moist and cold conditions, or for long aging under high pressure.   The liners of the caps are ground cork with vinyl disks or elastomer plastic.   Cork and plastic liners appear to work equally well.

Natural cork is the closure preferred by most producers of medium- to high-priced sparkling wine.   The dimensions of corks are 31 ± mm in diameter and 48 ± mm in height.   The upper part of the cork is composed of cork particles, 2–6 mm in size, bonded together with a polypropylene resin.   There are two or three whole cork disks, 6 mm thick, bonded to the bottom of the cork.   Agglutinated corks are less expensive and more consistent in performance than corks constructed of 3–7 whole pieces.   One or two small wineries still use whole corks.   Most of the corks are cylindrical in shape, but some are preshaped.   A preshaped cork has a top with a rounded upper edge, and a reverse tapered shank which forms a 1±- mm shoulder under the top dome.   This shoulder helps limit the depth the cork is inserted into the bottle to about 23 mm.   Corks have a light band of paraffin about 18 mm wide around the body.   Some suppliers vacuum-clean corks and then spray them with a silicone emulsion (Dow Corning 40 Emulsion).   This makes them easier to insert and remove from the bottle.   Corks are received in paper bags inside burlap sacks, or in plastic bags of 1000–5000 corks.   Sulfur dioxide gas occasionally is injected into the plastic bags to prevent mold.   Storage in plastic bags also prevents the corks from drying out.

Bottles of competitively priced sparkling wine are sealed with polyethylene plastic stoppers.   Stoppers from different manufacturers vary in shape.   All have a dome-shaped head 31–33 mm in diameter and a hollow shank 18–18.5 mm in diameter and 30–35 mm long.   On the shank are 4–6 raised rings 0.2 mm high.   The shank fits into the bottle and the rings act as gas seals.   Plastic allows for slow passage of gases, and the wine has a shorter shelf life than does wine sealed in a bottle with a cork.   Occasionally, plastic stoppers vigorously eject from the bottle when the containing wire hood is removed.   As a safety precaution, some wineries have a relatively low level of $CO_2$ in their product.   They also may have a precautionary note on the label to warn the consumer to be careful in removing the closure.   Because of the hollow shank, more air, 4–5 mL, can be trapped in the bottle with a plastic closure than with a cork.   Plastic stoppers are much less expensive than natural corks and are satisfactory for inexpensive wines consumed when they are young.

Small bottles, 187 mL, are closed with crown caps or roll-on aluminum caps.   For special customers such as airlines, these closures are used also on 750-mL bottles.   The roll-on or ROPP closure is the more popular of the two.   These are aluminum cups, 30 mm in diameter and 22 mm high, with an inner elastomer plastic seal.   After the caps are placed on the bottle, rotating dies roll the aluminum over the threads of the bottle.   Bottles for these caps have a specially designed thread finish.

Wire hoods are used to secure the cork or plastic closure to the bottle.   Wire hoods 36 mm high with dome-shaped tinplate disks 29 mm in diameter are used for natural corks.   The disks fit over the cork to prevent excessive indentation of the wire into the cork.   Wire hoods without disks, 32 mm high, are used for plastic stoppers.   Wire hoods have various designs with either four posts of twisted wire or two narrow metal straps, and have a lower wire loop.   One winery uses a special aluminum hood of their own design and manufacture.   When the wire hood is placed over the closure, the wire loop fits under the lifting ring on the neck of the bottle.   The wire loop is drawn tight by twisting.

*Analyses of Product*

Kochendorfer and Quinsland (*18*), in 1980, analyzed California sparkling wines purchased from retail stores. The wines were produced by wineries that market over 95 percent of all California sparkling wines sold. Table IV reports the results of these analyses. The author offers these observations: The low average ethanol content, 11.5% v/v, of the bulk process wines indicates use of early harvested grapes from the warm interior valley. Total acidity and pH vary with grape variety, degree of ripeness, and still wine preparation. For these reasons, no comment is made on acidity other than that some of the wines have too high a pH value (over 3.4). The volatile acidity levels of the wines are very good except for a few samples (over 0.55 g/L as acetic). This indicates sound grapes and clean

**Table IV. Analysis of California Sparkling Wines (*18*)**

|  | Traditional or Transfer | Bulk Process |
|---|---|---|
| Ethanol, percent volume |  |  |
| Number of Samples | 8 | 12 |
| Range | 11.5–13.0 | 10.2–12.7 |
| Average | 12.2 | 11.5 |
| Total Acidity, g/100 mL (tartaric) |  |  |
| Number of Samples | 10 | 14 |
| Range | 0.73–0.98 | 0.76–0.94 |
| Average | 0.88 | 0.84 |
| Volatile Acidity, g/100 mL (acetic) |  |  |
| Number of Samples | 10 | 14 |
| Range | 0.032–0.068 | 0.040–0.088 |
| Average | 0.046 | 0.053 |
| Total $SO_2$, mg/L |  |  |
| Number of Samples | 10 | 14 |
| Range | 67–202 | 120–238 |
| Average | 135 | 156 |
| pH |  |  |
| Number of Samples | 10 | 14 |
| Range | 3.20–3.85 | 3.09–3.76 |
| Average | 3.41 | 3.42 |
| $CO_2$, g/100 mL |  |  |
| Number of Samples | 8 | 12 |
| Range | 0.795–1.124 | 0.756–0.990 |
| Average | 1.010 | 0.806 |
| Reducing Sugar, g/100 mL |  |  |
| Number of Samples | 8 (Brut) | 14 |
| Range | 0.21–1.98 | 1.45–4.16 |
| Average | 0.88 | 2.65 |

primary fermentations.    The $CO_2$ content of the bottle-fermented wines are excellent, average 1.010 g/100 mL, but many of the bulk process wines have an exceedingly low level of carbonation.    This is a major defect.    The samples of bottle-fermented wines analyzed are all "Brut" and this is reflected by the low sugar content, average 8.8 g/L.    Bulk wines produced for the mass market are generally sweet, average 26.5 g/L.    The copper (0.01–0.11 mg/L) and iron (1.4–6.1 mg/L) contents are quite low, reflecting use of stainless steel equipment and possibly treatment of the wines to remove metals.    The $SO_2$ content of many of the wines appears to be too high for the best quality.

*Equipment*

Many of the machines used in the sparkling wine industry are specialized.    These include machines for transferring, riddling, neck freezing, disgorging, dosage syruping, corking, and wire hooding.    Most of these machines are imported from Europe.    Other machines such as vacuum and pressure fillers, filters, pumps, bottle conveyors, and case loaders and unloaders are used for both still and sparkling wines.

The important change since 1960 in the California sparkling wine industry —except for small producers—has been from manual to more automatic operations.    Hand operations of stacking bottles, riddling, and disgorging are being replaced and thereby are reducing labor cost of producing bottle-fermented sparkling wines.    The increased capacity of pressure tanks and the production rate of machines have decreased the cost of producing bulk process sparkling wines.    Stainless steel has replaced other metals in tank and equipment construction, thereby reducing metal contamination of the wine and facilitating sanitation.    Wineries will become more efficient in the future as new machines and processes are introduced.

*Comment*

The quality of California sparkling wine has improved greatly since 1960.    This has been attributable to several factors, including a more abundant supply of better grape varieties, better still wine production, and better secondary fermentation processes.    Doubtlessly, the products will further improve in the future.    The author believes that many of the producers can improve their sparkling wines by putting into practice techniques already known.    Some traditional and transfer method producers can increase the quality by using only free-run and gently pressed juices for cuvée wines; learning more about the art of blending; fermenting and aging in the bottles at a temperature less than 15° C; and aging on yeast a minimum of eighteen months.    Some bulk sparkling wine producers could improve their product by selection of cuvée wines that are more resistant to browning, and relying less on $CO_2$ and $SO_2$.    The level of carbonation of many bulk process wines is too low.

*Acknowledgment*

The author thanks the many people in the California wine industry, the University of California at Davis, and suppliers who generously shared their knowledge with him.

*Literature Cited*

1. U.S. Treasury Department. "Wine, Part 240 of Title 27, Code of Federal Regulations," *U.S. Government Printing Office, Washington, D.C.*, **1976**.
2. Bohr, C. "Kulsyrens oploeselighed i alkohol mellem/670 g + 45° C. In-og evasionskoefficient ved 0° C," Kj/obenk., Overs.: 1899; pp. 601–614. (Also *Ann. Phys.* **1900**, *1*, 244–256.)
3. Agabal'iants, G.G. "Khimiko-Tekhnologicheskii Kontrol' Proizvodstva Shampanskogo" Pishchepromizdat: Moscow, 1954.
4. Jaulmes, P. "Relation entre la Pression et la Quantité d'Anhydride Carbonique Contenu dans les Vins Mousseux," *Ann. Falsif. Expert. Chim.* **1966**, *66*, 96–128.
5. Lonvaud-Funel, A.; Matsumoto, H. "Le Coefficient de Solubilité du Gas Carbonique dans les Vins," *Vitis* **1979**, *18*, 137–147.
6. Brusilovskij, S. A.; Mel'nikov, A.I.; Merzhanian, A. A.; Sarishvili, N.G. "Proizvodstvo Soveskogo Shampanskogo Nepreyvnym Sposobom" (Production of Soviet Champagne in a Continuous Procedure)" Pishch. Promy'shle: Moscow, 1977.
7. Klyatchk, N.A.; Schoumilova, L.A.; Sareschvili, N. "6 on the Nature of $CO_2$ Fixation in Sparkling Wine (transl.)," *Vinodel. Vinograd. SSSR* **1979**, *39*(3), 52–53.
8. Reed, G., private communication (1980.)
9. Amerine, M.A.; Joslyn, M.A. "Table Wines. The Technology of Their Production," 2nd ed.; Univ. of California Press: Berkeley and Los Angeles, 1971; p. 794.
10. Amerine, M. A.; Berg, H.W.; Kunkee, R.E.; Ough, C.S.; Singleton, V.L.; Webb, A.D. "The Technology of Wine Making," 4th ed.; Avi: Westport, CN, 1979; p. 199.
11. Bidan, P. "Les Vins Mousseux," *Centre Documentation Inter. Ind. Utilisat. Prod. Agric. Ser. Synth. Bibliog., Paris*, **1975**, *7*, 1–166.
12. Reed, G.; Peppler, H.J. "Yeast Technology;" Avi: Westport, CN, 1973.
13. Baldwin, G., private communication (1980.)
14. Stang, F., private communication (1980.)
15. Brusilovskij, S.A. "O Sposobakh Osushchestvleniia Vtorichnogo Brozheniia v Proizvodstve Shampanskogo (On methods of accomplishing the secondary fermentation)," *Vinodel. Vinograd. SSSR* **1979**, *39*(4), 7–13.
16. Berti, L.A. "A Review of the Transfer System of Champagne Production," *Am. J. Enol. Vitic.* **1951**, *12*, 67–68.
17. Charmat, P. "Ten Tank Continuous Charmat Production of Champagne," *Wines Vines* 6(50), 40–41.
18. Kochendorfer, R.; Quinsland, D., private communication (1980.)

RECEIVED August 11, 1980.

# Production of Table Wines in the Interior Valley

ELIE SKOFIS

Guild Wineries and Distilleries, 50 Sansome Street, San Francisco, CA 94111

Major changes in distribution and consumption have taken place in the California wine industry in the past ten years. This change began around 1967–68 and became more evident by 1970 (1).

A tremendous increase has occurred in the shipment and sales of California table wines, which are those wines referred to in statistical studies as being not over 14 percent ethanol by volume. From 1967 to 1970, shipments (2) of this category of wines increased from 61.6 million to 111 million gallons, while in the same period the sale of wines over 14 percent ethanol (primarily dessert wines) decreased from 82.6 million to 70.5 million gallons.

Grape table wine has become the major segment of wine sold in the United States market in the past decade. By the end of 1978, it represented 69.9 percent entering wine distribution channels. Of this total, California table wine represented 76.6 percent or 230.5 million gallons. Included were 24.7 million gallons of flavored wines under 14 percent ethanol. There is no strong statistical data as to the percentage of apple or pear wine in this flavored wine class and, at the most, it would be no more than 10–12 million gallons.

The northern part of the Interior Valley (3) basically covers the grape growing area of Lodi–Modesto but includes Amador and Sacramento Counties. This represents the San Joaquin Valley north of Merced County. Then there is the very large area south from Merced that includes the southern part of the Interior Valley—the region embracing Merced, Madera, Fresno, Tulare, Kings, and Kern Counties. In California, a majority of the grapes crushed for table wines are produced in the Interior Valley as herein described. In 1979, 84.1 percent of all grapes crushed in California were crushed in the Interior Valley. Of the 1,721,587 tons of wine variety grapes crushed the past year, 1,309,000 tons were crushed in the Interior Valley. If the entire tonnage of all grapes crushed in California in 1979 is taken into account, over 2 million tons or 84.1 percent came from the Interior Valley. Three kinds of grapes come from here: the wine, raisin, and table varieties.

This area also accounts for the other segments of the wine industry—the dessert wines, vermouths, and brandies as well as grape concentrate and

0097-6156/81/0145-0123$05.00/0
© 1981 American Chemical Society

grape spirits other than brandy.   Based on Wine Institute production and shipment figures, there is a utilization of 1,100,000 tons of grapes for these products, virtually all of it originating in the Interior Valley.   The Wine Institute is a trade organization that assists its members in trade matters, including statistical surveys of sales and production.

Although this may appear to be a roundabout way to arrive at a tonnage usage of grapes for table wines, it is currently the only statistical way of so doing.   Based on the total of 2,193,000 tons crushed in the Interior Valley and approximately 1,100,000 tons utilized for other segments, it means that approximately 1,093,000 tons are crushed to produce table wines.   Using a yield of 170 gallons of table wine from each ton of grapes, we derive a potential production of 186 million gallons of table wine from the Interior Valley of California.

In 1979 (3), 379,600 tons of grapes were grown in the coastal counties and presumed to be crushed primarily in that area.   There also were 33,700 tons of grapes grown in southern California and crushed in that area.   There are no actual industry statistics on grapes crushed in a specific area that may not have been grown there.   It is known that many thousands of tons of Interior Valley grapes are trucked to coastal wineries for use in producing table wines, but the exact tonnage is not known.   Conversely, some coastal grapes are shipped to the Interior Valley for crushing.

The primary reason for this statistical presentation is to point out that the 380,000 tons grown in coastal areas could yield a maximum of 65–70 million gallons of table wine, whereas we have stated that some 230.5 million gallons of under 14 percent ethanol California wine entered distribution channels in 1978.   Assuming that the 70 million gallons are coastal-produced wines, then the balance, or 160 million, would have to be produced in the Interior Valley.

*Grapes*

Data (1977) show total bearing acreage to be 622,500 acres, of which 318,000 acres were wine varieties, 241,000 acres raisin varieties, and 65,000 acres table varieties (4).   In contrast, in 1970, the total bearing acreage was 448,000 acres, consisting of 132,000 acres of wine varieties, 245,000 acres of raisin varieties, and 71,000 acres of table varieties.   Thus, in this seven-year period, there has been a gain of 174,000 acres of all grapes.   In the same period, wine varieties increased by 186,000 acres whereas raisin varieties decreased 4000 acres and table varieties 8000 acres.   During this period, many acres of vineyards were removed from production and either the same or other varieties planted.   Grape crush statistics for California for 1979 (5) are shown in Table I.

Bearing acreage in California for 1977 was 622,520 acres; 494,800 acres of that were in the Interior Valley and 127,668 acres in other parts of the state,

### Table I. Grape Crush Statistics for California for 1979

|  | Tons | Percent of Total |
|---|---|---|
| *White wine varieties* | 592,755 | 22.7 |
| *Red wine varieties* | 1,128,834 | 43.3 |
| *Raisin varieties* | 700,227 | 26.9 |
| *Table varieties* | 184,035 | 7.1 |
| Total | 2,605,851 | 100.0 |

primarily the Coastal Counties.    In these coastal areas, only 7700 acres were not wine varieties, leaving 120,000 acres of wine grapes.    We have noted that there are 318,000 acres of wine varieties in the state.    The 198,000 acres of wine grapes in the Interior Valley therefore constitute 62 percent of the state's overall wine grape varieties.

In 1977, 2,341,000 tons were crushed in California in the following districts: Interior Valley, 2,052,300 tons, and coastal areas (including southern Californa) 288,700 tons.

The breakdown of varieties for the Interior Valley was as follows: wine, 1,205,900 tons; raisin, 569,800 tons; table, 277,100 tons; making a total of 2,052,300 tons.    The breakdown of varieties for the Coastal areas (including southern California) was: wine, 265,600 tons; raisin, 21,200 tons; table, 1900 tons; making a total of 288,700 tons.

Gross wine production in California for 1977, as reported by the Wine Institute (5), indicates the following gallonage: Interior Valley, 323,000,000 gallons, and coastal areas (including southern California), 54,300,000 gallons, making a total of 377,300,000 gallons.

Based on tonnage crushed, gross wine gallon yield per ton for coastal areas is figured at approximately 188 gallons per ton and for the Interior Valley, approximately 157 gallons per ton.

The figures for the Interior Valley do not reflect actual grape utilization into the various segments nor final gallonage of the various segments, that is, table and dessert wines, brandies, grape concentrate, and grape spirits.    The figures only serve to show a gross yield of 188 gallons per ton in production of table wine and that the tonnage crushed for table wines other than in the Interior Valley will not supply the present demand of California table wine.    Therefore, most of this table wine must be produced by Interior Valley wineries.

### Wineries: Number and Cooperage

On July 1, 1970, there were 240 winery premises in California.    By July 1, 1979, our latest data (5) indicate there were 406 winery premises, an increase of 166 in this nine-year period.

In the Interior Valley in 1970, there were 71 winery premises and 88 in 1979, an increase of 17, whereas in the coastal area there were 169 premises in 1970 and 287 premises in 1979, an increase of 118 wine producing and wine storage facilities.

Cooperage in the areas under discussion was as follows: for the Interior Valley in 1970, 385,400,000 gallons and in 1977, 628,300,000 gallons; in the coastal area (including southern California) in 1970, 89,800,000 and in 1977, 150,000,000 gallons. The total cooperage for the state in 1970 was 475,200,000 gallons and in 1977 it was 778,300,000 gallons (5). This was a 64 percent increase in cooperage, or 303,100,000 gallons, from 1970 to 1977.

The tremendous expansion of cooperage that took place in the Interior Valley during this period was a direct result of the large increases in table wine demand. A general rule is that one ton of grapes yields approximately twice the volume of table wine compared with dessert wine, which explains the need to increase storage cooperage in addition to the other winery equipment necessary to handle this increased volume of production.

**Types of Cooperage.** The latest data on wine storage cooperage shows 778.3 million gallons. Of this, 37.3 percent is stainless steel and 31.4 percent is coated metal. Concrete cooperage constitutes 14.8 percent of the total. There has been no increase in concrete; rather a small decrease since 1970. Oak cooperage is 2.7 percent or 20.8 million gallons and this has doubled since 1970, indicating a trend to age fine table wines in this type of cooperage. Redwood cooperage is 13.7 percent. There has been a very small decrease in redwood capacity since 1970.

The increase in cooperage today in California primarily is in stainless steel. With improvement in engineering and metallurgical techniques, large stainless tanks with capacities from 350,000 to 400,000 gallons can be built. See Figure 1. In the Interior Valley, tanks range in size from 50- to 350,000-gallon capacity, and some metal-coated cooperage has been constructed with a capacity of 600,000 wine gallons.

The largest wineries in California are situated in the Interior Valley, although some comparatively new, large wineries are now established in the coastal regions as well.

### Production: Wine Types in the Interior Valley

The big change in the California wine industry, as stated earlier, was that the dessert wine segment of the industry lost its number one position, held during 1968–69, to the table wine segment.

Dessert wines reached a peak in 1955, then started to lose ground to table wines. In 1955, dessert wine shipments were 91 million gallons compared with table wine shipments of 26.5 million gallons. By 1969, dessert wine shipments had declined to 76 million gallons and table wines had reached 87.6 million gallons. In this year, table wines assumed the number one position. In

Valley Foundry and Machine Works

*Figure 1. 176,000-Gallon stainless steel tanks*

the following nine years, table wine shipments (wines under 14 percent ethanol) to all markets increased to 230.5 million gallons while dessert wine dropped to 49.2 million gallons. (This included under 14 percent specialty wines.)

The demand for larger volumes of table wines, accompanied by reduced consumer demand and reduced production of the dessert wines, required changes in crushing and handling of grapes in the Interior Valley wineries. Previously, the volume demand for Interior Valley table wines permitted these wineries to utilize only a part of their free-run juice from grapes, since the balance of the must (or fresh juice and pulp) would be used in the production of dessert wine, brandy, or grape spirits. But with large increases in demand for table wine, there had to be a change in the equipment and handling methods to maximize wine gallon production from the grapes used. The majority of the Interior Valley wineries had been designed to produce dessert wine, which required less than 100 gallons of free-run juice per ton, with the balance of the grape used for grape spirits, a major element in the production of dessert wines. Dessert wines have been called "fortified" wines since wine spirits are added to develop the desired final ethanol in the wine.

Interior Valley wineries primarily designed to produce dessert wine used pomace removal methods which were not acceptable for table wine production both from the quality and sanitary viewpoints. Pomace removal meant the use of water to sluice the drained pomace out of the fermentors on to draining screens, followed by additional water washes and final pomace pressing.    In this system, maximum recovery of the grape sugar and ethanol from the pomace was achieved.    The pomace washes were designated as distillery material and used in grape spirits production.

**Equipment Problems.**    However, in table wine production every effort is made to maximize the amount of juice or wine from the must, followed by removal of the pomace without using water.    The pomace flows out of tanks with steep bottom floors, then is removed by internal screw conveyors, or falls through a bottom opening in coned tanks onto screw draining screens.    See Figure 2.    In expanding Interior Valley facilities for greater volumes of table wine production, equipment was designed and installed to remove the pomace easily.    California wine equipment manufacturers were well acquainted with the equipment used in smaller- or medium-sized table wineries.    But the manufacture of larger equipment to handle large tonnages of grapes, which often in one day equaled the seasonal crush of a smaller winery, was a real challenge.    It was even more difficult since most available European equipment was designed to handle smaller tonnages in table wineries. Engineering ingenuity enabled the manufacturers of winery equipment to design large-tonnage fermenting and crushing tanks, and pomace removal and pressing equipment that have resulted today in maximizing the production (in gallons of table wine) per ton of grapes crushed.    The largest-sized wineries can easily handle 2–10 thousand tons of grapes per day in production of table wines.

Wineries using this new equipment are able to produce up to 180–190 gross gallons of juice and wine per ton of grapes crushed.    Individual crush-

Valley Foundry and Machine Works

*Figure 2. Pomace drainer*

ing equipment can crush up to 300 tons per hour.   Pomace pressing equipment can press pomace 100–150 tons of grapes per hour, and discharge a pomace cake at low moisture content (ranging from 55 to 65 percent depending on type of grape and whether or not the pomace was fermented prior to pressing).

**Available Grapes.**   A grape imbalance exists in the Interior Valley for wine varieties.   The tonnage crushed for wine is now in a general ratio of two tons of black wine grapes for each ton of white wine grapes.   The current large demand for white table wines is shown by the latest shipment of California table wine, where white wine sales represent 52.8 percent of the 216 million wine gallons of California grapes table wine shipped to U.S. markets in 1979.   The remaining shipments were 24.5 percent rosé wines and 22.7 percent red wines.

A statistical breakdown of table wine by color categories was reported for the first time in 1979 (6, 7) and covered shipments from 1974 to 1979.   The trend towards white wine is shown clearly.   In 1974, white wine shipments were 38,600,000 gallons and, in 1979, shipments had reached 114,200,000 gallons.

All of this illustrates that other white grape varieties are needed to produce the required volumes.   There are no statistical data as to this tonnage.   In 1978, some 563,600 tons of white wine varieties were crushed that, based on 170 gallons yield per ton, would produce a maximum of 96,000,000 gallons.   These figures as noted are possible volumes.   The main point brought out is that the imbalance of grapes is not only in the Interior Valley but elsewhere in the state.   This is a known fact in grape growing, since it has caused havoc in the marketing of black grape wine varieties, as pointed out in the leveling off of sales of red table wines from 49,900,000 gallons in 1974 to 49,100,000 gallons, while at the same time the black grape acreage in the state increased because of the large plantings that took place in the late sixties and early seventies.   We stated in the introduction that the grape wine variety acreage increased from 132,000 bearing acres in 1970 to 318,000 bearing acres in 1977, a 186,000 acre increase.

We also have stated that there were two tons of black wine grape varieties produced for each tone of white varieties.   Based on equal tonnage per acre, this indicates that there are some 212,000 acres of black wine grape varieties and 107,000 acres of white wine grape varieties.   Recent 1979 weighted average grower returns in the state show that white wine varieties returned an average of $293 per ton compared with $167 per ton for red (or black) wine grape varieties.   These prices are the average for the state and do not reflect the range for various growing areas.   For instance, in the Napa area, white varieties averaged $4659 per ton and black varieties, $486.

*Grape Harvesting*

A recent report (8) of the 1979 crush season by the State of California Wine Grape Inspection Agency, which inspects grapes for soluble solids, defects, and material other than grapes (canes, leaves), shows that in the state, approximately 74.4 percent of all grapes inspected were hand picked and 26.6 percent were harvested mechanically.    In the coastal districts, only 7.4 were harvested mechanically.

The harvested grapes are delivered primarily to the wineries in gondola tanks on a truck flatbed.    The size of these containers ranges from two tons up to eight tons per container.    There is no standard size for these grape containers.    The size of grape load delivered also varies.

In the same State Inspection Agency reports, the average per truckload for the Interior Valley was 21.54 tons as compared with the coastal district, which averaged 8.81 tons.

The harvest season in the Interior Valley in 1979 (9) started slowly in the second week of August and was 95 percent completed by October 13, 1979.    In an eight-week period, August through October, 1979, 92 percent of the crush was finished.    The trend in recent years is that most grapes are harvested and crushed in an eight-week span.

The average degree Brix of all grapes purchased and crushed was 21.5° in 1979 and 20.9° in 1978.    The white wine variety grapes averaged 20.4° Brix in 1979, and the black wine varieties averaged 21.9°.    Listed below are the 1979 Brix averages for the more important white and black varieties.

| *White Varieties* | *Tons Crushed* | *Average 1979°Brix* |
|---|---|---|
| Burger | 15,219 | 17.3 |
| Chardonnay | 31,873 | 22.3 |
| Chenin blanc | 145,963 | 19.7 |
| Emerald Riesling | 21,256 | 20.7 |
| French Colombard | 225,305 | 20.6 |
| Palomino | 25,288 | 19.2 |
| Sauvignon blanc | 16,118 | 22.1 |
| Sémillon | 13,749 | 19.5 |
| White Riesling | 30,496 | 21.1 |
| *Black Varieties* | | |
| Barbera | 137,286 | 23.1 |
| Cabernet Sauvignon | 82,131 | 22.7 |
| Carignane | 186,022 | 22.7 |
| Carnelian | 19,914 | 23.5 |
| Gamay-Napa | 23,951 | 21.2 |
| Gamay Beaujolais | 14,431 | 22.2 |
| Grenache | 158,017 | 21.1 |
| Mission | 24,302 | 23.5 |
| Petite Sirah | 49,615 | 23.7 |
| Pinot noir | 32,810 | 22.2 |
| Rubired-Royalty | 97,268 | 23.1 |
| Valdepenas | 13,924 | 22.7 |
| Zinfandel | 106,195 | 23.1 |

*Grape Crushing*

Harvested grapes are delivered to the wineries within a few hours after harvesting to ensure that the fruit is in sound condition.   The wine industry, recognizing the importance of sound fruit in winemaking, instituted a wine grape inspection program with the State of California.   This voluntary program was initiated in 1957.

In 1979, this agency inspected 86 percent of all the grapes crushed in the Interior Valley.   Grape inspection tests are for soluble solids, defects, and material other than grapes (leaves, canes).   Figure 3 shows a typical station and grape sampler.   The oscillating grape sampler is lowered into the grapes in the gondola.

After grape inspection of the grapes and weighing of the truckloads, the grapes are unloaded by tilting the hinged gondola truck tank and dumping the grapes into a hopper.   These hoppers are made primarily of stainless steel, but a few epoxy-lined metal and concrete hoppers are still in use.   The grapes in the hopper are conveyed to the crusher for destemming and crushing.   See Figure 4.

Valley Foundry and Machine Works

*Figure 3. Grape sampling station and grape sampler*

*Figure 4. Stainless steel conveyor*

In the Interior Valley, crushing of grapes is done predominately with the Garolla-type crusher–destemmer.   This type of crusher (*see* Figure 5) consists of a large revolving horizontal screen cylinder.   The cylinder is perforated to permit the crushed grapes to fall through to the hopper, where they are pumped by a piston or centrifugal type pump through large-diameter stainless

*Figure 5. Garolla-type crusher–stemmer*

Valley Foundry and Machine Works

*Figure 6. Continuous press*

lines into the fermenters. A shaft within the revolving perforated screen cylinder has arms, or paddles, that beat the grapes off the stems and also convey them out of the perforated cylinder.

One of the main objections to the Garolla-type crusher is that a small amount of the stems passes through the one-inch-diameter cylinder perforations with the crushed grapes. The crushed grape mass is the must. Operation of the shaft with the paddles at a lower speed reduces the stems going in with the must.

Today, most crushers are made of stainless steel, although some constructed of black iron are still in use. Though there is some iron pickup in the must, the iron generally will drop out with the suspended grape solids and yeast cells during fermentation and is not a major source for iron pickup in the wine.

Also, today in the Interior Valley, the must may be pumped directly to juice predrainers (Figure 2), which rapidly separate the juice, primarily from white grapes. The drained pomace is conveyed to continuous presses (Figure 6) for further pressing of the remainder of the juice. In this type of separation, many winemakers claim that more suspended solids (pulp and skin material) pass through draining screens, usually with 3/32-inch-diameter perforations with the various juice fraction. In some screen systems, it is possible to get up to 8–10 percent suspended solids by volume.

In the case of black variety grapes used for red or rosé wines, the must is pumped to the fermenters since it is desirable to have fermenation of the juice with the skins, which contain the color pigments.

**Must and Wine Yield.** The wine gallon yield per ton varies with type of grape, whether white or black. Total wine gallon yield is composed of three fractions. The main volume is the free-run juice that flows from the crushed grape; second is the drain screen juice that separates from the pomace, which already has had the free-run juice removed; and third is the press juice from the tight squeezing of the screen-drained pomace that was conveyed to the grape press.

Also, free-run juice yield varies with method of handling, particularly in white grapes.   White grapes that are crushed into a crushing fermenting tank and that have had some contact with the skins and pulp may yield up to 140–150 wine gallons free-run per ton.   Grapes crushed directly to draining screens will yield lower volumes, usually 110–125 wine gallons.   The juice also is higher in suspended solids, depending on the type of screening equipment and from subsequent grating action of the draining grape pomace being conveyed over the screen.

Many winemakers add pectic enzyme to the crushed grapes to aid an additional free-run yield.   Many wineries have stated they get ten to fifteen wine gallons more free-run yield per ton; again this depends on grape type and grape maturity.   The juicier wine varieties yield more free-run juice.   Higher sugar grapes will yield less free-run juice.   Use of pectic enzymes to give additional juice has increased greatly in Interior Valley wineries.

Many wineries claim the yield with latest equipment to be approximately 175–180 net gallons of white wine or juice, and 180–190 gallons of red wine or red juice.   Yields are proprietary information and as such there are no published reports; only ranges can be quoted.

### Grape Pressing

Today in the Interior Valley table wine production, the presses used to squeeze out the balance of juice from pomace are of a continuous type.   The presses are constructed primarily of stainless steel.   (*See* Figure 6.)

Most presses used in California are built now by California manufacturers but are of European design.   Because of large tonnages handled daily, the presses are generally 800-mm-diameter screws revolving within sturdily built perforated or slotted screens.   The largest presses generally will handle fresh unfermented pomace from 100 tons of grapes per hour, and the same press will handle fermented pomace that has less slipperiness from 150–175 tons of grapes per hour, depending on the initial degree of juice drain from this pomace.   Today, presses with 1000-mm-diameter screws are being built or imported into California.   These larger presses will handle at least 50 percent more capacity than the 800-mm-diameter screws.

The moisture of the discharged pressed pomace varies with type of grapes, seeds, and whether or not the pomace had been fermented.   Certain no- or low-seeded grapes yield slightly higher moistures, generally 60–63% than seeded grapes, which may be at 55% moisture.

After pressing, the pomace may be either given a water wash to extract any further alcohol and grape sugar or discarded.   Most Interior Valley wineries have distilling facilities and will use these washes in the production of grape spirits.   Generally four to six proof gallons of grape spirits (ethanol) may be recovered per ton of the pressed pomace, and most Interior wineries do make this recovery.   Some recently built wineries have not installed distillery facilities and steam generating plants, as they believe the large capital investment can't be justified economically, particularly at the high capital cost of this recovery equipment.

At a market cost of $2.50 per proof gallon of grape spirits, recovery of the ethanol and sugar from the pressed pomace is economically sound.   Recovery costs today, even with higher fuel costs for established distilling facilities, are in the range of $1.00 per proof gallon, thereby recovering $1.50 and reducing the product cost of the table wine by four to six cents per gallon.

### Fermentation

**White Table Wines.**   The free-run grape juice is the most important fraction used in white table wine production.   To the juice will be added $SO_2$ at 75–150 mg/L, depending on the grape condition.   Most winemakers prefer to add not over 100 mg/L.   The primary purpose of the $SO_2$ is to prevent browning and retard growth of wild yeasts and other undesirable microorganisms.

Pure yeast starter at 2–4 percent volume level is added to the grape juice to initiate the fermentation sooner and to prevent wild yeasts from developing.

In the Interior Valley, wineries now ferment white grape juice at a lower temperature range to develop wines with more bouquet and aroma.   Fermentation at colder temperatures results in white wines with a noticeable "fermentation bouquet," which makes the wines more pleasing.   Much of the increase in demand for white wines is undoubtedly attributable to these characteristics.   Certain white wine grape varieties, particularly Chenin blanc, develop more of this bouquet when fermented slowly at the colder temperatures.   Research studies in South Africa have confirmed this development of fermentation bouquet.   Studies are being continued to determine why some of this particular odor is lost during cellar storage. Storage at colder temperatures reduces this loss.

As noted earlier, white wine grape varieties generally are crushed at a lower °Brix range than red varieties.   Winemakers prefer to ensure a higher total acid.

At the cooler temperature, 10°–15° C, it takes from ten to fifteen days for fermentation, and at very cold temperature, 7° C, it may take up to twenty to twenty-five days.

Most enologists prefer the cooler temperatures and slower fermentation to develop more flavor and bouquet.   Yeast at lower temperatures produces more esters and other aromatic constituents.

**Rosé Table Wines.**   Rosé table wines are becoming more popular and shipments have been growing at a good rate, but not as spectacularly as white table wines.   In recent reports (6, 7) on table wine shipment by color categories covering the years 1974–1979, rosé table wine shipments went from 33.6 million gallons in 1974 to 53.0 million gallons in 1979, or a 58 percent growth, while in the same period, red table wine shipments went from 49.9 million gallons to 49.1 million gallons, a slight decrease. Rosé wine is popular because it has a lighter flavor than red table wines and probably because it is served chilled. Production of rosé, or pink, table wines is similar to that of white table wine with a few exceptions. First, the time of fermentation of juice with skins and pulp is less than twenty-four hours, and the pink juice is free drained as soon as the enologist is satisfied with the rosé color intensity. After the free-run is drained, the pomace is pressed and this fraction may or may not be used for rosé wine; if too dark, it will be used in red table wine production.

Basic rosé grape varieties in the Interior Valley are Grenache Barbera, Carignane, Gamay, and Zinfandel.

Rosé table wines also may be produced by using a white table wine colored with a dark red table wine. Many enologists prefer this method, as the white table wine base may be fruitier and fresher with more fermentation bouquet.

The other similarity of rosé table wine to white table wine is its cooler fermentation to develop more fermentation bouquet and flavor.

**Red Table Wines.** As stated, shipments of red table wines from 1974 to 1979 showed no increase, rather a slight decrease.

Prior to 1970, sales of red and rosé table wines were generally three times the volume of white table wines. In 1970, the table wine market share was 49 percent of the 196 million gallons shipped from California (*10*) or 96 million gallons. Of this total, red and rosé table wine shipments were around 74 million gallons, and white wine shipments in the 50-million-gallon range.

In production of red table wine, the winemaker ferments the entire grape mass—juice, pulp, skins, seeds—at 24°–29.4° C until the °Brix drops from the 21°–23° Balling range down to 4°–6° Brix. At this point, the juice is free drained. This free-run fraction is higher in wine gallon yield; generally it is in the 150–165-gallon range.

After free draining, the pomace is removed and pressed. The press wine, which yields 30–45 gallons per ton, is dark red, high in tannin, and heavy bodied. This press wine generally is segregated from the free-run fraction and, after separate clarification to reduce the astringency caused by polyphenolic compounds, may be blended in with the main free-run volume.

The purpose of fermenting the juice with the skins is to develop the color, flavor, and aroma that are characteristic of the grape.

During fermentation, juice is drawn from the bottom of the fermenting tank and sprayed over the top of the pomace cap, which has developed and risen to the top, to extract more color and flavor and immerse the cap with the fermenting juice. This is an important procedure in red table winemaking.

The fermentation temperature is controlled for 24°–29.4° C and preferably at 24°–26.7° C. At these temperatures, the fermentation practically is completed in five to seven days.

In the Interior Valley, red wines are generally in the 3.4–3.7-pH range, which is more favorable for the malo-lactic fermentation that takes place within a few months after production. It is primarily a decarboxylation of malic acid to lactic acid. This results in a decrease in the acidity of the wine and an increase in pH. Generally, malo-lactic fermentation of Interior Valley wines decreases their quality.

### Clarification

After completion of fermentation, the table wines are racked (transferred) via pipeline or hoses into storage tanks. Many winemakers may rack the wines while in their final fermenting stages and permit the fermentation to be completed in storage tanks. As noted earlier, it is at this early storage stage that the wine generally starts to undergo its malo-lactic fermentation.

This newly fermented wine is cloudy from suspended materials such as yeast, protein, colloids, and fine grape cellular solids. In storage, a natural clarification, or gravity settling out, of these materials takes place.

In most Interior Valley winery operations, the wines are racked once. After this racking, the wines are fined. This is a clarification process carried out by use of certain fining agents that cause flocculation and settling out of any cloudiness in wine. In addition, certain colloidal and proteinaceous soluble solids are absorbed by the fining agent. If not removed by fining, these soluble materials may later precipitate out in the bottle and cloud the wine.

Commonly used fining agents in the Interior Valley are bentonite, gelatin, and certain proprietary agents. The major fining agent is bentonite, which is used as a slurry at the rate of four to ten pounds per 1000 gallons of wine.

After fining and settling for a few weeks, the wine is racked out of the storage tank and filtered, then returned to storage tanks, which are filled to the top. The wines may be cooled en route to the storage tank, then stored at cool temperatures.

Many Interior Valley wineries centrifuge the wines after the first racking and before any fining. See Figure 7. As stated earlier, red table wines undergo malo-lactic fermentation soon after production, and many winemakers will not fine these wines until after completion of this fermentation.

Rosé wines are clarified and stored the same as white table wines.

### Stabilization

One of the major requirements in clarification is to fine wines to remove certain proteins that may cause instability in wines. These unstable proteins, if not removed from the white and rosé wines, may precipitate out of the wines after bottling, causing cloudiness and sediment. This precipitation is more likely where the pH of the wine is near to the isoelectric point of

Westfalia/Centrico

*Figure 7. Centrifuge*

the wine proteins.    Though this cloudiness does not indicate a spoiled wine, the consumer views such appearance unfavorably.

     Wines are stabilized to prevent cloudiness from a number of causes, such as proteins, metals, colloidal materials, and bitartrates (natural salt of wine).

     Protein stability is achieved best with bentonite fining of the wine.    Amerine and Joslyn (11) state that other possible advantages of bentonite fining besides protein removal are prevention of copper cloudiness, reduction of possibility of iron cloudiness, absorption of growth factors, and absorption of oxidases and other materials.    They point out that the disadvantages are the possible exchange from the bentonite into the wine of sodium, potassium, calcium, magnesium, and other ions, absorption of red colors, and removal of vitamins.    However, most enologists favor use of bentonite as the major fining agent.

     Stabilization of wines is described by enologists as hot or cold stabilization. Hot stabilization is the term primarily used to describe removal of constituents such as proteins and colloidal materials that may precipitate out of the wine, particularly if the wine is subjected to elevated temperatures such as that used in pasteurizing.    Hot stabilization doesn't mean actual use of heat to accomplish this.

     In cold stabilization, cold temperatures are used to cause precipitation of excess potassium acid tartrate out of the wines.    If allowed enough storage time at very cold winter temperatures, this precipitation will take place.    Under California winter conditions, this reduction of excess tartrates is very slow, and the enologist resorts to refrigerating the wines at low temperatures. Generally, table wines are kept cold at −5.5° to −3.9° C for seven to fourteen days. After this cold holding period, the wines are filtered while cold to remove suspended tartrate crystals. The majority of the tartrates will precipitate and settle out to bottom of this cold holding tank during the cold holding period.

Other possible methods of cold stabilizing wines such as ion exchange are used infrequently in California because of industry concern about an increase of sodium in the wine, or increase in acidity if the hydrogen cycle only is used. There is some limited use of the hydrogen cycle ion exchange in conjunction with refrigeration by a few wineries to cold stabilize, but most of the wineries use only refrigeration for stabilization. However, a number of wineries use hydrogen exchange to lower the pH for taste and color considerations.

Other stabilizing procedures employed are the removal of excess metallic ions, particularly copper and iron. In recent years, with the wide use of stainless steel in construction of tanks, crushing and pressing equipment, pipelines, pumps, filters, and other major processing equipment, the problem of metallic copper and iron contamination has been reduced greatly. Should a metal removal fining agent be necessary, the proprietary compound Cufex, denoting "copper–iron extraction" from wine, generally is used. This is a legal compounded ferrocyanide preparation that leaves no cyanide residue in the wine.

Another major fining procedure in Interior Valley table wine production is use of the compound PVPP (polyvinylpolypyrrolidone) (12). This reacts principally with tannins and is used to reduce browning in white wines. This results from its affinity for catechin, the main substrate for browning reactions. This compound also is used widely in the brewing industry.

*Aging*

In the Interior Valley, the majority of the cooperage, as noted earlier, is stainless steel, coated metal, or concrete. The majority of tanks, except wood cooperage, consist of large sizes.

Aging of wine implies changes in flavor and bouquet believed attributable to slow oxidation, particularly so during aging in wood with a relationship of wood surface area to volume of wine. In a small oak cask or barrel, there is more wood surface area per gallon of wine than in a larger cask or tank.

The question arises as to how much aging can take place in an air-impervious container such as metal or concrete. In a wooden tank, the air transfer through the wood pores to the wine takes place slowly, but in a metal or concrete tank there is essentially none. How does aging take place? Is aging necessary or desirable for Interior Valley table wines? First, we note that the present day enologist in California produces table wines from grapes that have properly matured and with no or minimal deficiencies.

Grapes are picked at optimum °Brix/acid ratio to ensure that the fruit has the best quality characteristics as to sugar, acid, and, in the case of black grapes, color. The intent is to receive the fruit in the best possible condition.

The enologist then processes the grapes, utilizing the most sanitary equipment, fermenting the juice into wine under controlled temperature conditions. He uses pure yeast culture in fermentation and follows the fermentation process daily.

Upon completion of fermentation, the wine is transferred to storage tanks for settling and, after the first racking, is clarified by fining or centrifuging. In handling the white and rosé table wines, they are maintained at cooler cellar temperatures to preserve the fermentation bouquet.

By careful processing, the winemaker brings the wine to a finished state. The white and rosé wines will have maintained their bouquet and aroma and flavors. The red table wines will have been softened by careful fining with such agents as gelatin and PVPP, will be fruity, and will have distinctive varietal aromas and flavors with minimal astringency.

In the Interior Valley, the majority of table wines are produced for consumption while young. The white and rosé table wines are meant to be consumed within 1½ years and red table wines within 1½–2 years.

The same chemical principles presented by the speakers on red (p. 59) and white table wine (p. 29) production are applicable to table wine production in the Interior Valley. Differences in the size of the winery operations and grape maturity are attributable to regional climatic conditions. With modern viticultural practices, the grapes grown for winemaking in this interior region now produce quality wines and they also comprise the largest volume of table wines produced in California.

Interior Valley enologists can be proud of their product as evidenced by the large increase in its consumption in the United States.

*Literature Cited*

1. Anonymous, "1978 Wine Industry Statistical Report, Part II. Distribution and Consumption," *Wine Inst. Econ. Res. Rep.* **1979**, *43*, 1–23.
2. Anonymous, "Annual Report 1978," *Wine Inst. Bull.* **1978**, *1865*, 9.
3. Anonymous, "Final Grape Crush Report 1979 Crop, March 10, 1980," *Calif. Dept. Food and Agric.*, Sacramento, CA, 95814.
4. McGregor, R.A.; Cain, M.; Seckert, J.C. "1978 California Fruit & Nut Acreage," *Calif. Crop and Livestock Reporting Service*, Sacramento, CA, 95814.
5. Anonymous, "1978 and 1979 Wine Industry Statistical Report, Part I. Production and Inventory," *Wine Inst. Econ. Res. Rep.*, ER 44.
6. Anonymous, "Color Breakdown of Shipments of Bottled California Grape Table Wine to U.S. Markets," *Wine Inst. Econ. Res. Rep.* **1979**.
7. Anonymous, "Statistical Items," *Wine Inst. Bull.* **1980**, *80, 81, 82*, 1–10.
8. Anonymous, "1979 Wine Grape Inspection Annual Report," *Calif. Dept. Food and Agric., Fruit and Vegetable Quality Control: San Francisco, Wine Institute, Grape and Wine Quality Committees*, **1980**.

9. Anonymous, "California Wine Report," Bulk wine information bulletin No. 49, Federal–State Market News Service, *Fruit and Vegetable Market News* 1979, 55, 1–3.
10. Anonymous, "California Wine Report;" Bank of America: San Francisco, CA, 1978.
11. Amerine, M.A.; Joslyn, M.A. "Table Wines: The Technology of Their Production," 2nd ed.; Univ. of California Press: Berkeley and Los Angeles, 1970.
12. Amerine, M.A.; Berg, H.W.; Kunkee, R.E.; Ough, C.S.; Singleton, V.L.; Webb, A.D. "The Technology of Wine Making," 4th ed.; Avi: Westport, CN, 1980; p. 794.

RECEIVED July 28, 1980.

# Production of Baked and Submerged Culture Sherry-Type Wines in California 1960–1980

PHILIP POSSON

Sierra Wine Corporation, Tulare, CA 93274

S herry-type wines were one of the most important wine types during the dessert wine era in California, roughly from 1933 to about 1960.    There continues to be a demand for high quality sherries.    New processes, possible changes in state and federal regulations, and the continuing evolution of consumer preferences should give sherry a promising future in California.

*Varieties*

The Palomino has been the preferred grape variety for production of drier sherry-type wines in California.    It bears well and the fruit reach the winery in very good condition.    Its juice and wine are neutral in aroma.    In California, the variety enjoys a prestige that partially derives from its use as a sherry grape in Spain.    There its hardiness, freedom from disease, and development of a high sugar content make it popular.    Actually, any white grape that is neutral in flavor can be, and is, used in making sherry-type wines in California.    These varieties include Palomino, Thompson Seedless, Tokay, and Sultana for drier-type wines.    Mission, Grenache, Pedro Jimenez, and Feher Szagas are used in sweeter sherry-type wines.

Since sherries can be made from many grapes, the areas where sherry-type grapes are grown are determined by economic factors.    That is, the areas are favored where grapes can be grown at lowest cost.    This limits the production of sherry-type wines in California to the Sacramento and San Joaquin Valleys: the great Central Valley of California.    This is region IV or V area according to Amerine and Winkler's (1) climate classification—the warmest viticultural regions in the state.    Being cool in winter and hot in summer, it resembles the climate of the sherry areas of Spain.

**Harvesting.**    Harvesting starts in early August and is finished usually by October 15.    Picking is done either by hand labor or, more recently, by machine.    In hand picking, the grapes are picked into tractor-drawn gondolas, which are dumped into trucks for delivery to the winery.

0097-6156/81/0145-0143$05.00/0
© 1981 American Chemical Society

Machine picking is the preferred method of harvesting, but the vineyard and the variety must be suited to the requirements of the machines so that the machines will harvest efficiently.    Machine-harvesting costs are less than hand picking, but machine harvesting is less efficient in some varieties.    There are some varieties that cannot be picked by machine.    There is no consistent difference in wine quality between the two harvesting methods, at least as far as sherry-type wines are concerned.

**Crushing.**    Crushing is done at the winery in crusher–stemmers that crush the grapes and separate the stems.    Crushed grapes are pumped to fermenting tanks or to prejuicers.    Here there are two different methods of processing the crushed grapes.    Winery A may use only the free-run juice or combine free-run and press juice for fermentation.    Water is added to the pomace, which is fermented, pressed, washed, and repressed to produce distilling material.    This is converted to high proof alcohol for use in wine production.    This method uses energy in distillation and produces high BOD liquid wastes.

Winery B may operate under environmental restrictions or may not be large enough to justify a distillery.    Winery B presses the freshly crushed grapes and uses all the juice in wine production and discards the pressed sweet pomace as a by-product.    On a proof gallon recovered per ton of grapes processed basis, Winery A is more efficient.    However, Winery A must contend with continually escalating boiler fuel costs and must consider still slops disposal costs, whether it be to winery-operated land disposal or to municipal sewer systems.    In either case, energy and environmental considerations are becoming important factors in winery operations.

In both methods, it is important to separate the juice from the pomace as soon as possible to produce a juice low in tannin and harsh polyphenols, which are undesirable in wines for producing sherry (called shermats in the California wine industry).

*Fermentation*

In the alcoholic fermentation of juice to wine, $SO_2$ is added at the crushers at the rate of about one pound per one thousand gallons.    Pectic enzymes may be added to increase juice yields and clarity.    The fermentation is conducted with the native yeast of the grape or various pure culture strains of *Saccaromyces cerevisiae*.    Whether or not yeast cultures are added depends on the quality of the grapes and the winemaker's preferences.    Dehydrated wine yeast is in general use at the beginning of the crushing season.

I do not know of any wineries that use cultures of flor-type yeasts for the alcoholic fermentation.    (Strains of yeast that have a film stage after alcoholic fermentation are called flor types.)    In our winery, we are very careful to isolate the operations where the flor-type yeasts are used.    We also sterilize any residues produced from the flor-type yeasts.    We do not want the flor-type yeasts to become indigenous to our region since they may complicate production of table wines.

Fermentation temperatures are not critical in producing shermat; but, of course, temperatures should be below about 30° C to produce a sound wine. Fermentations are conducted in large tanks, usually over 40,000 gallons. Since very little heat is lost by radiation, cooling is necessary for processing shermats that are fermented to dryness.

**Preparation of Material.** California state regulations specify that wines labeled as dry sherry shall have 0–2.5 percent reducing sugar, standard sherry 2.5–4.0 percent reducing sugar, and sweet or cream sherry 4.0 percent or more reducing sugar. Sherry-type wines produced in California are marketed at 17–21 percent ethanol at present, with most being 17½–18½ percent. Prior to 1974, the limits were 19.5–21 percent ethanol.

The winemaker has several choices in producing the shermat. Some prefer to add spirits to stop the fermentation when it has reached the desired residual sugar level. Others may ferment to dryness and blend back with neutral, sweet, fortified wine material.

Wine spirits used in shermat production should be low (150 mg/L or less in higher-molecular-weight alcohols), but may contain 100 mg/L or more of aldehydes (or heads) without adversely affecting the quality of the wines. A muscat aroma should be avoided in shermat production. Muscat aroma is characteristically sweet like and flowery and is not compatible with sherry aromas, which tend to be dry and oxidized.

After addition of wine spirits, shermats are clarified with bentonite and rough filtered before the sherry conversion processes are started.

An important factor in sherry quality is the pH of the shermat. Berg and Akiyoshi (2) showed that lower pH material produced better sherry aromas. They preferred a material of 3.2 pH in laboratory trials. This low pH is seldom found in commercial shermats. Also, low pH material is more resistant to the sherry baking processes; it takes much longer to convert low pH shermats to sherry.

High pH shermats (3.7 or higher) give smokey, rubbery, or generally unpleasant aromas on baking. High pH materials were responsible for much of the poor sherry-type wines produced in California in the early post-Repeal period.

I prefer a shermat of 3.4–3.6 pH for baking, and pH 3.4 or less for production of submerged-culture flor wines. The pH can be adjusted by addition of acids, by ion exchange in the hydrogen cycle, or by plastering. Plastering is the use of gypsum ($CaSO_4$) while crushing the grapes. A crude gypsum called yeso was used formerly in sherry production in Spain.

The addition of calcium sulfate to the freshly crushed grapes in warm low-acid regions has many advantages. First, of course, it reduces the pH without raising the total acidity, by changing KHTa to $H_2Ta$ (where Ta represents the tartrate radical). The reaction is:

$$CaSO_4 + 2KHTa \rightarrow CaTa + H_2Ta + K_2SO_4$$

A second factor is the effect of the addition of sulfate to the juice. Research workers have found that yeast reduces sulfates to sulfites in amounts from 10 to 30 mg/L during normal fermentation, and in sulfated media, some yeast strains may produce up to 120 mg/L during alcoholic fermentation.  Sulfate also adds a touch of bitterness and saltiness to the taste of wines.

It is interesting to consider that the old traditional warm-region winemakers, in their use of plaster, were adding acid and $SO_2$ to low acid musts just as we do today.

### Production Procedures

In California, sherry-type wines are produced by baking or by the use of submerged cultures of flor-type yeasts in the shermat.

The practice of baking sherries is thought to have been originated by a California winemaker who had to produce some sherry in a short time.  (It is similar to the modern method used for producing madeira in the Madeira Islands.)  Heating accelerated the sherry process.  Over the past twenty years, the baking process has changed from baking at a temperature of 57°–60° C for ten weeks to baking at a temperature of 49° C for four weeks.  A small amount of air also is being used in the process.  Changes in the taste preference of the consumer probably are responsible for the changes in processing.  Present processes produce a lighter-flavored sherry.

Many methods of heating wines for producing baked-type sherry have been used in California, such as storing the cooperage in the sun or in heated rooms, and steam or hot water coils in the tanks.  External heaters of several types also are used, from plate heat exchangers and tube-in-tube heat exchangers to large external pressurized tanks heated to about 81° C.  In the latter, the shermat is kept for only a short time.

Another interesting development in baking sherries is a patent issued to Warkentin (3) covering use of ascorbic acid or other reductive acids that function as reducing agents under anaerobic conditions or as autocatalytic agents under aeration.  This process is said to produce a superior sherry that ages quickly.  This process is energy efficient.

Various methods are used to judge when the baking process is complete.  Color changes attributable to caramelization of sugars and oxidation are used by some winemakers to judge completion of the baking process.  There is a gradual darkening of the color from yellow to light amber.  Others use sensory tests as criteria of completion.  The odor of baked sherries changes markedly shortly after cooling so the samples should be "aged" before tasting.  The desired oxidized–carmelized odor required is the command decision of the winemaker.

One winery uses levels of hydroxymethylfurfural to indicate completion of the baking process.  Hydroxymethylfurfural is formed by dehydration of fructose when heated in an acid solution (such as wine).

In making the drier sherry-type wines by baking, the shermats are baked with about the sugar content at which they will be marketed.   Caramelization of sugar and resultant flavors are an important part of the baked, madeirized odor and flavor of the baked wines.

Some shermats are baked dry (without sugar) for blending purposes.   The cream sherries are usually blends of a lightly baked sweet material and a heavily baked dry material.   This reduces the amount of caramelization.   However, at least one popular cream sherry is produced by baking a very sweet shermat.   After blending, the sweet blends are heated once more to "marry" the components into a balanced wine.

All sherries are improved by aging.   The young baked sherries are strongly flavored and rough in taste.   Oak chips are used commonly in competitive sherry types.   The better wines are stored in fifty-gallon American oak barrels for several months to several years.   American oak is favored because of the stronger aroma and drier taste of wines stored in it.   The richness in flavor imparted by European oak apparently does not fit well into sherry flavors.   It is interesting to note that American oak is favored also by Spanish winemakers.

### The Flor Process

The concept and technique of submerged-culture fermentations to accelerate what were originally surface reactions were first used extensively in the pharmaceutical industry.   It was apparent to enological researchers in several countries that the same principles could be applied to production of flor sherry.

In the traditional Spanish flor process, the flor yeasts grow on the surface of wine in partially filled barrels, that is, in contact with air. The yeast colonies growing on the surface often resemble flowers in shape and give the process its name ("flor" being the Spanish word for flower).

The yeast colonies growing on the surface produce aldehydes, and the development of flor character accompanies the growth of yeast and production of aldehydes.   The complex flavors of Spanish sherries are derived also from a fractional blending and aging procedure called a "solera."   This procedure is fascinating, but it is not at present pertinent to a discussion of California sherry production.   (Only a few small California sherry producers use a solera system of aging.)

The flor process for sherry-type wines long has been of interest to California winemakers because of the unique wines that it produces in Spain and other wine areas of the world.

One of the California pioneers urging flor sherry production was Cruess (4).   On his visits to Spain, Cruess was impressed with the range of types and qualities of Spanish sherries.   He felt that the quality of California sherries could be improved by adoption of Spanish processing methods. These methods did produce good flor-type wines in California, but the film process, as it is used in Spain, is labor-intensive and requires long periods of time with attendant costs, which made it impractical for large-scale use in California.

Our interest in flor was aroused in 1963 when we were selling baked sherry for 50¢ a gallon, wholesale in bond. The Spanish sherries were $5.00 a fifth retail. We felt that the fiftyfold difference in price was interesting, to say the least.

Several articles had been published on submerged-flor processing prior to 1963, and the flor process has been developed and adapted to large-scale operations as a result of research done in Australia, Canada, and the University of California at Davis.

Fornachon (5) in Australia found that a yeast suspension aerated and agitated in an alcoholic solution produced aldehyde. He reported his extensive research on flor sherry production to the Australian Wine Board (6).

Crowther and Truscott (7) in Canada reported they produced flor-type sherry wine by submerged culture. The process is still used there.

Ough and Amerine (8) at Davis showed that a good quality submerged flor could be produced rapidly in pressure vessels and recommended a semicontinuous process where part of the finished flor was removed periodically and replaced with new material.

DeSoto (9) reported on commercial production of submerged flor in a pressurized vessel in California. He found commercial production was more difficult than laboratory scale fermentations. Farafontof (10) found that flor could be produced commercially without the use of pressurized equipment, but at a slower rate than under pressurized conditions.

The bulk flor process as we use it is as follows:

The shermat should be a clean, neutral white wine. The ethanol content of the shermat can be 12–16.5 percent. However, 14.5 percent is a good level. Lower ethanol wines are susceptible to acetification. At the upper limits, the flor yeasts do not grow or grow very slowly. The pH can be from 2.9 to 3.6. We have found 3.2 is a good average. At a lower pH, yeast develops very slowly. At over 3.4 pH, there is a risk of the growth of lactic acid bacteria.

The $SO_2$ content can be from very low to 150 mg/L, with 100 mg/L being satisfactory. Lower $SO_2$ levels risk acetification. Above 150 mg/L, yeasts do not grow in 14.5 percent ethanol wines. The temperature can vary widely—from 14° to 24° C with 18° C being a good operating level. At lower temperatures, the process is very slow. At elevated temperatures, the yeast becomes inactive. Elevated temperatures also favor acetification.

The physical condition of the material should be brilliant. The process is adaptable to any size of container. We have used 5000-gallon to 60,000-gallon tanks and we see no reason why any convenient size tank could not be used successfully.

The shermat is inoculated with an active culture of *Saccharomyces beticus* or similar flor yeast.   [As of 1981, this will be classified as *S. cerevisiae*, Ed.]   Dehydrated flor yeast is not acclimated to ethanol and must be fermented to produce a yeast that will grow in 14.5 percent ethanol media.

Oxygen is supplied to the shermat as oxygen gas or by aeration with air. We use porcelain sparger tubes to secure small bubbles and supply about one volume of air per volume of wine per day.   Bubble size is very important.   There is a ratio of about one to twenty in comparing the surface area of a volume of air in bubbles of 10-mm-diameter compared with the same volume of air in bubbles of 0.5-mm-diameter.   There is also a time factor of about one to four.   Small bubbles do not rise as fast as larger bubbles and so are exposed to the liquid for a longer period of time.   Overall, the air in smaller bubbles has nearly eighty times the exposure to the liquid as the air in larger bubbles.   Excessive aeration will strip the aldehydes from the shermat.

The yeasts are kept suspended by suitable agitation; the yeast cells must be kept in contact with the oxygenated shermat.

We have found that turbidity measurements can be used as a routine test to keep track of the yeast cell population.   Fermentations routinely were examined microscopically for cell count and viability.   We use a 1% methylene blue stain to differentiate viable and dead yeast cells.   The dead cells take the stain.

Yeast cell counts vary greatly during the course of a fermentation.   In the latter stages of a flor fermentation, the yeast agglomerates into clumps of three up to several hundred cells and settles out in spite of agitation.   There are generally about two plateaus in aldehyde production versus time graphs.   These may be where new generations of yeast are developing, where less resistant cells are dying, or where the yeasts are acclimating to higher levels of aldehyde.

In all fermentations, a maximum in cell count is reached and cell count declines just before, or in conjunction with, the maximum in aldehyde content.   The maximum aldehyde level is from about 750 mg/L to 1200 mg/L.   It is interesting that the slope of the aldehyde curve—how fast aldehydes develop—appears to be an individual constant for each fermentation.   The curve may be interrupted periodically, but it will go back to the same slope after the interruptions.   Fermentations that develop aldehyde most rapidly also reach the highest levels of aldehyde.

An active flor fermentation that is deprived of its oxygen supply immediately ceases aldehyde production.

The combination of oxygen and flor yeast in a suitable shermat results in yeast growth and production of acetaldehyde.   The wine passes through many taste and aroma phases during this process.   The process is very flexible and can be used to produce anything from a pleasantly aromatic wine at 200 mg/L aldehyde to a strongly flavored flor sherry at 700 mg/L aldehyde to an intensely flavored flor with a long aftertaste at 1000 mg/L aldehyde.

After the process is completed to the winemaker's satisfaction, the wine is fortified to 17–19 percent ethanol, is clarified, and the yeasts are filtered out.    The addition of ethanol seems to intensify the flor aroma.

The light flor wines may be blended with baked sherry-type wines or aged as is.    The heavier, higher aldehyde wines are used in baked sherry-type blends to improve their short aftertaste and to give more complexity and character to blends.    There appears to be an opportunity to produce and market a low alcohol, very light flor as an appetizer wine.    This has a low aldehyde content, under 14 percent ethanol, and has a light, almost fruity aroma.    This is a very pleasing light wine with possibilities as a new wine type for California.

Fornachon (6) states that a successful surface-film flor requires a surface area of nine to thirteen square inches per gallon.    This relationship obviously would limit the depth of a successful surface flor container.

Ough (11) reported that several nonfilm-forming varieties of S. cerevisiae will produce acetaldehyde and flor character, but that these nonfilm yeast fermentations developed off flavors on aging.

Webb and Noble (12) reported on the aroma constituents of the four general types of sherry.    Fino, oloroso, submerged culture, and baked sherries have significant differences in aroma constituents.    Many constituents were identified, but much more research is needed to correlate volatile components with sensory perceptions.

Castor and Archer (13) investigated the amino acid requirements of flor yeast growth and suggested more work should be done since the experiments were not conclusive.    This is still true.    Submerged flor production is still an art.    All of the necessary conditions for a successful flor fermentation are not known, or at least they have not been published.    We still have failures for unknown reasons.

Webb et al. (14) reported on a comparison of aromas of flor sherry, baked sherry, and submerged-culture sherry.    The same compounds were found in all three types, but baked sherry alone contained 2-furaldehyde.

In later investigations, Galetto et al. (15) found eight strongly flavored acetals in wines from submerged flor culture.    They suggest that the acetal to aldehyde ratio as a criterion of quality should be modified to reflect the species as well as the concentration of the acetal.

Recently Webb (16) explained the aromas of film sherries as by-products of an incomplete metabolic sequence where ethanol is being metabolized by film yeasts to carbon dioxide and water.    Webb also refers to Pasteur's *Etudes sur le Vin*, published in 1866, as the basis of the specialization of zymology, which recognizes different types of film formers that yield the wines of the Jerez district of Spain, *Vins jaunes* of the Jura region of France, and the flor wines of Australia, South Africa, the Soviet Union, and California.

Figure 1 shows the development of acetaldehyde content during twenty-five days of submerged culture without removal or addition.    The conditions in Figure 2 are the same, except that 50 percent of the wine was

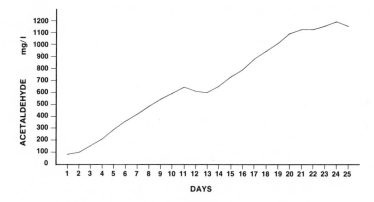

Figure 1. *Acetaldehyde content of a submerged culture over twenty-five days*

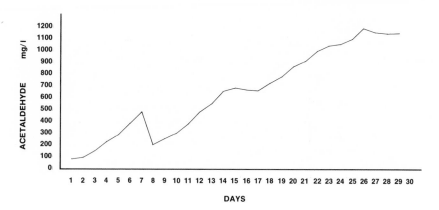

Figure 2. *Acetaldehyde content over twenty-nine days with a 50 percent transfer on the eighth day*

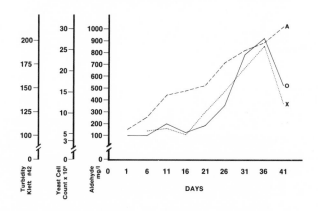

Figure 3. *Acetaldehyde, turbidity, and yeast count in a forty-one day period*

removed on day 8 and replaced with shermat.    Figure 3 indicates the turbidity (a measure of the yeast count), actual yeast count, and acetaldehyde content in a submerged culture tank over a forty-one-day period.    Yeast growth and acetaldehyde content during a seventy-day submerged culture are shown in Figure 4.    Note the 50 percent removals and additions on the thirty-eighth and fortieth days.

In conclusion, flor sherry is being produced successfully in California on a commercial scale by the submerged-culture process.

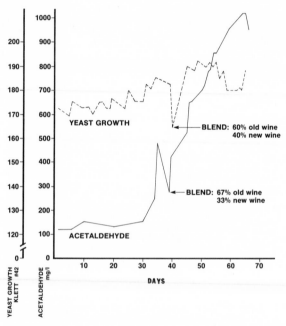

Figure 4. *Acetaldehyde and turbidity during a seventy-day period, with 50 percent transfers on the thirty-eighth and fortieth days*

### Literature Cited

1. Amerine, M. A.; Winkler, J. A. "Composition and Quality of Musts and Wines of California Grapes," *Hilgardia* **1944**, *15*, 493–675.
2. Berg, H. W.; Akiyoshi, M. "Tasting of Experimental Sherries," Report to TAC, Wine Institute: San Francisco, CA, Aug., 1956.
3. Warkentin, H. U.S. Patent 3 518 039, 1967.
4. Cruess, W. V. "Investigations of the Flor Sherry Process," *Calif. Agric. Exp. Stat. Bull.* **1948**, *710*, 1–40.
5. Fornachon, J. C. M. "The Accumulation of Acetaldehyde by Suspensions of Yeast," *Aust. J. Biol. Sci.* **1953**, *6*, 222–223.
6. Fornachon, J. C. M. "Studies on the Sherry Flor," Australian Wine Board: Adelaide, Australia, 1953.

7.  Crowther, R. F.; Truscott, J. H. L. "Flor type Canadian Sherry Wine," *Rep. Ont. Hort. Exp. Stat.* **1955–56,**72–83.
8.  Ough, C. S.; Amerine, M. A. "Studies on Aldehyde Production Under Pressure Oxygen and Agitation," *Am. J. Enol.* **1958,** *9,* 111–112.
9.  DeSoto, R.T. "Commercial Production of Flor Sherry by the Submerged Culture Method," Report to TAC, Wine Institute: San Francisco, CA, Aug., 1961.
10.  Farafontof, A. "Studies to Determine the Feasibility of Flor Sherry Production in California," *Am. J. Enol. Vitic.* **1964,** *15,* 130–133.
11.  Ough, C. S. "Aldehyde Formation in Submerged Cultures on Non-Film Forming Species of *Saccharomyces* such as Wine Yeast and Bread Yeast," *Appl. Microbiol.* **1960,** *9,* 316–319.
12.  Webb, A. D.; Noble, A. "Aroma of Sherry Wines," *Biotechnol. Bioeng.* **1966,** *18,* 939–952.
13.  Castor, J. G. B.; Archer, T. E. "Nutrient Requirements for Growth of the Sherry Flor Yeast *Saccharomyces beticus,*" *Appl. Microbiol.* **1957,** *5,* 55–60.
14.  Webb, A. D.; Kepner, R. E.; Galetto, W. G. "Comparison of the Aromas of Flor Sherry, Baked Sherry, and Submerged Culture Sherry," *Am. J. Enol. Vitic.* **1964,** *15,* 1–10.
15.  Galetto, W. G.; Webb, A. D.; Kepner, R. E. "Identification of Some Acetals in an Extract of Submerged Culture Flor Sherry," *Am. J. Enol. Vitic.* **1964,** *17,* 11–19.
16.  Webb, A.D. "Enology as an Interdisciplinary Emerging Science," *Interdiscip. Sci. Rev.* **1980,** *5*(1), 1–16.

RECEIVED July 22, 1980.

# Wine Production in Washington State

JOEL K. KLEIN

Chateau Ste. Michelle, Woodinville, WA 98072

The beginnings of the grape and wine industry in Washington State are found in the Puget Sound area. According to Somers (1), the first grapes were planted by Lambert Evans in 1872 on Stretch Island. By 1890, a grape nursery had been established in the same area by Adam Eckert. Because of the relatively high rainfall of thirty-six inches per year in western Washington, these vineyards were confined to *Vitis labrusca* cultivars.

## Other Areas

In contrast to the relatively wet areas of western Washington State, the area to the east of the Cascade Mountain range is a desert region. Average annual rainfall is less than ten inches per year in the Yakima Valley of south-central Washington. In 1906, the first of a series of irrigation canals was completed in the Yakima Valley. This was the beginning of the large-scale, commercial planting of *V. labrusca* cultivar Concord in Washington State. Today there are almost 22,000 acres of Concord grapes planted in the state.

The remnants of a very old, dry-farmed *V. vinifera* vineyard near Union Gap, in the Yakima Valley, still exist. It is reported to have been planted in the 1880s. The first documented planting of *V. vinifera* grapes in the Yakima Valley were planted in 1930 by W. P. Bridgeman. The first *V. vinifera* wines produced were made by Mr. Bridgeman at the Upland Winery in Sunnyside in 1936. A White Riesling wine was produced for several years before being discontinued.

Subsequent to Repeal, the wine industry in Washington State blossomed to forty-two wineries. Dessert, fruit, and berry wines were a major portion of the production of these facilities. Most of these wineries continued in business until the postwar slump of the late 1940s. In 1950, the first of the current *V. vinifera* vineyards was planted to Grenache and White Riesling cultivars. These were marketed as Grenache Rosé and Johannisberg Riesling. At this early time in Washington State's wine development, there was insufficient interest in varietal wines to sustain their production. Consequently, these grapes were used to produce generic white and rosé wines for a number of years.

0097-6156/81/0145-0153$09.50/0
© 1981 American Chemical Society

**Research and History.**　In 1960, Washington State University began wine grape research under the guidance of Drs. Walter Clore and Charles Nagel. These efforts are continuing today under the guidance of Drs. Mohammed Ahmedullah and Charles Nagel and are expected to be expanded significantly in the next few years.

The current *V. vinifera* table wines offered from the State of Washington have their beginnings in the wines offered by Associated Vintners and Chateau Ste. Michelle in 1967. In 1969, a major revision of the state's liquor laws encouraged a significant increase in the importation of wine into the state. With this came a very rapid increase in the interest in table wines in Washington State. This broadened availability of table wines brought about, in one five-year period in the mid 1970s, an increase in consumption of from 1.5 gallons to 3 gallons (5.68 liters to 11.36 liters) per capita.

Paralleling this interest in *V. vinifera* table wine, a separate industry and market has developed devoted to fruit and berry wines. Sweet loganberry, blackberry, and currant wines have been available from the Northwest for many years. Recent interest has developed for fruit wines such as rhubarb, cherry, and apricot. These newer fruit and berry wines are offered both as aperitif and dry table wines.

Of the 11,474,869 gallons (434,324 hL) of wine sold in Washington State in fiscal 1979, only 5.5 percent were produced by fourteen Washington State wineries.

*Viticulture*

The current interest in wine-grape growing in Washington State is centered in the south-central portion of the state. There is also a small cottage industry beginning in the Puget Sound area. This area is not yet developed and will not be reviewed here. Oregon's wine regions have a similar climate.

South-central Washington is in the rain shadow of the Cascade Mountain range and is a desert. Average annual rainfall is seven to eight inches (18 to 20 cm). Rainfall is illustrated in Figure 1 (2). Therefore, irrigation is a necessity for the growth of vineyards. Table I shows the average monthly minimum and maximum temperatures as well as the average monthly rainfall.

Because of the very cold winter temperatures that are possible, consideration must be given to their potentially disastrous effect in choosing the cultural practices prescribed for vineyard management. This single issue, winter hardiness, is the single most important factor in growing *V. vinifera* cultivars in south-central Washington. This will be discussed in greater detail in conjunction with viticultural practices.

To utilize as much of the sun's energy as possible, most of the vineyards in Washington State are planted on south-facing slopes. The benefits of this exposure have been described by Amdur (3). While no advantage

Table I. Average Monthly Rainfall and Minimum and Maximum Temperatures in South Central Washington State (Yakima Valley)

| | Jan. | Feb. | March | April | May | June | July | Aug. | Sept. | Oct. | Nov. | Dec. |
|---|---|---|---|---|---|---|---|---|---|---|---|---|
| Average Monthly Rainfall (inches) | 0.85 | 0.7 | 0.5 | 0.5 | 0.5 | 0.5 | 0.15 | 0.15 | 0.35 | 0.7 | 1.0 | 1.0 |
| Mean temp. (°F) | 30.1 | 36.3 | 44 | 51.1 | 58.7 | 64.9 | 70.4 | 69.3 | 62.7 | 51.3 | 39.8 | 33.3 |
| Minimum temp. (°F) | 5 | 12 | 18 | 25 | 32 | 38 | 42 | 42 | 35 | 28 | 19 | 14 |
| Maximum temp. (°F) | 55 | 60 | 67 | 77 | 88 | 94 | 98 | 97 | 91 | 78 | 64 | 65 |

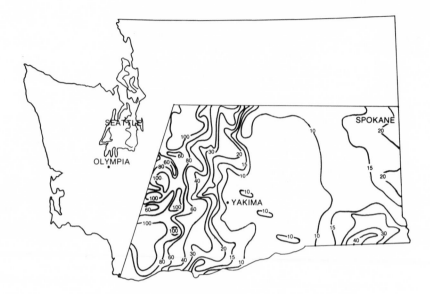

*Figure 1. Distribution of rainfall in Washington (in inches)*

exists for any particular slope during cloudy weather, in this desert environment there is very little cloud cover during the growing season. This is illustrated in Figure 2. These benefits are illustrated in Tables II and III, which show the increased amount of horizontal radiation received with increasing slope angle and the greater effectiveness of a 15° slope at more northerly latitudes, respectively. In addition to using south-facing slopes wherever

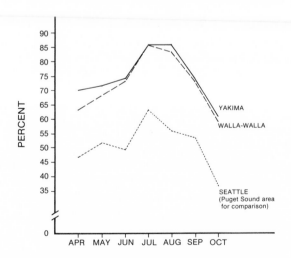

*Figure 2. Mean percentage of possible sunshine by months*

Table II. Percentage of Horizontal Radiation Received
by Various Slopes at 45° N

| Slope | June 21 | September 23 |
|---|---|---|
| S 15° | 107.0 | 122.5 |
| S 10° | 105.3 | 115.7 |
| S 5° | 103.0 | 108.2 |
| level | 100 | 100 |
| N 5° | 96.3 | 91.2 |
| N 10° | 91.7 | 81.2 |
| N 15° | 86.5 | 70.7 |

possible, Washington, because of its more northern latitude, literally has more day per day. It has been pointed out by Wagner (4) that in June, during the period of rapid cell division in the fruit, Washington State has 17.4 hours of daylight while California averages only 15.8 hours of daylight per day (*see* Figure 3). Coupling this with the understanding that increases in sugar are dependent upon temperature and light reception, while decreases in acidity are almost entirely dependent upon temperature (5), it is easier to understand why, in its 160- to 200-day growing season, Washington State tends to produce *V. vinifera* fruit of both high sugar and high acidity.

It is generally agreed among researchers in Washington State that the difference in day length has a marked effect on the resultant fruit. The degree to which this affects fruit quality and precisely which characteristics are affected by the longer day length from bloom until well after veraison are not clear.

In regard to the high acidity found in many of Washington's *V. vinifera* grapes at harvest, Nagel (6) has shown that, in general, in musts the malate concentrations were higher than in the same varieties in California, whereas tartrate levels were very similar. The effect of this is most noticeable in red wines when they undergo malo-lactic fermentation. Because of the large percentage of the acidity contributed by the malate, its conversion to lactate can reduce the acidity and increase the pH dramatically.

Table III. Radiation Effectiveness of Slope in Various Latitudes (150° Slope)
(Radiation on Horizontal Surface = 100)

| Latitude | June 21 | | September 23 | |
|---|---|---|---|---|
| | N Slope | S Slope | N Slope | S Slope |
| 50° | 83.7 | 109.5 | 65.7 | 127.5 |
| 45° | 86.5 | 107.0 | 70.7 | 122.5 |
| 40° | 89.0 | 104.2 | 75.0 | 118.2 |
| 35° | 91.5 | 101.5 | 78.8 | 114.5 |
| 30° | 93.5 | 99.5 | 81.7 | 111.5 |

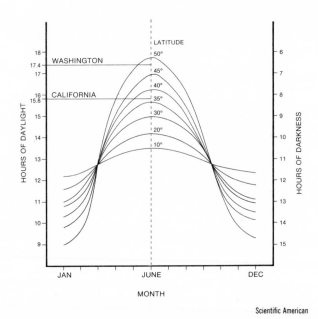

*Figure 3. Hours of daylight and darkness in California and Washington (4)*

In regard to the composition of Washington grapes and wine, Nagel and his co-workers have done a considerable amount of research in this area (7–15). Figures 4 and 5 illustrate ten-year minimum and maximum temperature isotherms for Washington. Figure 6 illustrates the degree–day as described by Winkler et al. (5). These illustrative figures for Washington State are temperature and heat summations (degree–days) from Ledwitz (2).

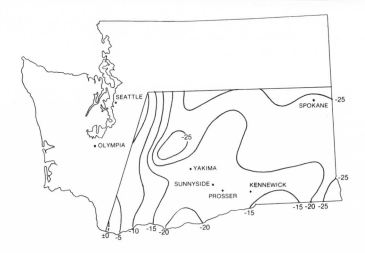

*Figure 4. Minimum temperature isotherms for Washington*

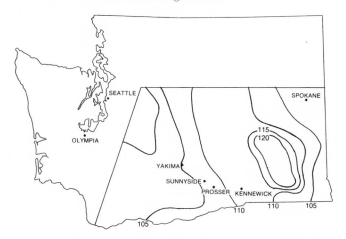

*Figure 5. Maximum temperature isotherms for Washington*

Soils are loessial sandy loams in most areas, with some alluvial deposits. It is not uncommon to find hard calcarious layers at depths of ten to forty inches. These require fracturing before planting for both water and root penetration. In many places, the soil is underlaid with basalt. Many areas show basaltic outcroppings. Yet, because of the nature of the weather, these are not degraded sufficiently to produce volcanic soils in any significant amount. Soil depths vary from less than twenty inches in some vineyards to more than ten feet in others.

The low levels of rainfall in south-central Washington make irrigation a necessity. Rill, solid-set overhead sprinkler, drip, and center-pivot irrigation systems are all being used to some extent in the vineyards of the Northwest.

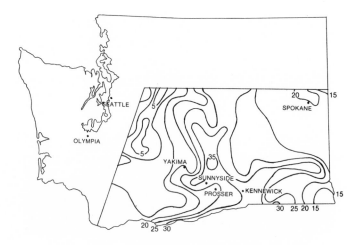

*Figure 6. Heat summations for Washington (× 1/100)*

Rill, or furrow irrigation, is being used less and less as new vineyards are established.    The solid-set overhead sprinkler is the most widely accepted system in V. *vinifera* vineyards today.    The newer systems are on a forty-eight by fifty-foot diamond pattern.    A 9/64 orifice operating at 40–60 psig is used almost ubiquitously.    An exception is the end sprinkler on the upwind edges of vineyards, where larger orifices often are used.

Some vineyardists are installing drip irrigation systems.    Insufficient data exist to assess their utility.    One major vineyard is investigating the possible use of a combination of solid-set sprinkler and drip system.    The solid set would be used to maintain a cover crop and for applications of waterborne pesticides, herbicides, and nutrients.    The drip system would be employed for deep irrigation of the grape vines.    Such a combination system is not yet installed in a vineyard.

Center-pivot or "circle" irrigation is new to the wine industry.    The first vineyards were planted under a center-pivot system in 1978.    Figures 7 and 8 illustrate this system.    The towers are approximately 130 feet apart.    The entire pivot system is one-quarter of a mile long.    This will irrigate 138 acres of the 160 acres in the one-quarter square mile area the system occupies.    The area between circles is not lost because of the overlapping or staggered arrangement of the circles.    The remaining area between circles is used for equipment storage, tanks for nutrient and pesticide additions to the irrigation system, utility connections, and so forth.    The wheels track true in a path less than two feet wide.    The variable-speed drive motor on the wheels allows the operator to complete a revolution in from eight to thirty-six hours.    The orifices are varied in size along the boom to produce a uniform irrigation.    The maximum rate of irrigation is 0.48 inches of water per twenty-four hours.    This level of irrigation may be a limiting factor in the use of center-pivot irrigation.

*Figure 7. Center pivot or circle irrigation*

*Figure 8. Center pivot or circle irrigation*

In hot weather, evaporation pans lose up to one-half inch of water per day.    Vineyards with cover crops lose up to 75 percent of evaporation pan losses.    Up to 25 percent of the irrigation water can be lost through wind drift and evaporation.    This results in a situation that is within 4 percent of a theoretical break-even input and output.    To accomplish this break-even situation requires constant, twenty-four hour a day irrigation.    While this concern is yet to be tested, past history with other crops has proved eminently successful.    In 1978, 500 acres of *V. vinifera* grapes were planted under center-pivot irrigation.    Since that time, an additional 1500 acres have been planted under center-pivot systems, so that today 2000 of the state's estimated 4500 acres of *V. vinifera* are utilizing center-pivot irrigation.

A major advantage of this method of irrigation is cost.    Solid-set sprinkler irrigation is estimated to cost in excess of $1100 per acre, or $151,800 for 138 acres.    A center-pivot irrigation system is estimated at less than $60,000 for the same 138 acres.    In both instances, an adequate water source at the site is presumed.

In the past, it was considered necessary to apply thirty inches of water to a vineyard each year.    Today, these requirements range as low as twenty-four to twenty-six inches per year.    It has been only in the past few years that the grape growing community has begun to incorporate the data from evaporation pans, hygrothermographs, anemometers, and soil moisture measurements into its irrigation decisions.

Irrigation is begun in April to aid in herbicide activation and to bring the soil moisture to capacity wherever possible.    Soil depth and method of irrigation will determine the frequency of irrigation. Rill systems may be applied only three times in a season. Solid-set sprinklers may be used as often as every two weeks. It is common practice to stop irrigation in mid August to allow the soil to begin to dry out. This is done so that as harvest is completed the soil moisture is at such a low level that it helps induce dormancy in the grape vines.

The drying out of the soil is assisted by a cover crop planted in mid row. The most popular cover crop is creeping red fescue. This grass is low growing and needs little attention. Furthermore, it goes dormant when the soil is dry and recovers rapidly when irrigated. In fact, it is not uncommon to apply shallow irrigations through September in vineyards with red fescue to keep it growing. A cover crop helps reduce vine damage and soil loss through high winds blowing the sandy loam soil. Wolfe (16) has stated that the cover crop acts as an insulator and assists in protecting vine roots from winter cold damage.

Another factor that can significantly affect the grape vines' ability to withstand cold winter temperatures is the soil moisture content. To gain the significant benefit of the heat of fusion of water (1436 cal/mol) wherever possible, a postharvest irrigation to a depth of two to three feet is applied. Areas that rely on irrigation canals often are denied this protection because of the water in the canals being shut off prior to the vineyardist's need for it.

The need for winter protection of V. vinifera also has had an influence on vine training techniques. Until the early 1970s, the most common pruning system employed was an adaptation of a Soviet development known as the "Fan System." This system uses four primary trunks per vine, each brought up from ground level. These were tied to a two-wire vertical trellis supported by posts of four to ten inches (10 to 25 cm) diameter every twenty-four feet (7.3 m). The wires were located at thirty-six and sixty inches (0.9 and 1.5 m). Two trunks were tied in an arch to each of these wires. A fan-trained vine is illustrated in Figure 9. Each fall the vines were spur pruned to from 60 to 100 buds (buds per spur varied markedly from vineyard to vineyard) per vine. When pruning was complete, the vines were cut free of the trellis and laid on the ground in the vine row. They then were covered with soil from mid row. As vineyard size grew, it was no longer feasible to continue this practice of insulating the grape vines. As an alternative, the vines were left on the trellis and soil was mounted up around the base of the trunks to a height of twenty inches (0.5 m). In the event of a hard freeze, it was felt that this soil mound would protect dormant buds in the trunks that, in the event of dieback of the upper trunk, would push and allow rapid reestablishment of the vineyard. Wolfe (17) feels hilling is beneficial to one- and two-year-old vines and that the benefit to older vines is insufficient to justify the time and expense required.

The most hardy varieties include White Riesling, Gewürztraminer, Pinot noir, and perhaps Chardonnay. Least hardy are the Grenache, Sauvignon blanc, and perhaps Cabernet Sauvignon. The Sémillon, Chenin blanc, and

*Figure 9.  Fan-trained vine*

Merlot are intermediate.   It should be noted that hardiness is very dependent on cultural practices and environment.   Excess yields or vigor can
greatly reduce hardiness.   Proper manipulation of water, nitrogen, and crop
can greatly increase hardiness.   It is Wolfe's (18) opinion that cultural manipulation under our climatic conditions will minimize differences in hardiness
attributable to genetic factors; that is, hardiness between varieties is more
directly physiological rather than genetic in nature.

   A large percentage of the new vineyards are being established with
single-trunk, cordon-trained vines.   The vine spacing is being reduced from
the former eight by ten feet (2.44 × 3.05 m) to six by ten feet (1.83 × 3.05
m).   Trellising now is utilizing seven-foot (2.13-m) stakes at every other
vine.   The stakes are buried two feet (0.61 m) in the ground with a wire
strung at forty-six inches (1.17 m).   At the top of the stake, an eighteen-inch
(0.46-m) crossarm fourteen inches (0.36 m) above the cordon wire allows the
shoots to be caught, even in some of the windy vineyard locations.   This wide
spacing also assists in achieving a spreading of the foliage for better exposure
to the sun.   It is felt that, as these vineyards mature, modification of the
pruning systems will be required.   Varieties such as Gewürztraminer and
Sauvignon blanc have growth and cropping habits that may require a modified
cane-pruning technique.   Wolfe (16) has suggested the following number of
buds to be left at pruning: thirty-five to forty-five for Chenin blanc, Grenache,
and Sémillon; forty to fifty for Merlot and Muscat blanc; fifty to sixty for
Cabernet Sauvignon, White Riesling, Chardonnay, Pinot noir, and Gewürztraminer; and sixty to eighty for Sauvignon blanc.   These recommendations
are for mature vineyards.   Wolfe (18) has summarized the varietal characteristics of the *V. vinifera* wine varieties grown in Washington State as follows:

Cabernet Sauvignon: vigorous grower with moderate yields (3–6 tons/acre). Matures midseason to late midseason (mid October). Performs best on south- or southwest-facing slopes in warmer areas (recommend 2800 or more heat units). Best quality seems to be associated with heavier soils (silt loams). Ranked moderately cold-tender of V. *vinifera* varieties because of extreme vigor under high moisture and fertility conditions. However, established vines recover well from damage because of vigor.

Merlot: moderate vigor with higher yields than Cabernet Sauvignon (4–8 tons/acre). Matures early midseason (late September–early October). Fruit has a tendency to dehydrate on the vine when mature, resulting in high sugar content. Very difficult to machine harvest. Because of early maturity, adaptable to a greater range of slopes and soil types than Cabernet Sauvignon. Considered moderately cold-hardy of V. *vinifera* varieties.

Pinot noir and Gamay Beaujolais: low to moderate vigor (GB) with good yields (4–6 tons/acre). Buds tend to be very fruitful, producing three clusters per shoot. Matures early season (late September). Moderate to good cold hardiness (best of reds commercially grown). Because of hardiness, productivity, and early maturation, Pinot noir is adapted to a wide range of Washington's soils and microclimates. However, fruit quality has not been good for red wine production. This is probably attributable to cultural practices and selection of sites with excessive heat.

Grenache: very vigorous grower producing erratic crops (2–7 tons/acre). Grenache is most cold-sensitive commercial variety and frequent dieback is responsible for cropping behavior. Should be grown on the warmest sites (more than 3000 heat units) with longest growing season. Recommend light soils of moderate depth to control vigor. It matures in late midseason.

Other reds: there are several other reds that possibly could be grown in Washington. These include Petite Sirah, Malbec, Cabernet franc, and Limberger. Red varieties tend to be late maturing with high acids and more cold-sensitive than white. They should be planted in the warmer sites under low fertility conditions.

White Riesling: moderate vigor with good yields (5–8 tons/acre). Matures late season. Most cold-hardy of V. *vinifera* varieties and adaptable to a wide range of climatic and soil conditions. Buds are extremely fruitful (often four clusters per shoot), which can lead to overcropping. It is the most widely planted vinifera in the state. Sensitive to *Botrytis cinerea*.

Chenin blanc: very vigorous and prolific yielder (6–12 tons/acre). High acid, late maturing variety (end of October–early November). Although moderately cold-hardy, it is subject to damage because of vigor and a tendency to overcrop.   Should be grown on warm sites with low fertility.   Recovers well after damage.

Sémillon: vigorous with high yields (6–10 tons/acre).   Also, moderately cold-hardy, but tends to suffer damage from overcropping.   Midseason maturity.   Recovers well from cold injury.  Relatively easy variety for farmer to grow and is adaptable to a wide range of conditions.   Generally free of insect pests and fungal diseases, somewhat susceptible to thrips.

Gewürztraminer: low to moderate vigor with low to moderate yields (3–6 tons/acre).   Matures in early season.   Tends to be very low in acid and should be grown in the coolest sites (less than 2500 heat units).   Comparable with White Riesling for cold hardiness.   Because of hardiness and early maturity can be planted on less desirable sites (north slopes, fertile ground, etc.).   Because of low yields and bushy growth, may require cane pruning. Free of fungal diseases, it is somewhat susceptible to leaf hoppers.

Chardonnay: moderate vigor and yields (3–6 tons/acre).   It can be as hardy as White Riesling, but has behaved erratically. Although of early to early midseason maturity, the variety tends to be high in acid.   Recommend warm sites, possibly with western exposure.   This variety is very prone to powdery mildew.   Suggest low fertility conditions to keep vine open to combat acid and mildew.

Sauvignon blanc: very vigorous with moderate yields (3–5 tons/acre).   Midseason maturity.   Second most cold-sensitive variety after Grenache.   Young vines appear particularly cold-sensitive, with improved tolerance with vine age.   Suggest warm sites with low fertility sandy soils.

Other whites: many other whites could be grown in Washington.   Main deterrent is consumer acceptability (marketing).   Growers anticipate planting as many of the new German varieties in the future, particularly in low-heat-unit sites.

A problem that is somewhat unique to the vineyardists of the Northwest is 2,4–D damage.   This is a herbicide that is used widely by the wheat industry. Contamination of vineyards by herbicide drift or other means can be devastating. *V. vinifera* Caberet Sauvignon and Sauvignon blanc appear to be least affected while Gewürztraminer, Pinot noir, and White Riesling are most sensitive.

### *Harvesting*

The harvest season in Washington State is somewhat shorter than in California.   It generally begins during the third week of September.   To avoid potential damage or losses through frost or freeze damage, it is necessary to complete the harvest no later than the first week of November.   Wolfe

(19) has projected the approximate dates of harvest for popular V. *vinifera* cultivars in south-central Washington State. These are shown in Table IV.

The growing conditions, weather, and day length, previously described, combine to form a set of conditions at harvest time that are often quite different from those found in California vineyards. It is sometimes necessary to delay the harvest of certain varieties to the upper limit of the desired soluble solids content to allow the total acidity of the fruit to be reduced to the desired level. This results in a wine with a relatively high total acidity and potentially with a high ethanol content as well.

The picking of the fruit is done both by hand and by mechanical harvesters. Where mechanical harvesters are used, it is often in conjunction with field crushing equipment. The hand-picked fruit is picked into lug boxes containing 36 pounds (16.33 kg) of grapes or into half bins, which hold 400 pounds (181.41 kg) of grapes. These half bins are approximately four feet (1.22 m) and one foot (0.27 m) deep. These are stacked five high on a tractor trailer for transport to the winery. Utilization of these shallow half bins prevents the grapes from being crushed by the weight of the fruit in them. This virtually eliminates juicing and thereby reduces the potential for oxidation of the juice prior to receipt by the winery.

The cool nighttime temperatures and the relatively cool daytime temperatures during harvest yield fruit at the winery generally below 60° F (15.56° C). Ough and Berg (20) have shown that damage through oxidation caused by polyphenoloxidase is not a problem at temperatures below 72° F (22.22° C).

The pivotal striker-type of mechanical harvester has been used during the past five years in some Washington vineyards. The development of the horizontal impulse-type mechanical harvesters has caused some rethinking in regard to training practices in Washington vineyards. The majority of the older vineyards are on post and wire trellises consisting of a four-inch (10-cm) or larger diameter post, spaced on twenty-four-foot (7.32-m) spacings with

**Table IV. Projected Harvest Dates for Popular *Vitis vinfera* Cultivars in South Central Washington State (19)**

| | 15 Sep. | 20 Sep. | 30 Sep. | 10 Oct. | 20 Oct. | 30 Oct. | 9 Nov. |
|---|---|---|---|---|---|---|---|
| Chardonnay | | | — | — | | | |
| Chenin blanc | | | | | | — | — |
| Gewürztraminer | | — | — | — | | | |
| Muscat blanc | — | — | — | | | | |
| Sauvignon blanc | | | — | | | | |
| Semillon | | | | | — | — | — |
| White Riesling | | | | | — | — | — |
| Cabernet Sauvignon | | | | | — | — | — |
| Grenache | | | | | — | — | — |
| Merlot | — | — | — | — | — | | |
| Pinot noir | — | — | — | — | | | |

wires at thirty-six and sixty inches (0.91 and 1.52 m).   Many of the plantings of the last two years have utilized a stake and wire rather than a post and wire system to permit future use of the horizontal impulse-type mechanical harvesters.   These newer vineyards have ten-foot (3.05-m) rows and six feet (1.83 m) between vines in row, as previously described.

**Mechanical Harvesting.**   Where mechanical harvesting is used, if the winery is in close proximity to the vineyards, the grapes may be discharged from the harvester into lines, full bins.   These full bins are approximately four feet by three feet (1.22 m × 0.91 m) and have a plastic liner in them and a cover that is put on after they are filled.   If the grapes are to be hauled any distance, a crusher–stemmer is transported through the vineyard parallel to the harvester and receives the fruit directly from the harvester.   The crusher–stemmer discharges its must into a closed, stainless steel tank, which is carried directly below the crusher–stemmer.   These tanks may be picked up and dropped in the vineyard from the carrier upon which the crusher–stemmer is mounted.   These stainless steel transport tanks are four feet (1.22 m) wide and eight feet (2.44 m) long and domed on top.   They very much resemble a large mailbox.   On the top of them, at one end, is a six-inch (15.24 cm) diameter door and on the other end, a fifteen-inch (38 cm) diameter manway.   Prior to use, these tanks are inspected and filled with carbon dioxide gas.   They then are transported to the field and distributed with a large fork truck.   As needed, they are picked up by the crusher–stemmer and carried through the field where the grapes are discharged from the crusher–stemmer directly into the tank through the fifteen-inch (38 cm) manway.   As the must fills the tank, liquid sulfur dioxide is metered in so that the full tank contains an average $SO_2$ content of 80 mg/L.   To take advantage of the cool nighttime temperatures, mechanical harvesting to date generally has been confined to the hours from midnight to 10 A.M.

Use of the 920-gallon (34.82-hL) transport tanks for the must permits the winery to use these tanks for maceration of the juice in contact with the skins and pulp.   This is accomplished by allowing these tanks to stand for as many hours as is deemed appropriate for skin contact prior to transferring the must to dejuicing tanks and subsequently pressing.

While maintaining a picking crew for hand picking is always an effort, doing so in Washington is particularly difficult.   In most of the winegrowing regions of the world, the major agricultural endeavor during harvest is the harvesting of grapes.   In Washington, the grape harvest coincides with the apple harvest, a major industry in this area.   The future will see more and more mechanical harvesting as well as mechanization of other aspects of vineyard management.

### Crushing

The Garolla-type crusher–stemmers are used widely in this viticultural area.   They are employed in a variety of sizes—very small ones, which are used in the field in conjunction with mechanical harvesters, to medium or large crushers used at the wineries. The addition of $SO_2$ is done at the crusher in almost all wineries. Most wineries prepare a solution from either potassium metabisulfite or liquid $SO_2$ and add this at the crusher. In some cases, potassium metabisulfite crystals are sprinkled over the grapes prior to being crushed. The field crushing units use liquid $SO_2$. This is measured into a high pressure glass cylinder and then metered into the portable receiving tanks as the grape must is crushed into the tanks. The $SO_2$ levels used vary from winery to winery. Most wineries are adding 50–70 mg/L $SO_2$ to sound grapes and up to 100 mg/L $SO_2$ when the grapes show some signs of mold or degradation. There has been a trend at some larger wineries to employ lower levels of $SO_2$ addition at the crusher. Levels in the range of 20–50 mg/L have been utilized. Current thinking is that minimum levels of 40–50 mg/L should be added to the fresh must.

An exception to the full utilization of the Garolla crusher–stemmer is the case of V. *vinifera* cultivar Pinot noir. In many wineries with this variety, the stems that are separated from the grape by the crusher–stemmer are added back to the must. In general, the entire amount of stems removed from the grapes is not returned to the must. Rather, a measured percentage is added back. If the stems are chopped into small pieces, a level on the order of 10–30 percent generally is added back. However, up to 80 percent chopped stems have been returned to the must by one winery. Where whole stems are added back to the must, up to 100 percent of the stems have been utilized by some wineries.

## Dejuicing

For the production of white wine, it is almost universally accepted that a relatively clear juice of 0.5–2.0 percent suspended solids is desired for fermentation. This is achieved by separating the juice from the skins, pulp, and seeds. Many of the small wineries use a horizontal basket press to receive their fresh must. These presses utilize either an inflatable bladder or a movable piston to press the crushed grapes. In many cases, the must is pumped directly to these presses from the crusher–stemmer. An exception to this method of operation in small wineries is the case where skin contact is desired. Several wineries will allow maceration for from four hours to twenty-four hours for V. *vinifera* cultivars Chardonnay and Gewürztraimer.

An alternate method, which is used for a large percentage of the white wine made in Washington State, is to pump the fresh must to a dejuicing tank. Many of these are the Winery Systems design (as illustrated in Figure 10). Typically, the musts of the fresh fruity varieties such as White Riesling and Chenin blanc are held in the dejuicing tank only long enough to allow adequate separation of the pulp and juice prior to draining and pressing. As

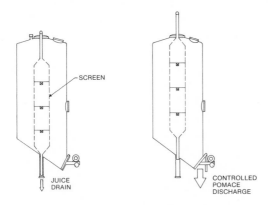

*Figure 10. Dejuicing tanks*

mentioned above, Chardonnay, Gewürztraminer, or heavily botrytized must would be allowed to macerate up to sixteen hours in these dejuicing tanks. These are large stainless steel tanks of approximately ten-foot (3.05-m) diameter with a central screened area of two-foot (0.76-m) diameter running up the center of the tank from the bottom to almost the top of the tank. This design allows the screened portion in the center to receive juice that has had to filter through the solid particles in the must. These skins, seeds, and pulp particles are an adequate enough filter to produce a juice of less than one percent solids as it is drained from the tank. This juice is considered clean enough to be fermented without further treatment to remove additional solids.

The larger wineries utilize horizontal screw presses to remove the remaining juice from the must. The juice collected from the horizontal presses is divided into three fractions. The first section is the juice collected in the unpressurized section of the press. This juice is allowed to settle in refrigerated tanks, racked (decanted), and centrifuged. This juice then is added to the juice that was drained from the same lot of grapes in the dejuicing tanks. These are fermented as a single lot. The juice collected from the intermediate section of the press, where pressure is beginning to build and tannin levels are noticeably higher, is settled in refrigerated tanks, racked, centrifuged, and fermented as a separate lot of wine. The juice collected from the highest pressure section of the presses is interblended among all white varieties and fermented out as a single generic lot of wine.

In using the centrifuge to clarify white juice, it is preferred to achieve solid levels in the discharge of from 0.5 to 2 percent solids. Experience has shown that below 0.5 percent solids, the possibility of incomplete fermentation exists and above 2 percent solids, off odors can develop. The use of centrifuges is increasing in this viticultural region, as it is in other parts of the world.

*Fermentation*

Fermentation in this new viticultural region is carried out in a diverse array of fermentors.    Many small wineries have found they can successfully use jacketed dairy tanks.    These are used either with cold water in the jacket or in conjunction with a small refrigeration system.    One winery is using 500-gallon (18.93-hL) fiberglass open tanks for fermentation of their red wines.    There is one winery using 10,000- and 12,000-gallon (378.5- and 454.2-hL) open-top cement fermentors that have been epoxy lined and fitted with stainless steel cooling coils.    The more modern facilities employ the now common jacketed, closed, stainless steel fermenting tanks.

Refrigeration systems are either freon used to cool glycol, which is pumped to low pressure jacketed tanks, or flooded ammonia systems in high-pressure jackets.    The most innovative system in the state employs ammonia refrigeration pumped directly to the double wall jacketed section of the stainless steel fermentors.    This not only allows very efficient control of the cooling necessary during fermentation but, by an additional steel pipeline to the fermenting area from the compressor, these jackets can be utilized to heat the tanks where their must is received very cold or during malo-lactic fermentation.    This is accomplished by desuperheating the compressed ammonia gas from the compressor and utilizing the fermentor jackets as condensers.    A common suction return line collects this condensate as well as the mixed liquid–vapor return from the jacketed tanks using liquid ammonia for refrigeration.

**Yeasts.**    The yeast strains used are similar to those commonly employed in the California wine industry.    Several of the small *V. vinifera* wine producers utilize a commercially available lyophilized form of the University of California Davis strain #595.    Other strains that are maintained and utilized are Pasteur Institute's white and red wine strains and the Steinberg strain from Geisenheim, Germany.    Sparkling wine has been made in Washington State using either the Berkeley Yeast Laboratory strain from Scott Laboratories or a Moët strain from Épernay, France, for the secondary fermentation.    These yeasts are all strains of *Saccharomyces cerevisiae.*

**Temperature Control.**    Wineries with adequate refrigeration control utilize this capability to maintain their fermentations either by setting a control temperature or by controlling the rate of fermentation. That is, in the case of white wines, if they are fermented by utilizing temperature control, a maximum temperature is set during the early parts of fermentation of 55° F (12.78° C).    If they are using rate of fermentation, they are fermenting their white wine at a rate of 1–1.5 percent sugar per day by controlling the temperature of fermentation as a secondary consideration.    When the fermentation has reduced the sugar content to 6–8 percent soluble solids, the thermostats are raised to 60°–63° F (15.56°–17.22° C) and the fermentation is allowed to proceed at as fast a rate as the yeast can accomplish under the highly competitive conditions that exist for the remaining sugar.   This is done in an effort to ensure that the fermentation will not stick.

Many of the fresh, fruity style white wines of the Northwest are marketed with residual sugar content.   Many of the wineries accomplish this by stopping the fermentation and leaving a certain portion of the sugar from the original must as the sweetening agent in the wine.   This is done for several reasons.   It is felt that a superior wine quality results by using this method.   Additionally, a tendency toward relatively high sugars in the grapes of this region, coupled with the current interest in low alcohol wines, adds to the desirability of leaving a certain portion of the grape sugar unfermented to reduce the alcoholic strength of the wine.

To accomplish this, the smaller wineries will begin racking and chilling the wine two or three days before they plan to stop the fermentation.   As an individual tank approaches a point at which it is felt it should be stopped, the winemaker will taste it several times each day.   When it is felt that the tank has achieved a proper sugar/acid balance for the desired style of wine, the winemaker may add 50–100 mg/LSO$_2$ and rack the wine in an effort to stop the fermentation.   This racking may be followed with a rough filtration, if possible.

In the wineries equipped with a centrifuge, the procedure for stopping the fermentation is slightly different.   As the tank is fermenting normally, when it achieves the desired sugar/acid balance, the cooling jacket thermostat is set to a low temperature to induce an initial slowdown of the fermentation.   The wine is centrifuged as cleanly as possible, as soon as possible.   Suspended solids are generally less than 0.1 percent subsequent to this centrifugation.   Sulfur dioxide is added immediately after centrifugation to further inhibit the activity of any yeast remaining in the wine as well as to prevent oxidation.   These wines generally are maintained in jacketed tanks and held at 40°–50° F (4.44°–10° C).   White wines, which are fermented dry, would receive similar racking and centrifugation treatments subsequent to completion of the fermentation.

**Red Wines.**   The fermentation of red wines is quite different.   To extract color from the skin of the grapes, the bulk of the fermentation is carried out with the solid matter in contact with the juice of the grapes.   During the early stages of the fermentation, it is controlled by assessing the maximum temperature in the fermentor.   The phenolic constituents in wine are more soluble in warm solutions than cool and more soluble in ethanol than water.   Therefore, it is general practice to ferment quite warm during the early stages of fermentation and then begin cooling the fermentation so that, at the time of separation from the pomace, the wine in fermentation has slowed enough so that it can be completed in an unjacketed tank.   The hottest location in the red fermentor is in the center of the tank just above the liquid layer in the "cap."

Because the yeasts used begin to suffer thermal death at temperatures close to 100° F (37.78° C), a maximum fermentor temperature of between 80° and 90° F (26.67° and 32.22° C) is accepted generally. As the fermentation proceeds from an initial 23–24 percent soluble solids, down to approximately 18 percent soluble solids, the temperature rises quite rapidly. The lesser density of the pomace, coupled with the floatation effect caused by the generation of $CO_2$ by the fermentation, causes the pomace to float above the juice. This is known as the "cap."

To extract color from the skins, it is necessary to either wet them with the juice periodically or to remix them with the juice. This apparently subtle difference can make a dramatic difference in the style of wine produced. One Washington winery is using small open fermentors and is punching the cap down in the time-honored traditional fashion. Others either are pumping over by drawing juice off at a racking valve and pumping it over the top of the tank to break up the cap and cause it to remix with the liquid, or are pumping over at a lower rate to just moisten and refresh the cap and allow the fermenting juice to percolate down through the still intact cap. Most Washington wineries are pumping over twice a day, with 20–50 percent of the juice in the fermentor being pumped over each time. During these pump-over periods, the temperature of the juice is measured. One major winery attempts to achieve a maximum temperature of 85° F (29.44° C) in the juice during pump-over as the fermentation proceeds from 18 percent to 12 percent soluble solids.

During this time, the yeasts are in an active growing stage with little or no competition for the sugar available. At 10–12 percent soluble solids, cooling of the must is begun so that at the time of draw-off the temperature is between 70° and 75° F (21.11° and 23.89° C). Some wineries begin draw-off of the wine from the pomace when the fermentation has proceeded to 5–8 percent soluble solids. Others wait until the fermentation has gone to completion before separating the wine from the pomace. Fermentation on the skins generally takes from four to seven days.

In some cases, fermentation is much longer because of the grapes being received in a very cool condition. It is not uncommon to receive V. vinifera cultivar Cabernet Sauvignon at temperatures of 40°–45° F (4.44°–7.22° C). In one instance, the grapes were received in a frozen state so solid that they sounded like marbles going through the crusher–stemmer. Where ammonia is used directly in the jackets of the fermenting tanks, it is the practice of the winery, when grapes are received very cold, to set the jacket on the heating cycle at a temperature of 65° F (18.33° C). Generally, allowing this condition to exist overnight will warm the must sufficiently to allow it to be inoculated with yeast and begin a more typical and rapid fermentation.

Removal of the red pomace from the fermentor is accomplished by a number of different methods. In some wineries, it is shoveled directly to a portable press located in front of the tank. In other cases, the pomace is shoveled into a chain conveyor and, in other cases, either a receding vein or piston pump is used to pump pomace to the presses.   In this latter case, a certain amount of wine is recirculated to the fermentor to keep the cap moist enough to allow it to flow freely to the pump.

The small wineries in this area generally use horizontal basket presses for both red and white pressing.   The larger wineries currently are using horizontal screw presses.   The red press wine is separated into two fractions generally considered soft and hard press wine.   The hard press wine is kept separate and interblended from several lots of fermenting red wine.   This is allowed to ferment to completion as a separate lot of wine.   The soft press may be fermented out as a separate lot of wine or it may be blended back with the free-run wine drained from the fermentor.   In one winery, the soft press has been centrifuged to approximately 5 percent solids and blended immediately with the free-run juice.   It has been deemed necessary by this winery to blend this centrifuged pressed wine with the free-run wine to raise the yeast cell population to a sufficient level to allow the fermentation to proceed to completion rapidly.

Many of the Washington red wines tend to have a high tannin content subsequent to fermentation.   Total phenol content in new red wines in excess of 3000 mg/L, as gallic acid, is not uncommon.   Table V lists flavonoid and total phenol content for *V. vinifera* cultivar Cabernet Sauvignon from 1969 to 1977 produce by one Washington winery.

**Yeast Cultures.**   Most small Washington wineries are using lyophilized yeast for starters.   These generally are added by using a weighed amount of yeast per ton of grapes crushed, soaking it in warm water to rehydrate, then adding to the tank of juice or must.   Where fresh yeast cultures are utilized, a laboratory culture collection is maintained.   One large winery is maintaining a culture collection on sterile, unglazed berl saddles according to the method of Pilone (*21*).

For each strain of yeast used, at about ten-day intervals, a fresh culture is started in sterile media.   This is grown up until a quantity of five to twenty gallons (18.93–75.7 L) is obtained.   This active culture is then added to juice that has been centrifuged to less than 2 percent and greater than 0.5 percent solids, heated to in excess of 170° F (76.67° C), and allowed to cool.   This culture is grown until the yeast population is such that an inoculation of a fresh tank of juice or must can be made at six million cells per milliliter.   Subsequently, this tank and future inoculations made from this tank will be used until the next ten-day cycle has begun.   Inoculums are taken from tanks that are between 18° and 12° Brix.   This is done in an effort to be assured that the yeast are in an actively growing state rather than in a competitive stage of fermentation.   This allows the winery to presume that a cell count, run under a microscope on a hematocryte, consists primarily of viable cells.   These cell counts are made within four hours of the time of inoculation.   Inoculations are maintained at the six-million-cell-per-milliliter level.   A benefit of using

Table V. Analyses of *Vitis vinifera* Cultivar Cabernet Sauvignon Vintages 1969 through 1977: Flavanoid and Total Phenol (as Gallic Acid), Color, Total Acidity, pH, and Ethanol Content

| Wine | Flavanoids | Total Phenol | Color | | Total Acidity | pH | Ethanol Percent Volume |
|---|---|---|---|---|---|---|---|
| | | | OD 420 + 520 nm 1 cm path length | OD 520 nm OD 420 nm | | | |
| Cabernet 1969 | 2615 | 2885 | 5.9 | 1.1 | 0.84 | 3.16 | 12.37 |
| Cabernet 1970 | 2615 | 2925 | 10.2 | 1.2 | 0.77 | 3.25 | 13.09 |
| Cabernet 1971 | 2425 | 2720 | 8.8 | 1.2 | 0.79 | 3.20 | 12.80 |
| Cabernet 1972 | 2220 | 2500 | 8.5 | 1.2 | 0.76 | 3.22 | 13.38 |
| Cabernet 1973 | 1837 | 2175 | 9.4 | 1.4 | 0.80 | 3.15 | 12.83 |
| Cabernet 1974 | 2292 | 2535 | 7.5 | 1.3 | 0.69 | 3.34 | 12.64 |
| Cabernet 1975 | 2611 | 2895 | 10.4 | 1.4 | 0.64 | 3.51 | 12.43 |
| Cabernet 1976 | 2265 | 2530 | 8.0 | 1.2 | 0.57 | 3.54 | 12.99 |
| Cabernet 1977 | 2150 | 2390 | 5.4 | 1.2 | 0.64 | 3.59 | 13.38 |

actual cell counts for inoculation is that the winery is forced to examine its yeast cultures on a regular basis.   This permits the winery to assess for any potential gross contamination by a wild yeast culture.   While it is not certain that a wild yeast culture or other organism will appear sufficiently different under the microscope to be identified, this is often the case.

### Secondary (Malo-Lactic) Fermentation

The organism used for malo-lactic fermentation in Washington is *Leuconostoc oenos* (University of California Davis, ML 34).   Until 1974, the malo-lactic fermentation was not carried out with any regularity in Washington.   In that year, a sample from the culture collection maintained by Dr. R. E. Kunkee at the University of California at Davis was obtained.   This was cultured in Regosa broth.   Through a series of inoculations, a successful culture was established in *V. vinifera* cultivar Cabernet Sauvignon.   From this initial culture, additional cultures were produced and maintained in several laboratories and distributed to many of the other Washington wineries.

In recent years, the use of pasteurized apple juice as a growth medium for the initial inoculum of *L. oenos*, ML 34, has become common.   This is readily available, requires no preparation, and allows the malo-lactic organism to grow rapidly.   Where possible, the inoculation of a lot of wine is accomplished at a level in excess of 10 percent inoculum.   Once the initial lot of wine shows completion by paper chromatographic analysis, as described by Kunkee (22), it is used to inoculate a larger lot of wine, again at a 10 percent level or higher.   This procedure is followed in subsequent inoculations.

**In the Winery.**   To maintain the malo-lactic culture in an active state in wine, it has been found necessary to have the wine at a temperature in excess of approximately 65° F (18.33° C).   In red wines, this is accomplished most often by inoculating the wine immediately after separation from the pomace (skins, pulp, and seeds).   This separation generally is performed at five percent to eight percent soluble solids as indicated by a Brix hydrometer. There is often enough heat of fermentation generated to allow completion of the malo-lactic fermentation.

There has been some innovative technology applied by some wineries to maintain the wines in a warm condition.   Several wineries have been visited where small tanks, puncheons, or barrels were covered with electric blankets to maintain an adequate temperature for the malo-lactic fermentation.   Larger wineries utilize an external heat source to warm the storage tanks in which the red wine is held.   Where wineries are using ammonia refrigeration systems directly in the jacketed portion of the fermentors, these systems can be used as a heat pump.   The hot ammonia gas from the compressors is desuperheated and the tank jacket used as a condenser to condense this gaseous ammonia.   This has proven to be a very effective means of warming a tank.

The length of time necessary to accomplish a malo-lactic fermentation, which appears complete by paper chromatographic analysis, varies widely.   It has been found that this fermentation can be accomplished in as little as three days in tanks as large as 16,000 gallons (605.6 hL). The level of the inoculum for this rapid malo-lactic fermentation was 20 percent of the volume of the tank. In other cases, it may take as long as several months to achieve completion of the malo-lactic fermentation. Because of the cool cellar temperatures during the winter months, it is sometimes the following summer before malo-lactic fermentation is completed in some wines.

In addition to the use of malo-lactic fermentation in red wines, it also has been tried in V. *vinifera* cultivar Chardonnay. In the experiments known to the author, the use of the malo-lactic fermentation in Chardonnay has not proved successful from a sensory point of view. In general, the rise in pH was too great and the buffering capacity of the wine too great to permit adequate adjustment with tartaric acid. However, this work is continuing in conjunction with a number of variations in the local viticultural practices to produce Chardonnay of a lower total acidity. In addition to the use of malo-lactic fermentation for the reduction of the acidity, considerable work has been done in Washington on the use of acid reduction with calcium. Both calcium carbonate and the double salt precipitation, as described by Steele (23, 24), have been utilized. Some very significant successes have been achieved, particularly with the double salt method.

*Clarification of Wine*

Clarification of wine subsequent to fermentation relies on some combination of settling, fining agent(s), chilling, heating, filtration, and centrifuging. The handling of the wine can be subdivided into three basic categories: these are the handling of white wines that are fermented to dryness, white wines that have a residual sugar in the final product, and red wines.

To assess the completion of a fermentation of a dry white wine, it is common practice to use the Dextrocheck (25) method to assess the amount of residual reducing sugar in the wine. When the residual sugar is less than 0.2 percent, and no fermentation activity is visible in the fermentor, the wine is considered to be fermented "dry." In the past few years, it has not been uncommon for some of these fermentations to proceed very slowly in their latter stages. Under these circumstances, it is found to be beneficial to rack the fermenting wine from its gross lees. This is done to minimize the chance of formation of reductive compounds such as hydrogen sulfide in the resultant wine.

When fermentation is complete, the small wineries will rack the new wines as soon as possible. The larger wineries will utilize a centrifuge and immediately reduce the suspended solids content to less than 0.1 percent. At this point, the $SO_2$ content of the wine will be adjusted. The means of assessing how much $SO_2$ is to be added vary from winery to winery. Some add a set amount to each tank, others will adjust the free-$SO_2$ content, and others will raise the total $SO_2$ in the wine to a predetermined level.   With few exceptions, all of these methods produce a total $SO_2$ content in the wine, after adjustment, of 60–100 mg/L.

**White Table Wines.**   White table wines with a residual sugar are stopped in their fermentation process when the winemaker feels that the sugar/acid balance he perceives when tasting the wine is at the desired level for the end product.   This is done on a lot-by-lot basis.   Analyses have shown that the reducing sugar in individual lots of wine for a given wine type will vary quite widely.   However, the interblending of these individual lots yields a surprisingly consistent end product.   The means by which the fermentation is stopped varies with the capabilities found in a given winery.   One winemaker adds three pounds (1.36 kg) or more of bentonite when he judges it to be one to three days prior to the time at which a lot of wine is to be stopped.   When he achieves the proper sugar/acid balance, 75 mg/L of $SO_2$ is added.   The wine is racked and chilled to stop the fermentation.

In the larger wineries, when it is desired to stop a fermentation, the thermostat on the jacketed fermentor is set to reduce the temperature of the wine to between 35° and 40° F (1.67° and 4.44° C).   The effect of this action is to cause maximum cooling of the fermentor.   This appreciably slows the rate of fermentation.   The wine is centrifuged as soon as possible after the decision is made to stop it, generally within a matter of a few hours.   Residual suspended solids, at this point, are well below 0.1 percent.   Subsequent to centrifuging, $SO_2$ is added.   The level of addition is generally 50 mg/L, provided this yields an initial free $SO_2$ of greater than 60 mg/L and a total $SO_2$ of less than 100 mg/L.   Conditions outside these limits or special wines are handled on an individual basis.   It generally is found desirable not to add $SO_2$ until after centrifugation.   Addition of $SO_2$ prior to removal of the yeast tends to produce a higher bound-$SO_2$ content in the resultant wine.   One winemaker has reported that addition of $SO_2$ within one hour prior to centrifugation improves his wine quality.

White wines that are to be aged may be put into oak barrels and tanks at this point or they may be chilled to 28° F (-2.22° C) for ten to fourteen days, rough filtered through nonasbestos pads with a diatomaceous earth body feed, then aged in oak containers.   White wines that are to be bottled without aging are blended and finished at this point.

A number of different treatments are utilized for the handling of red wines subsequent to racking from the pomace and pressing.   Some wineries keep the free-run and press wines separate until after the completion of fermentation.   Others combine the free-run and press fractions immediately and allow them to complete fermentation as a single lot of wine.   One winery has lightly centrifuged the press wine to reduce the amount of suspended solids and then blended this press wine back with the free-run to allow completion of the fermentation.   This blending back subsequent to centrifugation ensures a high enough yeast cell count to ensure completion of the fermentation.

Most wineries in Washington are adding the malo-lactic starter at the point where the wine is separate from the pomace.   At completion of malo-lactic fermentation, the wine is racked from its lees and often aerated.   This aeration is accomplished by racking into a sump or racking the wine through the top door of the receiving tank.   The total $SO_2$ content is adjusted to a minimum of 60 mg/L at this time.

Red wines generally are racked twice more for a total of three rackings prior to the end of January.   Some wineries age their wines in oak cooperage at this point.   Others will perform a light gelatin fining at the level of 0.125–0.75 lbs/1000 gal (1.5–9 g/hL).   The wine will then be chilled to 38° to 40° F (3.33° to 4.44° C) for seven to ten days, racked, and rough filtered to oak tanks and barrels for aging.   Additional clarification and stabilization are done in conjunction with finishing the wine in preparation for bottling.

### Aging

In this new winegrowing region, with its unique combination of geographical location, weather conditions, and soil types, it has been found that the wines age differently than those from other regions of the world.   Because of the differences that are seen in these "new" wines, a number of wineries are taking a fresh look at which types of wood cooperage are best suited to individual wines.   As an illustration of this experimentation, one winery has acquired French oak barrels from four separate French coopers.   Each of these coopers has prepared barrels from oak from four separate French forests.   These barrels will be prepared similarly and filled with wine from a given lot.   The different lots of wine will be assessed carefully to determine which produces the most desirable end product.   At least one small winery, which has had to take cost considerations into account, is using recoopered used whisky barrels exclusively.

**Oak Barrels.**   Currently Chardonnay and Sauvignon blanc are being aged primarily in French oak from Limosin and Allier at one major winery, while another is using primarily Nevers oak for aging of these wines.   Very little white wine other than Chardonnay and Sauvignon blanc currently is being aged in wood cooperage.

V. vinifera cultivars Cabernet Sauvignon and Merlot are being aged predominantly in eastern United States white oak of mixed origin.   Some wineries are beginning to incorporate French oak barrels for the aging of red wine.   In one winery, the French oak barrels from Nevers represent up to 80 percent of their red wine barrel cooperage.   Another major winery is using up to 30 percent French oak barrels for the aging of their red wines.   In addition, this winery is now purchasing French oak tanks for their larger wood cooperage aging requirements.

An area that will see further work in the near future is identification of difference in aging potential of oak from different regions in the United States.   There is interest in having a major U.S. cooper produce barrels from wood of specific regions such as Wisconsin, Virginia, and Arkansas.   The wine aged in these barrels would be assessed carefully to determine if the oak from one region has a tendency to produce a superior wine over the oak from other regions.   The United States Department of Agriculture has expressed a desire to find a use for the white oak growing in Oregon.   This currently is considered a trash wood in the logging operations of the conifer forests of Oregon.   Some of this Oregon white oak has been harvested and is being air dried in preparation for the coopering of wine barrels from it.

The vast majority of the oak aging done in Washington is accomplished in barrels.   American oak barrels of 52 gallons (197 L) and European barrels of 60 gallons (227 L) are the most common containers used for aging.   In addition, European puncheons of 135 gallons (511 L) are being used.   Oak tanks of 1500-, 2000-, 4000-, and 8000-gallon (56.77, 75.7, 141.4, and 302.8 hL) capacity also are used in the aging of some Northwest wines.

Because of the small size of most of the wineries in Washington, only one winery has large redwood tanks for the storage of young red wines.   These are of 8000-, 16,000-, and 24,000-gallon (302.8, 605.6, and 908.4 hL) capacity.   These redwood tanks have been used for the holding of wines during malo-lactic fermentation.   It has been demonstrated that, in a number of cases, there is now a sufficient malo-lactic starter in these large tanks that it is not necessary to inoculate a lot of new red wine to have a malo-lactic fermentation go to completion.   Investigation of the organism responsible has indicated that it is *L. oenos*, ML 34.

**Barrel Storage.**   Many of the wineries of Washington are storing their barrels in barrel racks.   This permits them to roll the barrels to one side so that the bung may be kept below the liquid level to minimize losses.   The use of racks also permits the barrels to be removed between fillings to be rinsed or washed thoroughly if necessary.   The racks also permit removal and re-coopering of any barrels that develop a leak.   Most wineries top (fill) their barrels on a regular basis.   The frequency of topping varies from once a week to once a month depending upon the winery.   To minimize evaporative losses, at least one major winery is in the process of incorporating humidity control in addition to temperature control in its wood cooperage aging cellars.   Work by Guymon (26) has shown that losses during wood aging can be reduced substantially by maintaining the humidity in the aging cellar in the range of 70 percent to 80 percent relative humidity.

A problem common to many wineries in this area is an overabundance of new or almost new wood cooperage.   It is often not possible to allow the wines to remain in wood to achieve the level of maturity desired by the winemaker.   Rather, it is necessary to remove the wine prior to it becoming too astringent and having too predominant an oak aroma.   In lieu of a long wood aging cycle, a number of wineries are bottle aging their wines for an extended period of time prior to release.

Only one winery currently is offering a dry, aged style of wine from V. *vinifera* cultivars White Riesling and Gewürztraminer.   It is the author's belief that in the future we will see more of these dry or slightly off-dry, mature styles of white wines coming from the Northwest, in addition to the currently popular fresh, fruity, slightly sweet styles most common today.

### Finishing

The finishing of a wine consists of any necessary final blending, the elimination of any properties considered adverse to the wine's general quality, and ensuring that the wine is stable against breakdown through exposure to excessive heat or cold.    In most wineries, the finishing of the fresh, fruity style of white wine as *V. vinifera* cultivars White Riesling, Chenin blanc, Sémillon, and Gewürztraminer begins as soon after the completion of fermentation as is feasible.    In assessing individual lots of wine to be blended into a master blend, any specific treatment required for an individual lot would be performed on that lot of wine prior to master blending.    This might include removal of excess tannins or elimination of a reductive condition. Most commonly, once a master blend is made of the fresh, fruity white wine varieties, the only treatment given the wine is to ensure heat and cold stability.

**Fining.**    Generally used fining agents are bentonite (a montmorillonite clay), gelatin, PVP, and egg white.    Also considered are isinglass, activated carbon, and sodium caseinate.    The degree of stabilization necessary is assessed in the laboratory by adding varying levels of bentonite, which has been soaked at least overnight in hot water, to samples of the wine.    The treated samples are allowed to settle overnight, filtered, and placed in a 120° F (50° C) environment for two days.    After two days at 120° F (50° C), the samples are removed and observed both hot and after they come to room temperature. These same samples then are placed in refrigerated storage at 28° F (-2.22° C) for two days.    At this point, they are removed from the cold storage and observed both cold and again at room temperature.    Freedom from any deposit or haze at this point is considered to indicate a stable wine.    The minimum amount of bentonite necessary to achieve this clarity is added to the blend of wine under study.

**Refrigeration.**    At least one major winery minimizes the amount of wine movement necessary by cold stabilizing the wine at 28° F (-2.22° C) in a jacketed tank until laboratory evaluation shows the wine to be cold stable.    The wine is allowed to warm to 30°–32° F (-1.11°–0° C), then a slurry of bentonite, which has been soaked at least overnight in hot water, is added to the wine at the level prescribed by the previously described laboratory procedure.    When the bentonite has settled to the bottom of the tank, the wine is racked off the bentonite lees and filtered to a holding tank.    The wine is now ready for polish filtration and bottling.

A number of small wineries in Washington do not have the refrigeration capabilities to achieve cold stability by chilling to 28° F (-2.22° C).    These small wineries achieve cold stability by opening their wineries in the winter time and allowing the entire cellar to be chilled through the winter months.    This is their sole source of cold stabilization.    A number of wineries in the Northwest have been adding dry bentonite to the wine rather than slurrying it in hot water twelve to twenty-four hours prior to use.    These wineries often require more bentonite to achieve heat stability than those winerires that are first hydrating the bentonite prior to use.

Cold stabilization of white wines in Washington at 28° F (-2.22° C) often is achieved within ten to fourteen days.    Bentonite levels rquired to achieve heat stability often run higher than typical California levels.    In Washington, four to eight pounds per 1000 gallons (48–96 g/hL) of white wine is a typical range of bentonite addition.    Addition of the hydrated bentonite to the wine is accomplished either by slow addition to the tank while the tank is agitated or by means of a suction device on the inlet side of a centrifugal pump as the lot of wine is pumped from one tank to another.    It is important in the addition of all fining agents to have an intimate mixing of the fining agent in a proportional manner throughout the entire lot of wine.

Work is currently in progress to assess the benefits of adding bentonite to white juice prior to fermentation rather than waiting until the wine has finished fermentation to add bentonite.    It is currently the practice of one winery to add approximately three pounds per 1000 gallons (36 g/hL) of bentonite to their white juice prior to fermentation.    Other wineries are experimenting with this concept.    Where bentonite is added prior to fermentation, a difference in the sensory effect on the wine may be achieved by removal of the bentonite prior to fermentation versus leaving the bentonite in contact with the juice or wine throughout the fermentation.    These studies are being conducted with levels of bentonite lower than those generally required for complete heat stability.    This results in a requirement for a light bentonite addition subsequent to the completion of fermentation.    Initial sensory evaluations have shown the bentonite-treated wine is preferred by the panel to wine produced without bentonite addition prior to fermentation.

**Aged Wines.**    In the case of aged wines, when it is determined that they have been in wood cooperage for a sufficient period of time, they are pumped out and blended.    In at least one major winery, the winemakers smell each barrel individually prior to being emptied.    Any barrels that are felt to be atypical are marked and set aside.    These atypical barrels generally exhibit an off odor attributable to some form of microbial contamination.    Wines from these barrels are blended separately and assessed for any needed treatment.    Often this sub-blend is found to be acceptable for addition to the master blend.    To feel more secure about the future of the wine, any $SO_2$ addition deemed appropriate for the entire master lot of wine will be added to this small lot of atypical barrels.    This small lot will then be interblended with the remaining portion of the wine that was removed from wood cooperage, thereby reducing the $SO_2$ content to the desired concentration.

A common treatment, subsequent to aging in many of the Washington red wines, is a light egg white fining.    The majority of the egg white additions utilize fresh egg white at a level of 0.5–1.5 lb/1000 gal (6–18 g/hL)of wine. The fresh egg white is felt to be superior to either frozen or dried egg white for the purpose of fining premium red wines.   The egg white is prepared by first partially beating the egg white, then adding a small amount of wine to this and further beating it.   A very low level, a "pinch"or 2.5 g/kg of egg white, of salt (sodium chloride) is added at this time.   This egg white material then is mixed intimately with the lot of wine to be treated in a manner similar to that described for bentonite addition.   Subsequent to this, the heat and cold stability of the wine will be rechecked and any necessary final adjustments will be performed.   The wine is then racked and, in some cases, filtered to a holding tank prior to bottling.   In at least one major winery, the red wines are racked to oak tanks of 2000–4000 gallons (757–1514 hL) to be held for a period of four to eight weeks prior to polish filtration and bottling.

   **Filtration.**   Filtration in Washington wineries is performed almost exclusively with plate-and-frame filter presses.   In some cases, these filters have wide frames so that they are capable of performing diatomaceous earth filtrations.   There is only one stainless steel, screened, diatomaceous earth, pressure-leaf filter in use in the Washington wine industry.   Two major wineries have found they can utilize a paper septum over a medium pad in their plate-and-frame filters.   This allows them to precoat and body feed with diatomaceous earth as the wine is filtered.   This accomplishes both a coarse and medium filtration in one movement of the wine.

   It is believed that the future will see a significant increase in the popularity of pressure-leaf filters in this region.

### Bottling

   As in any other winegrowing region in the world, the array of bottling equipment in this area is diverse.   The small wineries generally do not prepare their new glass in any way prior to filling.   These wineries use either a gravity or vacuum filler and single head corkers without vacuum capabilities.   Labeling is often semiautomatic or hand labeling is employed.   All wineries polish filter their wine prior to bottling and several use membrane filters just ahead of the filler.   The smaller wineries pump their wine to the filler; one major winery polish filters to a bottling tank, then uses nitrogen pressure to push the wine through a membrane filter to their pressure filler.   White wines are membrane filtered through 0.45-micron filters.   Where red wines are membrane filtered, a 0.65-micron membrane usually is employed.

   The vast majority of Washington wine is filtered through nonasbestos filter pads.   In preparing the wine for bottling, the $SO_2$ levels employed will vary depending upon whether or not the winery utilizes membrane filtration and/or some other form of wine sterilization.   One major winery bottles its wine at 35 mg/L free $SO_2$ with the addition of 200 mg/L of sorbate followed by a membrane filtration.   Many of the small wineries lack a source of steam or hot water for sterilization. Instead, chemical sterilization is performed in the bottling area prior to bottling. Most of the wines of Washington are cold-sterile bottled.

A major winery rinses its new incoming glass with water that has been heated in excess of 185° F (85° C). To avoid the potential buildup of resistant microorganisms, this water is not recycled. As the bottles drain they enter an enclosed room containing only the filler and corker. The air in this room is circulated through a nominal 0.3-micron HEPA air filter every one to two minutes. The bottles enter a filler and are pressurized with nitrogen gas to displace the air in the bottle. The wine is filled against this nitrogen pressure in the bottle.

The bottle exits the filler and enters the corker where it is corked with a natural cork that has been exposed to a high $SO_2$ content atmosphere prior to being fed to the corking machine. In the corker, as the bottle is put into place, a vacuum is drawn of approximately twenty-seven inches (680 mm) of mercury on the bottle headspace. The cork then is inserted into the neck of the bottle against this partial vacuum. The bottle leaves the enclosed room, a foil is placed on the neck, it is labeled, cased, and stored neck down until ready for release by the winery.

The entire bottling line, including membrane filters, piping, filler, and corker, is sanitized daily. The primary means of sanitation is use of 192° F (89° C) hot water and circulating it through the wine contact areas and the corker vacuum lines for a minimum of twenty-five minutes each day. In addition, the corker jaws are sprayed with 70 percent ethanol solution at least twice each day. To further ensure cleanliness, the facility is shut down mid afternoon each Friday and the balance of the day devoted to an in-depth cleaning using chlorine or idophor solutions. Attention has been paid to such details as covering the corners of the room for easy cleaning and ensuring that all drains drain from sanitary areas to the outside areas rather than vice versa. Prime areas of sanitation difficulty are the bottling line chain conveyor and the corker.

**Sanitation Check.** To further check the sanitary integrity of the system, it is monitored daily. Each morning and any time a membrane filter is changed, a sample of approximately 400 mL is pulled from the inlet and discharge of the membrane filler. A one percent sterilized, peptone broth medium is used in conjunction with sterilized cotton swabs. These swabs are used to check half of the corker jaws and four of the forty filler spouts each day. After swabbing the piece of equipment to be checked, the swab is placed in a sterile container of peptone broth and the handle of this swab broken off so that no portion that has been touched by the person running the test enters the peptone broth. These samples are shaken and the peptone broth filtered through 0.45-micron membrane filters, which are subsequently cultured for seventy-two hours at 86° F (30° C). In addition to these samples, two bottles of wine are pulled at random from the bottling line each hour during operation.    Each of these samples is filtered through a 0.45-micron membrane filter and cultured for three days to check for microbial activity of either yeast or mold.    A typical cell count for viable yeast or mold in these sixteen samples would be three to five organisms for the twelve liters of wine.

This same winery also maintains the bottled wine in the warehouse for a minimum of thirty days prior to being released for distribution.    Prior to release, samples are pulled at random from the warehouse, assessed visually, and tasted.    In addition, a random selection of these wines is filtered through 0.45-micron filters and cultured for seventy-two hours to ensure that yeast or mold activity has not increased while in the warehouse.

While the above description adequately describes the bottling of V. vinifera table wines, the majority of the fruit and berry wines are bottled without membrane filtration.    Virtually all of these fruit and berry wines have potassium sorbate added to them to ensure microbial stability.

*Bottle Aging*

The care and development of a wine is by no means terminated when the wine is bottled.    Once bottled, the development of the wine is evidenced first by the disappearance of "bottle sickness" followed, over a longer period of time, by the development of maturity and complexity of the wine within the bottle.    Having the wine in the winery during its early stages of development also affords the winemaker the opportunity to be assured of the sterility of cold-sterile bottled wine.

In bottling wines, enologists almost always note a disturbance of the character of the wine between the bottling tank and the recently bottled wine.    This detrimental quality effect seems to be caused by the large amount of handling in terms of pumping, filling, general agitation, and potential aeration that the wine is exposed to in being bottled.    The "bottle sickness" effect dissipates rapidly during bottle aging.    In most cases, it is almost unnoticeable in wine thirty days after bottling.

**Checking Samples.**    In sampling bottles for sterility at the time of filling, a viable cell count of yeast and mold of zero per bottle is desired. However, it is sometimes found that bottles will have a viable cell count of between zero and ten cells per bottle.    To be sure that these organisms will not grow in the acidic, aqueous ethanol solution we call wine, it is best to recheck random samples of the wine at a minimum of thirty days after bottling.    This has been found to be the minimum period of time to allow for these microorganisms to acclimatize themselves to the conditions in the bottle.    If this recheck of sterility shows a significant decline in viability of cells within the bottle, one can be reasonably assured of sterility.    However, if the cell count has maintained itself at its former level or shown signs of increasing, there is a strong possibility of significant contamination.    In the latter case, it is best to hold the wine for a minimum of ninety days before rechecking for sterility.

The development of maturity and complexity of the wine is a relatively slow process.   While we occasionally observe significant increases in these characteristics in as little as three months, it is more common to find increases in maturity and complexity over time spans measured in years.   Some of the white wines of the Northwest are allowed to mature in the bottle for up to one year prior to release for sale.   These wines are usually either sweet or are truly dry white wines.   Typical examples would be botrytized or late harvest White Rieslings and Chardonnays.   The red wines of the Northwest generally are aged in the bottle for one year or more prior to release.   A notable exception in recent years has been wines of the *V. vinifera* cultivar Merlot, offered by several wineries in Washington with six months or less bottle age.

Most wineries store their wine in a standard warehouse type of building.   One major winery stores its white wines in an insulated, temperature controlled (both heated and cooled) warehouse to maintain conditions as close to 55° F (12.78° C) year round as is possible.   This same facility stores its red wine in a standard warehouse type of building to allow some temperature change throughout the year.   It is felt that this small amount of temperature change will allow the wine to mature somewhat more quickly in the bottle.

*Speciality Products*

The development of the wine industry in Washington subsequent to Prohibition had as its foundation the production of dessert, fruit, and berry wines.   The dessert wines were produced primarily from *V. labrusca* grapes and the berry wine from those berries that were common in the region.   Most popular have been loganberry, blackberry, and currant.

Dessert wines, as they developed in the Northwest, took two divergent approaches.   One was the production of high ethanol wines through fermentation rather than through fortification.   This was done to avoid the need to put the word "fortified" on the label.   At that period in Washington's wine industry development, this word was considered a detrimental term with respect to quality.   Production of these wines was accomplished by the slow and continuous addition of sugar until an ethanol content of up to 18 percent was produced.   This type of dessert wine, known as "high fermentation" wine, has not been produced since the early 1960s.   The balance of the dessert wines were produced in the more traditional fashion by addition of high-proof grape spirits to wines fermented to 12–14 percent ethanol.

The use of *V. labrusca* grapes in the production of dessert wine caused a need for amelioration.   This is because of the low sugar content of approximately 16 percent soluble solids, and the high acid levels on the order of 1.0 g/100 mL, as tartaric.   These wines are fermented to 12–14 percent ethanol.   Other wine designated for distillation is produced, distilled, and added back to these wines.   The fortified dry wine is held in storage until ready for finishing and bottling.   At this point, sweetening of the wine is accomplished through addition of sugar either as dry sucrose, dry dextrose, or liquid fructose solutions. The marketing of these wines produced in Washington and Oregon generally is confined to the northwestern states.

**Berry Wines.** The berry wine industry was very active in the 1960s. There was a decrease in this market in the late 1960s and early 1970s, followed by a recent resurgence of interest in these wines. Within the last five years, there have been at least three wineries founded in Washington to produce fruit and berry wines. The fruit and berry wines of the 1960s were of an aperitif type. The soluble solids content ranged from 6 percent to 14 percent. The recent interest in these wines has been as a table wine in addition to use as an aperitif. We recently have seen the widespread availability of dry and almost dry fruit and berry wines. In addition, the use of fruits such as apricot and bing cherry has become popular.

Production of berry wines differs considerably from production of table wines made from grapes. To pick the fruit at optimum maturity, it is often necessary to pick as many as six to eight times. This differs markedly from optimal maturity for other uses such as frozen fruit or pie making. The fruit, as harvested for winemaking, would be considered overmature for these other uses. The fruit is often very soft and will break apart to some extent at the level of ripeness desired for winemaking purposes. The fruit is picked clean and put into fifty-gallon open top drums with $SO_2$ added. These berries then are stored in a refrigerated warehouse as frozen fruit until required. When a lot of wine is to be produced, the berries are removed from storage, allowed to thaw, and pumped to a fermenting tank. The acidity of these fruits is often in excess of 20 g/L and the sugar content will be less than 10 percent. Amelioration is a necessity to produce a palatable product. Once this is accomplished, a standard wine yeast strain of *S. cerevisiae*, such as montrachet, is introduced and the wines are fermented to dryness. Fining of these wines also differs from grape wines. The compositions of these fruits are different enough that the handling has to be tailored to the individual fruit. Some fruits, such as cherry, tend to produce large quantities of lees, which must be compacted to achieve an economical yield. In some fruits, their acid constituents can change to an isomeric form to such an extent that they are no longer completely soluble in the aqueous ethanol solution (wine). This requires specialized stabilization techniques in preparing the wine for bottling. Subsequent to fining, these wines may be sweetened and then are bottled. Most berry wine producers use potassium sorbate as an insurance against microbial growth in the bottled product. Unlike the majority of the grape table wines, the berry wines do not tend to improve with bottle age. It is more common for them to show a decline in quality within one year's time in the bottle. For this reason, it is common practice to make individual lots of fruit and berry wines throughout the year to maintain a fresh supply in the marketplace.

**Specialty Wines.** There have been a number of specialty products produced from *V. vinifera* grapes in the Northwest in the last several years. In 1974, the first blanc de noir wine was produced and bottle fermented by the classic méthode champenoise.   This sparkling wine has been produced every year since in increasing quantities with modest success.   Knowledgeable members of the industry have encouraged the growth of this infant sparkling wine trade.   With the exception of one cuvée, which was 25 percent *V. vinifera* cultivar Chardonnay, all the sparkling wine in Washington has been made 100 percent from *V. vinifera* cultivar Pinot noir.   The grapes have been pressed in a vertical, hydraulic basket press with no precrushing or stemming being performed.   The juice has been fermented dry and then bottled with either a Berkeley Yeast laboratory strain or a French champagne strain of *S. cerevisiae*.   The wines have remained on the lees a minimum of three years prior to hand riddling and disgorging.

There have been a number of botrytized wines produced in the Northwest.   While most of these have been produced from naturally occurring *Botrytis cinerea*, one winery has cultured this organism in the laboratory and then sprayed in the vineyard.   Under this latter circumstance, the vineyard was sprinkler irrigated twice a day to maintain higher than normal humidities for seventy-two hours.   To the author's knowledge, botrytized wines have been produced in Washington from *V. vinifera* cultivars White Riesling, Gewürztraminer, and Chenin blanc.   In addition to the botrytized wines, there also have been a number of late harvest wines produced.   These include wines from *V. vinifera* cultivars Sauvignon blanc and White Riesling.   Perhaps the most exciting specialty wine of these latter types has been the production by two separate wineries of botrytized Ice Wine.   These have been produced from *V. vinifera* cultivar White Riesling grapes harvested early in November after freezing weather—down to temperatures of 18° F (-8° C).   The quality of these Ice Wines has been good enough that they have been compared favorably with their German counterpart.

### Future

It is the author's belief that the infant wine industry of Washington has a long and exciting road to travel in the future.   There will surely be an increase in the number of wineries well beyond the fourteen bonded wineries in this state at the end of fiscal 1979.   The *V. vinifera* acreage in this state will exceed 20,000 acres by the year 2000, with a potential for in excess of 200,000 acres sometime in the future.

In the vineyard, a far greater understanding of what is required for cold hardiness and which varieties best exhibit this capability will be demonstrated.   Cultural practices will be found that will circumvent the present apparent cold tenderness of some cultivars.   We will see widespread use of mechanical harvesters and the introduction of mechanical pruning.   As we increase the number of irrigated acres and our understanding of the ecological factors involved, we will see changes in our irrigation systems.   There will be an increase in drip irrigation, and drip–sprinkler irrigation combination systems may well be developed.

In the winery, we will see improvements in our crushing techniques. Better understanding of stemmer–crushers versus crusher–stemmers versus partial destemming followed by crushing will evolve. Pressing techniques and our knowledge of their effects on the wine will improve. The use of presses that generate less suspended solids will be more widespread in the future. Along with the improvements in pressing techniques, we will become more knowledgeable in the areas of achieving a cleaner juice for white wine fermentation. The use of centrifuges, especially in the small- and medium-sized wineries, will become much more widespread. We will begin to see a diminution in the numbers of filtrations to which individual wines are subjected and increased use of pressure leaf filters in lieu of the current widespread use of plate-and-frame filters.

As the winemakers become more knowledgeable in regard to the specific characteristic of the grapes of the Northwest and of the style of wines they are producing, we will see changes in the techniques employed in the winery. For example, more careful selection of yeast strains for particular wine types may develop. Fermentations will be controlled more carefully in the future. Control of fermentations by rate of fermentation rather than by temperature of fermentation will become more prevalent. A more in-depth understanding of the use of the wide array of fining agents available to the winemaker will be seen. We will see a "fine tuning" of the use of these fining agents. In the bottling of these wines, a greater use of cold-sterile bottling techniques will develop.

Finally, as the industry and the winemakers' knowledge grow, we will see more specialty wines produced. Perhaps a separate industry devoted to sparkling wine production will evolve. High quality botrytized and late harvest wines will appear with greater regularity. Finally, the future will see the beginnings of a competitively priced table wine industry evolve from "premium" V. *vinifera* grapes.

### Literature Cited

1. Somers, H., personal communication.
2. Ledwitz, M. W. In "Technical and Economic Assistance in Fostering the Economic Development of the Wine-Grape Industry of Washington;" Washington State University, College of Agriculture Research Center: Pullman, WA, 1976; pp. 210–270.
3. Amdur, E. "Comparative Climatology and Vineyard Microclimatology for Northern Area;" A posthumous condensation, Macgregor, David, Ed.; Lake Sylvia Vineyards: South Haven, MN, 1978.
4. Wagner, P. M. "Wines, Grape Vines and Climate," *Sci. Am.* 1974, 230(6), 107–115.
5. Winkler, A. J.; Cook, J. A.; Kliewer, W. M.; Lider, L.A. "General Viticulture;" Univ. of California Press: Berkeley and Los Angeles, 1974.
6. Nagel, C. W.; Powers, J. R.; Atallah, M. T.; Sawaya, W. N.; Carter, G. H. "Malate and Tartrate Contents of Musts and Wines from Grapes Produced in Washington," *Am. J. Enol. Vitic.* 1972, 23, 144–151.

7. Nagel, C. W. "Comparison of French, California, Oregon, and Washington Musts," Washington and Oregon Wine Societies, 1975.

8. Clore, W. J.; Nagel, C. W.; Carter, G. H. "Ten Years of Grape Variety Responses and Winemaking Trials in Washington," *Wash. State Univ. Agric. Res. Center Bull.* **1976**, *823*, 1–30.

9. Johnson, T.; Nagel, C. W. "Composition on Central Washington Grapes During Maturation," *Am. J. Enol. Vitic.* **1976**, *27*, 15–20.

10. Nagel, C. W.; McElvan, K. R. "An Analysis of the Influence of pH and Titratable Acidity in the Scoring of Wine," *Am. J. Enol. Vitic.* **1977**, *28*, 69–73.

11. Munyon, J. R.; Nagel, C. W. "Comparison of Methods of Deacidification of Musts and Wines," *Am. J. Enol. Vitic.* **1977**, *28*, 79–87.

12. Wulf, L.W.; Nagel, C. W. "High Pressure Liquid Chromatographic Separation of Anthocyanins of *Vitis vinifera*," *Am. J. Enol. Vitic.* **1978**, *29*, 92–96.

13. Ong, B. Y.; Nagel, C. W. "Hydroxycinnamic Acid-Tartaric Acid Ester Content in Mature Grapes and During the Maturation of White Riesling," *Am. J. Enol. Vitic.* **1978**, *29*, 277–281.

14. Nagel, C. W.; Wulf, L. W. "Changes in the Anthocyanins, Flavanoids and Hydroxycinnamic Acid Esters During Fermentation and Aging of Merlot and Cabernet Sauvignon," *Am. J. Enol. Vitic.* **1979**, *30*, 111–116.

15. Nagel, C. W.; Baranowski, J. D.; Wulf, L. W.; Powers, J.R. "The Hydroxycinnamic Acid-Tartaric Acid Ester Content of the Musts and Grape Varieties Grown in the Pacific Northwest," *Am. J. Enol. Vitic.* **1979**, *30*, 198–201.

16. Wolfe, W.H. "Minimizing Winter Damage: Site Selection, Vineyard Establishment and Maintenance," *Wash. State Grape Soc. Proc.* **1979**, *9*,67–75.

17. Wolfe, W.H. "Winter Injury to Grapes: How to Minimize It," *Wash. State Grape Soc. Proc.* **1979**, *9*, 44–47.

18. Wolfe, W.H., personal communication (April, 1980).

19. Wolfe, W.H., personal communication (January, 1980).

20. Ough, C.S.; Berg, H.W. "Simulated Mechanical Harvest and Gondola Transport. II. Effect of Temperature, Atmosphere and Skin Contact on Chemical and Sensory Qualities of White Wines," *Am. J. Enol. Vitic.* **1971**, *22*, 194–198.

21. Pilone, G.J. "Preservation of Wine Yeast and Lactic Acid Bacteria," *Am. J. Enol. Vitic.* **1979**, *30*, 326.

22. Kunkee, R.E. "Simplified Chromatographic Procedure for Detection of Malo-Lactic Fermentation," *Wines Vines* **1968**, *49*(3), 23–24.

23. Steele, J.T.; Kunkee, R.E. "Deacidification of High Acid California Wines by Calcium Double-Salt Precipitation," *Am. J. Enol. Vitic.* **1979**, *30*, 327–331.

24. Steele, J.T.; Kunkee, R.E. "Deacidification of Musts from Western United States by the Calcium Double-Salt Precipitation Process," *Am. J. Enol. Vitic.* **1978**, *29*, 153–160.

25. "Dextrocheck: Colorimetric Test for Reducing Sugar," Ames Co., Division Miles Laboratories, Inc., Elkart, IN.

26. Guymon, J.F., personal communication.

RECEIVED July 22, 1980.

# 8

# Grapes and Wine Production in the East

PHILIP WAGNER

Boordy Vineyards, Riderwood, MD 21139

It is often overlooked that winegrowing Europe is divided into two distinct areas. There is a good deal of overlapping, as there always is when two different ecological systems converge. But the division is sufficiently distinct to be traced on a map of Europe, blurred as the line may be at various points, from the Atlantic coast in northern Portugal, northeast through Spain into France and then on east all the way to the Black Sea and beyond. (*See* Figure 1.) This is the line that separates the influence of the Mediterranean basin, with its two-season climate, from the four-season temperate climate in its many variations that lies to the north.

## The Grapes

Along with the rest of its characteristic flora (olive trees, cork oaks), the Mediterranean region has its own grapes and its own viticultural and winemaking practices, and the wines have common characteristics. The grapes grown to the north of it, though nominally of the same species (*Vitis vinifera*), are different, and so are the viticultural and winemaking practices as well as the wines. Compare the wines of the Moselle Valley and the Champagne with those of eastern Spain, the French Midi, Algeria, and Greece. Climate is the controlling factor.

In North America, there is a similar but more drastic division—climate again being the controlling factor. But the line runs north and south with the Rockies rather than west and east as in Europe.

California with its Mediterranean climate of mild, wet winters and hot, dry summers is a home-away-from-home for the vinifera varieties of Europe. Add adjacent parts of Mexico, southern Nevada, Arizona, and protected parts of New Mexico and west Texas and Mediterranean-like conditions are spread across a broader range of latitude than the Mediterranean basin itself.

In most of the rest, meaning all that lying east of the Rockies except the subtropical segment in the Southeast, variations of the four-season climate generally prevail. But unlike the temperate climates of winegrowing Europe, most of them softened by maritime influences, these are subject to such continental extremes that even the hardiest and most disease-resistant European wine grapes are not really at home. Nowhere in this area has a

0097-6156/81/0145-0193$08.00/0

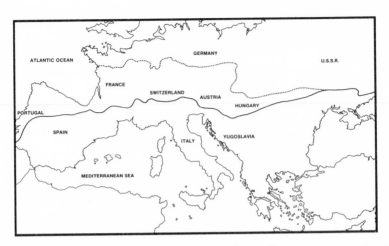

*Figure 1. Northern limit for vine growth and division between continental and Mediterranean climates*

commercially thriving winegrowing industry yet been established on the basis of the classic European grapes, despite centuries of effort.   Grape species, like all forms of plant life, have their requirements and limitations. This is less obvious in the case of the European grape than it is, say, in the case of the coconut palm and the pineapple and other such obviously exotic plant forms.   It took a long time to learn that eastern American conditions do not in general meet the prescription for V. *vinifera*.

The Learning Period.   The story of the colonial efforts and disappointments in trying to acclimate the European grape often has been told (1, 2) and will not be gone into in any detail.   Suffice to say that the early explorers and settlers were deluded by the presence almost everywhere of flourishing wild grapevines.   They assumed that where wild grapevines do so well, the cultivated European species would do well too.   True, the wild grapes are relatives (same chromosome number, 16, except for V. *rotundifolia*, 17, commonly called the Scuppernong, which is native to the Southeast).   But natural selection, being concerned with survival rather than wine quality, had altered them so drastically as to confound the assumption.   While the wild vines flourished around them, vines and cuttings brought from Europe failed repeatedly, if not in the first winter then after a few years of struggle, prey to the extremes of temperature and the indigenous mildews and insects.

What happened, though, was that the immigrant vines sometimes survived long enough to flower and hence to interbreed with the native wild ones of the same chromosome number, producing natural hybrids.   From time to time one of these natural hybrids showing distinct improvement in fruit quality was discovered and then domesticated by vegetative propagation; and by degrees the shrewder would-be winegrowers realized that the way to success would have to be through the "improvement" of the native species.

And so through natural hybridization, the basis of an eastern viticulture and winegrowing industry came into being.   The natural hybrids that provided this basis acquired names: Alexander, Isabella, Catawba, Delaware, Norton, and many others, including Concord.   A stumbling block was that the dominant, and showiest, wild species in much of the area of early settlement was V. *labrusca* with a pronounced aroma and flavor that came to be called foxy.   True, there were several other species in this area, notably V. *riparia* and V. *aestivalis*, and no doubt many wild vines represented crosses of various sorts.   But it was V. *labrusca* with its large edible fruit and pronounced flavor that was the native parent of most of the early hybrids brought into cultivation.

It was an easy step from these to artificial hybridization, and in the early nineteenth century it became a gentleman's hobby to improve the existing natural hybrids by crossing.   Hedrick's account (*1*) of this is a classic.   But with very few exceptions (Clinton, Delaware, Dutchess, Norton), the labrusca contribution was only too evident.   Wine carrying the labrusca aroma and flavor, no matter how refined, is different from the wines of Europe and, to many habitual users of wine, is not agreeable though a taste for it is acquired easily.   Ways of ameliorating the pronounced character of these grapes in the course of converting them into wine were developed, and they became and still are the basic material of the Eastern wine industry, despite the interlude of Prohibition (*2*).

**The Westward Movement.**   As new land was opened farther west, V. *labrusca* gave way to different wild species, V. *rupestris*, variants of V. *riparia*, V. *lincecumii*, V. *cinerea*, V. *monticola*, V. *berlandieri*, and others.   Their fruit lacked the labrusca foxiness, though some carried other rather obtrusive "wild" flavors and aromas.   These inspired another grape "boom" in mid nineteenth century, beginning with identification of species and discovery of desirable natural hybrids, but moving on swiftly to artificial hybridization.   Of this new generation of grape seekers, the names of Munson (*3*), Jaeger, Rommel, and the partners Bush and Meissner are most memorable.   Out of this came many new grapes, most of them since forgotten as producers of wine or fresh fruit, though a fair number of Munson's are still grown in the Southwest to a limited extent.   When it came to naming his productions, Munson was as fertile as the anonymous genius who used to think up names for Pullman cars.   Some of the Munson names: Armlong, Black Eagle, Captivator, Delicatessen, Enolian, Gold Coin, Hernito, Lomanto, Lukfata, Olivanta, Semendida, Ten-Dollar-Prize, Valhallah, and Wapanuka.

Though most of these names are forgotten, the efforts of these men coincided with the disastrous phylloxera epidemic, when that accidentally introduced American insect all but destroyed the vineyards of Europe (*4*).   *Phylloxera vastatrix* (also known as *P. vitifolii* and, if you prefer, *Dactylosphaera vitifoliae*, Shimer) in its subterranean form destroys by feeding on the vine's roots, and the European species has no immunity to it.   But the Europeans soon discovered that samples of the species sent to them by these Midwestern workers were highly resistant to phylloxera.   And so the most spectacular accomplishment of such men as Jaeger and Munson was to rescue the vineyards of Europe by providing resistant rootstock material on which the classic vines of Europe could be grafted and so survive.   Munson was awarded the equivalent of a knighthood for his contribution.   The Bush and Meissner catalog was translated and became a French viticultural classic.

In comparison, the impact on the American wine industry of the fruit-producing hybrids originated by these men was negligible.   By then, the Eastern industry, based mainly in New York and Ohio, but with a substantial offshoot in Missouri, was adjusted to the material it already had and remained so.   But in sending some of the hybrids they had produced to their French correspondents, they unwittingly laid a time bomb, the effects of which will be considered later on.

**Eastern Viticulture.**   In working with the varieties they had, eastern grape growers had developed culture practices quite different from those appropriate to California for *V. vinifera* varieties.   These were imposed by growth characteristics unlike those of vinifera grapes, and still more by climate.

The grapes, being for the most part first-generation interspecific hybrids, had abundant hybrid vigor.   They are rampant growers and require extensive training systems, and trellising is imperative.   Unlike most *V. vinifera* varieties, the basal buds of many of them are either unfruitful or not so fruitful as those farther out on the cane, another reason for extensive training.   Also unlike most vinifera varieties, their shoots and canes have a drooping rather than a vertical habit, which requires fairly high training for air drainage and access beneath the trellis for cultivation.

For the ubiquitous and ultravigorous Concord, the training method of choice today is the Geneva Double Curtain.   The essence of this is a trellis with two parallel wires about two feet apart at a height of four or more feet and supported by arms extending from each side of the trellis post.   Two trunks are led from the base of the vine, one to each wire; and from the head of each trunk canes of one-year wood or semipermanent cordons extend along the wire in each direction.   In the case of cordons, bearing canes are left to droop.   The number of fruiting buds left at pruning time is determined by a formula based on the weight of the "brush" that is removed by pruning.   For most other varieties, such exact pruning formulas have not yet been worked out.   The main advantages of the method are that maximum sunlight gains access to the center of the vine and that ventilation is improved.   Less vigorous vineyards are trained to a "single curtain."   At a given point in the growing season, the bearing canes are "combed" to distribute growth and weight evenly, a practice made possible by their drooping habit.

There exist many local training variants.   But in the four-season climates (for which the word "temperate" does not always seem appropriate) good practice everywhere requires full access to the vineyard floor throughout the growing season.    Under a two-season climate, the maintenance of a clean vineyard floor is easy, once spring rains have ceased.    In the East, irregular patterns of rainfall, much of it occurring during the growing season, complicate matters because weed growth is continuous and must be controlled.    For this purpose, cultivation beneath the row by means of one or another form of grape hoe largely has given way to the use of dormant herbicide sprays such as Karmex or Simazine, supplemented during the growing season by Paraquat or Princep.    Clean cultivation of the vineyard alleys is still general, but the use of herbicides for the entire vineyard floor is increasing.    A variation is to apply a dormant herbicide in alternate alleys in alternate years.

The one predictable thing about weather patterns in the eastern areas is their unpredictability.    The irregularity of rainfall and normally high humidity during the growing season that characterize these four-season climates (less rain and less humidity, of course, as one moves beyond the Mississippi) provide ideal conditions for fungus diseases that do not prevail in California. California must cope with powdery mildew (oïdium).    So must the eastern regions, but in the East the risk of devastation by downy mildew and black rot is even greater.    Strict adherence to the standard fungicidal spray schedule (preblossom, postblossom, and second postblossom) is absolutely vital.    But, depending on the conditions of the season, this must be supplemented often by one or more still earlier sprays as well as supplementary sprays later on.    Constant vigilance is necessary because the fungicides available in this country are preventive, not curative.    The new systemic fungicides, which give lasting protection and now are coming into general use in Europe's vineyards, are not approved for use here; and the cost of obtaining approval is so high that they are not likely to be available in the foreseeable future, even though at least one of these is the product of an American laboratory!

**Rainfall.**    In addition to intensifying the disease problem, heavy rainfall at certain seasons causes troubles of another order.    Thus, much rain and cloudy weather frequently occur during the blossoming season, with a consequent reduction in the set of fruit.    Heavy rainfall also must be anticipated from mid August through September and into October, precisely the period when no rainfall at all is the ideal.    In addition to favoring the "normal" diseases, this encourages rotting in the early ripening varieties, holds back further development of sugar, and by dilution even reduces the proportion of sugar already present in the later ripening varieties.    A premature harvest often is necessary to save the crop.    During this period, clashes of moisture-laden, low-pressure systems originating in the Caribbean with Arctic highs traveling southeast are characteristic of a broad belt of the East Coast throughout this period, frequently producing hail along with abundant downpour. September of 1979, for example, was punctuated by a series of such storms, the most severe one occurring on the night of September 4–5, when eleven inches of rain fell on a Baltimore County vineyard between the hours of 11:00 P.M. and 2:00 A.M. Nearby areas received hail as well, though fortunately this vineyard did not.    Laying a two-dollar bet at Pimlico is piker stuff compared with the gamble of growing wine grapes in hurricane alley.

Insects provide another difficulty.    One of the axioms of entomology is that in the Northern Hemisphere, insect populations are larger and more varied in the eastern parts of a continental mass.    In addition to its other problems, eastern viticulture must do constant battle against numerous voracious insect pests.    The rose chafer regularly appears just in time to nip off inflorescences as they are about to flower.    The Japanese beetle turns every leaf of a grapevine into a piece of lace, if allowed to.    In the Tidewater sections of the lower part, nematode infestation can be so severe as to make viticulture almost impossible.

When rainfall doesn't require premature harvesting, early frosts often do.    This is especially true of the short-season areas such as New England, New York, Michigan, and Wisconsin, but is not a problem for them exclusively.    North of 40° latitude (except in microclimatic situations) the attainment of optimum maturity for winemaking purposes, meaning an ideal sugar/acid balance, is always in question.    Except in the Southwest, the ratio is nearly always overbalanced on the acid side—exactly the reverse of what prevails in most California viticultural areas, where the problem is more likely to be overripeness than underripeness.

**Temperature.**    Eastern viticulture also is limited severely by the extreme fluctuations of winter temperature that prevail throughout, a problem virtually unknown to California viticulture, though familiar enough in the northerly extensions of the two-season area such as the Yakima Valley of Washington and adjacent parts of the Columbia River and Snake River drainage basins.    It is a much more complicated problem than it appears to be at first sight.

To begin with, there are minima below which none of the cultivated wine grapes, and most of the native species, cannot survive.    These cannot be stated exactly because they are dependent on so many variables.    Among these are their duration, the amount and duration of dehydrating winds, the nature of the soil (cold penetrates some soils more deeply than others), the amount of snow cover (even in severe cold, abundant snow cover usually protects enough of the vine to allow swift regeneration from the roots), fluctuations from abnormal cold to abnormal warmth and back again, the calendar (early winter or late), the species parentage ʃ a given hybrid, and the condition of the vines when they went into dormancy.    See Figure 2 for examples of damage to vines caused by winter killing of V. vinifera in France and New York.

This is not the place for a review of the widely scattered literature dealing closely with single aspects.    A few examples from experience will have to suffice.    Thus, we know that varieties of the species V. rotundifolia will not survive even the most moderate of winters north of southern

*Figure 2. Uprooted winter-killed vines of* V. vinifera *in Bordeaux (top) and results of winter killing in New York (bottom)*

Virginia. *V. vinifera* is exposed to severe damage if temperatures fall very far below freezing, though its chance of survival is much improved if its wood is well ripened and it is fully dormant prior to the first freeze. Since it must be grafted, it cannot regenerate if it is killed to the ground, as own-rooted varieties can. Vines of even the hardiest varieties become more susceptible to winter damage if they have been allowed to overbear or have lost some or all of their foliage, since their wood is not well ripened. Hard freezes once dormancy has been broken are equally lethal, even though there are no overt symptoms of the break in dormancy such as sap flow or bud swell. Abnormal cold may split cordons and trunks, and, though the vine may show normal bud-break, it is often weakened permanently. In the Northeast, even the reputedly hardy varieties have some degree of bud-kill and cane kill-back in all but the most exceptional winters.

The sum of it is that the ever present hazard of winter damage, even well down into Texas when an Arctic air current swings southward, is one of the two factors that limit the choice of varieties for eastern viticulture (the other being disease susceptibility). A winery cannot long exist without a reliable source of material. A vineyard farmer must be able to count on his vines for a living. The grapes currently dominating eastern viticulture do so as a result of economic selection, which is a sort of human corollary to natural selection. The many new grapes that are now being introduced, and that will be discussed shortly, are going through the same process of selection.

**Post-Prohibition.** The repeal of Prohibition found eastern viticulture, what there was left of it, in deep depression. Unlike California, it was not helped by the huge grape "deal" directed at home winemakers; and it had lost much of the fresh fruit market to Thompson Seedless, Flame Tokay, and Emperor from the Central Valley, short on flavor but long on shipability.

The wine industry was reduced to a handful of survivors, with run-down cooperage and equipment, no oncoming corps of winemakers, and a shortage of capital. As the wineries reopened, they picked up where they had left off. The emphasis was on sparkling wines, as it had been before when these easily dominated the market. Still wines were relatively unimportant, as likewise they had been before—except for the surprising appearance of a generalized nonethnic market for the so-called kosher wines; heavy, sweet, nonfortified wines produced mainly from the abundant Concord grapes.

**New Departure.** Then in the late 1940s and early 1950s, something unexpected happened: the appearance of an entirely new range of grape material. These are the vines commonly known as French hybrids. Though varying greatly, they have characteristics in common. They are much more winter-hardy and disease-resistant than the classic *V. vinifera* varieties. Yet their fruit and the wines made from it show little or none of the foxiness and other "wild" flavors associated with the American species. Their wines are much closer, flavor-wise, to European models.

They were then producing a substantial proportion of France's non-appellation wine, having proved their cultural value decisively during the wartime shortages of copper and sulfur for fungicides.   They were unknown to our eastern viticulture, though the New York Agricultural Experiment Station at Geneva had a small selection of these hybrids, and several other private and public varietal collections in this country contained specimens of others.

Ironically, the origin of these goes back to that same group of Americans whose work in providing rootstock material had been so important for the French vineyards.   Along with the species material, they sent samples of their various hybrids that wére intended for the direct production of fruit rather than for use as rootstocks.   Among these was a *Lincecumii rupestris* hybrid by Jaeger, originally known as Jaeger No. 70 but by him renamed Munson, in honor of his fellow hybridizer.

The main strategy in the French antiphylloxera battle was to graft their familiar varieties on resistant roots.   There was a parallel effort by others to avoid the need for grafting by breeding new varieties, which, ideally, would combine fruit of good wine quality with disease-resistant wine characteristics.   By accident, Jaeger No. 70 was given a key role in this.   A vine of Jaeger No. 70 came into the hands of an amateur named Contassot, a pastrymaker in Pezenas, a village in Ardeche so modest that it is not even listed in the Guide Michelin.   Contassot planted it in his garden alongside a few vinifera, Cinsaut, Gamay, and Raisaine (5).   He cross-pollinated them and saved the seeds.   The following spring he divided the seeds between two neighbors, Albert Seibel and Georges Couderc.   From some of these seeds came vines yielding wine acceptable to the French taste; and they became the first in the long line of hybrids associated with the names of Seibel and Couderc.   It should be noted that the hybrids from Contassot's seeds contained no *V. labrusca* ancestry at all, being crosses of (*Lincecumii* × rupestris) × *V. vinifera*.   One of them, C.7120, was an instant success and continues to be grown in substantial acreage throughout southern France. Much interspecific crossing and recrossing has continued to this day, almost entirely by private persons, devotees of limited means and little or no scientific training but a pronounced "feel" for their métier.   For descriptions of many of these see Galet (5, 6, 7) and Wagner (2).   The weight of the French viticultural establishment (academic, journalistic, legislative) is against the hybrids and favors grafted vinifera.   The establishment has clout, and in response to this pressure, the hybrids are currently in regression.   Yet the French acreage of hybrids is still enormous.

What does the word "enormous" mean in this connection?   Let me offer a comparison, necessarily inexact, but indicative.   In 1976, California's total acreage of the true wine grapes in bearing, excluding table and raisin varieties of grapes, was 292,646 (8).   In 1976, the total French acreage of the thirteen most generally grown hybrids was 487,400, or two-thirds greater than the total California wine-grape acreage (7). (California's wine-grape acreage has increased considerably since 1976 and France's hybrid acreage has decreased since 1976. The comparison is useful only as an indication.) See Table I for acreage of hybrids in France.

Although hybrid acreage in France is small compared with that of the main bulk-producing varieties (Aramon, Carignane, Grenache), another indication that their quantitative importance is not neglibible may be had by comparing the 178,800 acres devoted to the so-called cepages nobles with the 487,400 acres above. (Again, the acreage of cepages nobles has increased since 1976 while that of the hybrids has decreased.)

Interest in grape hybridizing is reviving in Europe again, if indeed it ever really lapsed. A series of international meetings has been devoted to the amelioration of the vine, which is to say grape genetics, most recently in 1980 at the University of California at Davis, California. Several series of hybrids from the German Geisenheim and Geilweilerhof Institutes, yielding "Riesling-like" wines, are now under extensive test in Germany. Among those being followed closely are the Geisenheim hybrids of the French Seibel 7053 × Riesling and (Sylvaner × Riesling) × Seibel 7053 and the French hybrid Leon Millot. The complexity of some of the hybrids being used in such work is indicated by the genealogy of the Seibel 7053 (see Figure 3). In connection with this new outburst of work, Professor Dr. H. Becker of the Geisenheim Institute has this to say (9) (in the rather awkward official translation):

> We continue our Geisenheim program to breed interspecific varieties besides our broad vinifera-breeding activities and clone selection . . . We are convinced that interspecific hybridization will be fundamental to vine improvement though the German legislation presently will not allow to recommend and plant grape vines which are not vinifera.

**Table I. Acreage of Most Popular Hybrids in France in 1976** (7)

| | |
|---|---|
| Baco blanc | 60,000 |
| Baco noir | 24,000 |
| Chambourcin | 12,000 |
| Couderc 7120 | 67,000 |
| Oberlin 595 | 7200 |
| S. 4986 | 7200 |
| S. 5455 | 79,200 |
| S. 8357 | 3600 |
| Seibel 7053 | 40,000 |
| SV 5276 | 4800 |
| SV 12375 | 64,800 |
| SV 18283 | 21,600 |
| SV 18315 | 96,000 |

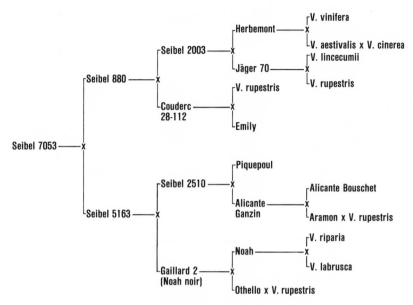

*Figure 3. Genealogy of Seibel 7053*

However that may be, the existing French hybrids represent a important addition to the resources of the Eastern wine industry. Much has been done, and far more remains to be done, in matching varieties with regions and sorting out the most promising of them in terms of both wine quality and cultural characteristics. Following is a list of those varieties so far most widely tested under climates ranging from those of New Mexico to New Hampshire and eastern Washington to Alabama: red wine hybrids: *Baco No. 1, Joannes Seyve 26205, Landot 4511, *Marechal Foch, *Leon Millot, *Seibel 7053, *Seibel 9549, *Seibel 10878, *Seibel 13053, and Seibel 18315; white wine hybrids: Ravat 51, Seibel 4986, *Seibel 5279, *Seibel 9110, *Seibel 10868, *Seyve–Villard 5276, Seyve–Villard 12375, and *Vidal 256. (Note that the above list overlaps but does not correspond with those in Table I—not surprising in view of the differences in North American and French climates and soils.) The old faithfuls such as Concord, Delaware, and Catawba continue to dominate commercial eastern viticulture, since they are reliable and already familiar to growers and the wineries are used to working with them. However, several of the new hybrids, indicated in the above list by asterisks, have entered the production pattern of the large wineries and several are being promoted as varietals. See Figure 4 for photographs of three of these promising hybrids.

An interesting development is that several of the present hybrids are being used at the New York Agricultural Experiment Station at Geneva as

*Figure 4. Three promising hybrids: Landot 2281 (left), Seyve–Villard 5276 (Seyval) (center), and Seibel 4986 (Rayon d'Or) (right)*

parents for yet another hybrid generation.    The leading idea is to back-cross them with the various cepages nobles in the hope of introducing specific European varietal flavors—much as is being done at the German stations.

Moreover, a whole new generation of small quality-minded wineries has come into being since 1960, oriented more toward the French hybrids than the traditional varieties.    At the same time, a number of these are giving some of the V. *vinifera* varieties another whirl.

Those taking another look at the possibilities of V. *vinifera* varieties in the East are entitled to a few words of mingled encouragement and caution.    Considering the history of past failures, it is gallant to challenge such a dismal record.    It may not be entirely impractical.    In the vast area loosely called the East, some parts are less hostile than others.    There is a chance of finding microclimates where the obstacles are not too great, and, of course, the armament against disease is improved considerably.

As for the warning, let it be said that the encouragement of such plantings has a large element of the romantic in it and comes mainly, though not entirely, from armchair vignerons.    Much has been published about prospects but very little so far about economic results.    Mendall, after a lifetime as an Eastern viticultural consultant, states that he knows of no single commercially successful vinifera enterprise in the East and considers experimental plantings north of 40° latitude to be quite impractical (*10*).    Munson, after his lifetime of experience with all species in the Red River Valley of Texas and thereabouts, placed the practical northern Texas limit for V. *vinifera* at 35°, just north of Amarillo, but added that isothermal lines are better guides than latitude (*3*).    Much will be learned from the work of current experimenters.    But those among them who want to have wine on the table every night will find it prudent to plant a few hybrids alongside their vinifera, as indeed the majority have done.

## Wine Production

In terms of volume, most wine production from eastern grapes is accounted for by a handful of large and medium-sized wineries, concentrated in New York State and the Midwest. A number of substantial enterprises, relying to a large extent on California juice, concentrates, and bulk wine, are excluded from this discussion. The remainder is produced by a large number of small wineries scattered over the entire area but concentrated in the northeast and north-central states. The maps, Figures 5 and 6, give a notion of their distribution.

Most of this new generation of wineries has come into being since the mid sixties. Most have been inspired by the challenge of the newly available wine varieties and, thus, represent a departure from eastern traditions. Many owe their being to the liberalization of laws in some states—passage of the so-called farm winery laws. In a high proportion of states, the laws affecting wine production and distribution are highly restrictive or even prohibitive, practically speaking. In part, this is a lingering reflection of Prohibition sentiment, the theory having been at the time of Repeal that a winery might become a focal point for the moral corruption of the populace. In part, it reflects simple or inadvertent ignorance. The coming into being of these small new wineries, under liberalized laws, is evidence of the American public's awakened interest in wine as a food beverage.

The large wineries are sophisticated enterprises with broad markets, thoroughly modern equipment and techniques, well-trained personnel, access to capital, and substantial vineyards of their own supplemented by close grower relationships. The wines they make are changing, but gradually and from an already existing base.

The small wineries range from the sophisticated to the primitive. Most of them are essentially one-man or family operations. Being uninhibited by tradition, they are highly experimental in their attitude toward both grapes and wine types. Their markets are primarily local, and where the law allows, they depend heavily on retail winery sales to regular customers and tourists and other transients. This is their means of building a market, and the full retail markup is vital when production is so small. Several institutions sponsor short courses, annual meetings, and other technical help, notably the Agricultural Experimental Station at Geneva. The stations in Ohio, Pennsylvania, Michigan, Missouri, Arkansas, and Texas have such programs, and the published "transactions" of these various short courses and meetings are frequently of high quality. The American Society of Enologists, which is the professional organization of American winemakers, now has an eastern branch. There are two area-wide, privately sponsored associations, the commercially oriented Association of American Vintners and the American Wine Society, which is a bridge between serious amateurs, institutional research, and the small new wine producers as well as

*Figure 5. Distribution of (W) wine production, (B) winery bottling, and (P) grape products production outside of California (23)*

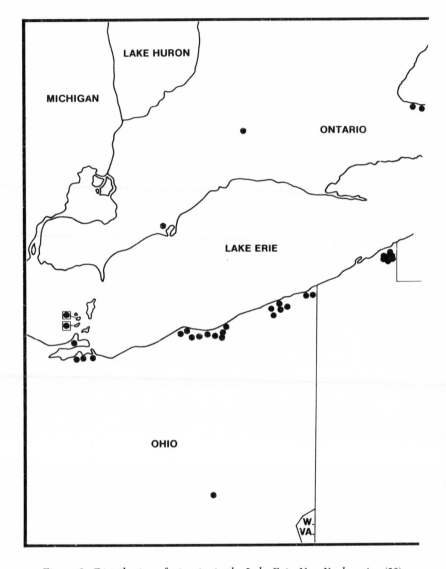

*Figure 6. Distribution of wineries in the Lake Erie–New York region* (23)

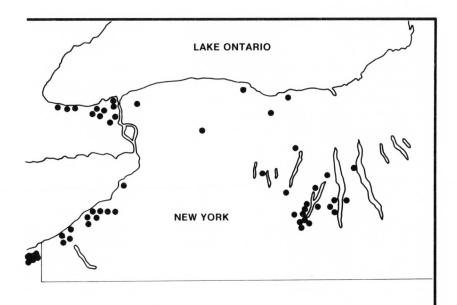

LAKE ONTARIO

NEW YORK

PENNSYLVANIA

numerous small private groups that are grower oriented rather than consumer oriented. There are also several periodicals. There is a need for modest laboratories, public or private, that can provide routine wine production analyses and recommendations, such as exist throughout winegrowing Europe and in California. The analogy is with established agricultural extension services, such as provision for foliar and soil analyses.

Because the eastern situation is so amorphous, the best that can be done in the following notes is to describe general trends where they are evident and divide attention between the large established wineries and the new generation of small ones. This description of "the state of the art" assumes to supplement a more technical paper by A.C. Rice (11), which emphasizes microbiological and biochemical aspects.

**Harvesting.** Except in the southwestern and southeastern quadrants of this huge area, ripening comes gradually. California's problem of avoiding overripeness (too much sugar and too little acid) is infrequently encountered. Quite the reverse is true. The eastern problem, in the greater part of the area, is to achieve maximum sugar and moderate acidity. Frequently, as in northern Europe, the ripening period is cut short before an optimum balance can be reached. And many (but not all) eastern varieties appear to be incapable of reaching the levels of sugar content common to the V. vinifera varieties grown in California. Further increase of sugar by dehydration (raisining) is rare indeed; rotting is more characteristic of overripeness when this occurs. On the other hand, in most parts, harvesting becomes a favorable factor in cool weather. Mechanical harvesting is now common in the larger vineyards. Machines are of the beater type with the removal of chaff by a blower. Hand picking is the rule among the small wineries, even where contract mechanical harvesting is available, and it eliminates the capital cost of a machine. Hand picking brings in the grapes in better condition, and mechanical harvesting is not practical in small vineyards of irregular shape and terrain. In the case of some of the superior and more fragile varieties [the now widely planted Seibel 5279 (Aurora) is a case in point], some of the large wineries are returning to hand picking. Field crushing has not yet taken on to any great extent.

*White Wine*

Stemming is now practically universal for white wine grapes as well as for red, though some of the smaller wineries continue to crush directly into the press without stemming. Dejuicers taking off around 60 percent of free-run are now normal in the large wineries and are beginning to be used in some of the smaller ones. The purpose may be to ferment and finish the free-run juice separately; more often, free-run and press juice are recombined in the fermentor and the function of the dejuicer is simply to increase press capacity and pressing efficiency.

**Pressing.**   Continuous screw presses as well as horizontal basket presses of the Vaslin and Willmes sorts are used by the larger wineries, and smaller sizes of the latter types are now general in the smallest wineries.   Some of these latter wineries use large Italian-style basket presses equipped with hydraulic pressing heads, more laborious but unrivaled as to juice quality.   Pressing problems with the traditional slip-skin grapes are eliminated by addition of bulking agents such as rice hulls or cellulose fiber, and pectic enzymes.   The old-fashioned, rack-and-cloth mechanical or hydraulic presses are now but a memory, though they continued to be used for some years after the repeal of Prohibition.   Of the numerous pectic enzyme products now available, of foreign and domestic origin and in both dry and liquid form, much experimenting goes on; there is no clear consensus.

**Preliminary Clarification.**   There is no consensus about this either. Centrifuges may be used at this point by the large producers.   Cold settling of the juice with 50–75 mg/L of $SO_2$, with or without pectic enzymes, is used by some wineries but is not nearly so general as in California.   Generally speaking, juice of the principal eastern varieties does not give sufficient separation to make it worthwhile.   Right or wrong, there is also a rather general belief among Eastern winemakers that such separation as does take place robs the ultimate wine of valuable flavor characteristics.

**Amelioration.**   This is the principal distinction between eastern and western winemaking, made necessary because in all but the most exceptional circumstances, a deficiency in sugar, low pH, and high acidity of eastern grapes requires correction if a well-balanced wine is to be made.   It is as necessary as the addition of acidity to some California wines, either direct or by ion exchange.   When the grapes are harvested, 18° Brix and 1.2 g/100 mL (as tartaric) are considered very good averages.   Sugar can be much lower (and acid higher) and is anticipated for the special crop called cold-press Concords, which is harvested in the Northeast.   This consists of immature Concords having negligible pigment and minimal foxy aroma and flavor, pressed fresh, and treated as white wine.   These are used in the lower grades of wine.

Amelioration means, first of all, the raising of sugar content to an appropriate level, about 22° Brix—a practice that also is used routinely in some of the most prestigious wine districts of Europe, when necessary.

Amelioration in the East also means the increase of pH and reduction of total acidity.   Total acidity is essentially the sum of the two principal acids of grapes: tartaric and malic.   The reduction of the two acids is obtained in different ways.

Reduction of tartaric is, of course, incidental to fermentation wherever wine is made.   This acid, mainly present in grapes as potassium bitartrate, is much more soluble in water (the principal ingredient of grape juice) than in alcoholic solutions.   Thus, as grape juice ferments and alcoholic content rises, it becomes supersaturated and a proportion of the bitartrate precipitates. This is further encouraged, chiefly by chilling of the new wine, to achieve tartrate stability and so avoid accidental precipitation after the wine is bottled. Its additional value in the East is the ameliorative effect of reduction in total acidity.

**Malo-lactic Fermentation.** For the sake of clear exposition, a discussion of this phenomenon is included at this point because of its pronounced effect on the reduction of total acidity, though it also has the same useful function in the preparation of red as well as white wines and though it has other effects besides the reduction of acidity.

In general, eastern grapes have a much higher proportion of malic acid than do western grapes because it is the typical acid of fruit grown in cool climates. High malic acid content is also characteristic of many of the grapes of temperate-climate Europe. This acid does not precipitate during fermentation, though some is destroyed by yeasts. Malic acid can be converted partially or entirely into the much weaker lactic acid with a large resulting increase of pH value and lowering of total acidity. The conversion (the malo-lactic fermentation) is done by members of a large family of bacteria (the lactic bacteria), some of which are nearly always present and multiply tremendously during the later stages of alcoholic fermentation.

In some cases, pure cultures of a desirable strain of bacteria are added during or after alcoholic fermentation. Some of these, which thrive in a low-acid medium, yield by-products exceedingly harmful to wine quality. They are a constant menace in the wines of warmer areas of California. Not being acid-tolerant they are rarely a menace in eastern wineries. On the other hand, the more acid-tolerant kinds normally present in eastern fermentations are highly beneficial ameliorating agents, as they are in temperate Europe and in some regions of California. At worst, they raise the volatile acidity slightly.

However, a difficulty is that if the pH is too low, these beneficial agents will not do their job. This is taken care of traditionally in the East (and was, long before the role of the lactic acid bacteria had even been associated with winemaking) by amelioration with a material that is, as previously noticed, already the principal ingredient of grape juice—namely, water. Amelioration in eastern winemaking is to a point where the benign lactic acid bacteria will take hold and do their work. That is around 1 g/100 mL (as tartaric). Ameliorating the acidity this way below 0.5 g/100 mL is illegal.

Several provisos should be mentioned here. The lactic bacteria are extremely sensitive to free $SO_2$ and are inhibited by its presence even in low concentrations. The bacteria become inactive at temperatures much below 18.3° C (65° F). The reduction of the total acidity of the juice is not directly proportional to the amount of water amelioration. On occasion, the natural increase of the bacterial population does not reach the critical point at which the malo-lactic reaction takes off.

Federal regulations have long authorized such amelioration up to 35 percent of the resulting volume, and even provide a gallonage table (paragraph 240.961) in the industry's winemaking "bible" (*12*). Amelioration to the full allowable extent may have been necessary under former winemaking conditions, before the ameliorating role of malo-lactic fermentation had been discovered and confirmed. Using contemporary techniques (avoiding the inhibiting effect of $SO_2$, holding the newly fermented wine at a minimum temperature of 18.3° C for a sufficient period, seeding with an active inoculum of malo-lactic bacteria of a correct strain, and delaying the first racking), full use of this ameliorating allowance, or "credit," is not necessary for this purpose.

Normal practice in large wineries is to use liquid sugar for amelioration, plus such additional water as may be required for correct balance. Small wineries use dry sucrose, mixing in the calculated quantity of water to make a thin syrup. Sucrose is, of course, converted to glucose and fructose on contact with the juice. Sugar/water amelioration, therefore, adds no ingredient to grape juice that is not naturally present as the two main ingredients. It simply corrects the proportions of these.

As already stated, the ameliorative effect of malo-lactic fermentation is equally important in the preparation of red wines—probably more so since a degree of tartrate not desirable in a red wine is often wanted in a white wine. It is also necessary to achieve "bacterial stability." So long as malic acid remains in the wine and there is any presence of lactic bacteria, there is a risk, however remote, of delayed fermentation in the bottle accompanied by hazes and gassiness. In former times, French Burgundies often were subject to this accident. Finally, the slight increase of volatile acidity that accompanies malo-lactic fermentation may help to heighten and improve aroma and flavor.

Another method of acid amelioration, used to avoid water amelioration, is the addition of calcium salts for the purpose of substituting calcium for potassium ions. The resulting calcium bitartrate salts, being less soluble, increase the precipitation of bitartrate. This raises technical problems, one being that if the malo-lactic fermentation should take place subsequently, the wine may contain insufficient acidity of any kind. Another is that calcium tartrate precipitates slowly and in more finely divided form, often causing persistent hazes that are hard to remove. Often, too, this precipitation is delayed, leading to the presumption that the wine is "tartrate stable." Only after it is bottled, the brilliant and supposedly stable wine may develop a delayed calcium tartrate haze and even a deposit. The calcium salt method in a refined form is used considerably in Germany but rarely here.

**Conduct of Fermentation.** The ameliorating material normally is added to the sulfited juice prior to the onset of fermentation and thoroughly mixed in. An actively fermenting yeast starter is added. The large wineries maintain a yeast generator for the propagation of a continuous supply originating from a selected strain. The starter may amount to as much as 2 percent of volume, and in its active condition, it is presumed to dominate random strains of wild yeast that may be present. Dominance of a good strain has been simplified by the industrial production of dehydrated or compressed yeast of well-known strains of *Saccharomyces cerevisiae* that are tolerant to $SO_2$ and ethanol. The most commonly used strains are montrachet and champagne, but several other strains are available, and some wineries maintain their own strains, which they either propagate themselves or farm out to industrial yeast producers. Small wineries often propagate anew for each batch, using dehydrated yeast. There is nothing like a fixed rule for the proportion of starter. Once a clean and vigorous fermentation is under way, the slapdash method of using it as a starter for subsequent batches is used more often than anyone cares to admit. In California, this would be hazardous. In the East, owing to low pH of the material even after the initial amelioration, the risk from undesirable spontaneous fermentations is much lower. This is similar to the practice in some parts of temperate Europe where a mixed culture of the local yeast flora may be considered preferable to a pure culture of a single strain.

Once fermentation has started, constant surveillance is maintained, with special attention to heat control. Fermentation causes an immense thermal buildup, and the object is to hold the fermenting temperature roughly between 21.1° and 26.7° C (70° and 80° F). In large wineries, the necessary cooling is done by circulating the fermenting wine through heat exchangers, by means of cooling jackets that circulate cold water or a refrigerant, or (where cold water is abundant as in the Finger Lakes district of New York) by maintaining a constant flow of cold water over the sides of the fermentors. In the East, cool weather is a great help. In the hotter parts, the combination of earlier ripening and high ambient temperatures can be troublesome unless anticipated by cooling equipment. Small wineries that cannot afford such equipment use small fermentors and get rid of much of the excess heat by radiation. Above 26.7°–29.4° C (80°–85° F) there can be a loss of quality. Above 32° C (95° F), the yeasts are progressively inactivated, with danger of a stuck fermentation, often hard to restart and always easy prey to spoilage organisms. There is a school that argues that highest quality is obtained from lowest possible fermenting temperatures. The case is not fully proved, the fermentation period may be unduly prolonged, and malolactic fermentation is inhibited. In normal practice, temperatures are held in the middle range, especially for reds.

To keep heat buildup under control and for other reasons, one of the largest wineries prefers to begin with nonameliorated juice that consists of mixed free-run and press juice without any preliminary clarification, with the addition of a minimal dose of $SO_2$ (20 mg/L) and a massive starter, and postpone amelioration until the fermentation has been brought down to 8° Brix. The rationale is that fermentation begins more swiftly with simple juice, a protective layer of $CO_2$ is formed immediately (reducing the chance of oxidative browning), and the load on the heat exchangers is reduced by spreading out heat buildup. However, it may be added that the rapid browning prior to fermentation of the juice of grape varieties rich in oxidase, though alarming, is rarely troublesome. Fermentation provides a reducing medium and the early oxidative reaction that causes the browning is reversible.

**Postfermentation Care.** For white wine, it is considered a good general rule that the less handling the better. Some fill the fermentor full as soon as primary fermentation is finished, leaving the wine on the lees at moderate temperature to make sure that malo-lactic fermentation can be finished swiftly. Others rack immediately but do not add $SO_2$ at this point, unless they wish to avoid the malo-lactic fermentation for some reason. It is rare that a $H_2S$ problem occurs if wine is left on the lees awhile because elemental sulfur is not much used in eastern vineyards for spraying or dusting, as it is in California. Should it develop, as it does occasionally, the wine is racked immediately in the presence of air and sometimes with the addition of a small dose of copper sulfate. The copper combines with the sulfide to produce an insoluble precipitate. A maximum addition of 0.5 mg/L of copper sulfate is permitted under Federal regulations.

The wine is racked when the malo-lactic fermentation has run its course, sometimes with centrifuging, a protective dose of $SO_2$ is added, and the wine is chilled thoroughly for bitartrate precipitation and to encourage natural clarification. The amount of $SO_2$ varies considerably depending on the nature of the wine and the purpose for which it is intended (a tendency to oxidize easily calls for a substantial dose, a wine to be used as a sparkling wine should have only a light dose, etc.) and the predisposition of the winemaker. Some aim for minimal use throughout processing and others prefer to play it safe by using more. A fair average at the time of this first racking would be 50 mg/L. In the East, chilling is easy: doors of the storage area are opened and the low prevailing outside temperatures do the job. Much the same routine is followed in both large and small wineries. Cold storage tank rooms or heat exchangers combined with insulated tanks are used in the warmer regions and also where production schedules require precise time/temperature control. Two weeks at -3.3° C (26° F) does a thorough job; if that temperature is not attainable, then a longer time is required for precipitation. An alternative is ion exchange (replacing the potassium ion of potassium bitartrate with sodium), but it is not much used in eastern winemaking.

The new wine usually is fined, or more tightly centrifuged, or given a preliminary filtration, around the first of the year. Bentonite is used most commonly, the amount being determined by laboratory-size samples of different concentrations. The average quantity is about 0.3 mg/L. The proprietary material Sparkalloid also is used a great deal, as is the classic gelatin–tannin combination.    Again, the proportions and quantities for a given lot of wine are determined by comparing laboratory-size samples.    The two latter types of fining function less swiftly than bentonite but give much more compact lees (precipitated material).    Keeping the storage containers full (topping) on a regular schedule is an indispensable routine, to take care of shrinkage and prevent exposure to air.    Once the wine is stable and brilliant, it may be bottled at the discretion of the winemaker, preceded normally by a polish filtration and a final addition of $SO_2$.    Total $SO_2$ for bottled wines destined for wide distribution may run from 120 mg/L to 300 mg/L.    Total for wines of limited local distribution may be considerably less.    The trend is toward early bottling of white wine to retain freshness. Aging of white wine in small cooperage is rare, more frequent in the small wineries than the large.

### Red Wine Production

The red wines of the East are less well known and in smaller demand than the whites.    This is not an unusual situation.    Germany is known as white wine country, though substantial quantities of red are made.    The same is true of the Champagne district and the Loire Valley of France, both better known for their whites than their reds, though the latter can be very good.

The pigments and most of the other natural ingredients that distinguish red wine from white are located in the skins primarily and may be extracted in two ways: by fermentation "on the skins" or by heat.    In the East, the traditional method in large wineries is by heat.    This is not unique.    Controlled heating, in advance of fermentation, of all or part of the vintage is often used in some regions of great prestige such as the French Côte d'Or.    See Ferré (13).    Various systems of "thermovinification" are used in southern Europe for large scale production and are not unknown in California.    Some pre-Prohibition heat-treated red California wines made by the Gundlach– Bundschu winery of Sonoma survived the ordeal of Prohibition very well.    This little hoard was released commercially after Repeal, and some of it even found its way as far east as Baltimore (author's testimony).

The eastern technique today is to put the stemmed grapes and their juice through a precisely controlled tubular heat exchanger, bringing the material up to a point that will provide full color extraction yet will not impart a "cooked" character.    For the coarser grapes such as Concord, the temperature is normally 62.8° C (145° F).    For varieties whose flavor (and sometimes color) is more likely to be distorted by the process, such as the new hybrids, the temperature is normally 48.9° C (120° F).    The material, with one or another of the comr..ercially available pectic enzyme formulations added, is held hot in a tank for about half an hour, with stirring, to complete the extraction.    It is then pressed while hot, with the addition of bulking agents.    These, together with the enzymes, greatly improve press-

ing efficiency.   Producers of the enzyme formulations provide specific recommendations as to amounts and holding times appropriate to various
temperatures.   This juice, with its full burden of skin extractives, then goes
to the fermentor, being cooled on the way.   The hot-press juice is obviously
different in composition from that of grapes pressed cold.   The function of
the enzymes is to break down the otherwise troublesome pectins.

**Hot Pressing.**   The hot-press method does cause flavor changes, as
anyone can discover by comparing the "Concord flavor" of Concord grape
jelly and wines with the original flavor of the fresh fruit.   They are quite
different.   But the changes have found acceptance in labrusca wines.   The
hot-press method gives the production advantage that the grape pomace
(skins, seeds, and stems) is eliminated immediately and only the juice is
involved from then on.   But in processing the new and more delicately
flavored grape varieties, many winemakers prefer the classic method of
fermentation on-the-skins, with pumping over during fermentation to encourage extraction and with the necessary control of temperature.   In the
small wineries, skin fermentation is universal, using open fermenters with
either twice-daily punching down of the "cap" of skins to improve maceration
or pumping over, which is a less laborious method of accomplishing the same
purpose.   In skin fermentations, heat buildup tends to be more rapid than
in juice fermentations.   Provided the danger point of $32.2°$ C ($90°$ F) is not
passed, a somewhat higher fermentation temperature than in white wines is
acceptable.   The length of time on the skins is variable—according to the
judgment of the winemaker, depending on the grape variety, the style of
wine aimed for, the ambient temperature, and other factors.   Usually, the
free-run is drawn off and the wet pomace pressed while the mass is still in
active fermentation, with $5°$–$6°$ Brix to go.   Usually the amelioration of red
wine is delayed until this time since it can be calculated more exactly on the
basis of juice than of crushed grapes.   Otherwise, there is approximate
amelioration prior to fermentation and final adjustment at this point.   In
addition to the advantages of better heat control and amelioration adjustment, a short skin fermentation tends to reduce astringency and give more
finesse.

**Maceration Carbonique.**   Experimental work with maceration carbonique has been done in the East, mainly by Beelman and McArdle (*14*),
with interesting results.   Experiments have given mixed results, including
a special flavor that may or may not be desirable depending on the grape
variety, a reduction of malic acid, and a tendency to increased volatile
acidity.   Much more work needs to be done.   But it is unlikely to become a
generalized technique because it ties up so much fermenting capacity.

Subsequent handling of red wine is not greatly different from that of
white wine: holding for a while at a moderate temperature (about $18.3°$ C)
($65°$ F) and without $SO_2$ to complete malo-lactic fermentation promptly, with
or without lactic bacterial inoculation.   Several rackings follow, the first one
usually with some aeration and always with addition of $SO_2$ once the malic

has been eliminated: then thorough chilling, fining, centrifuging or filtration.   Red wines ordinarily receive more prolonged bulk aging, and several more rackings, than the whites.   Barrel aging is used rarely except in the small wineries.   The fad for white oak cooperage of various species and exotic origins has affected only a few of the more sophisticated small wineries in the East.   Its excessive cost tips the scales in favor of good American white oak.   Subtle differences contributed by the various oak extractives do not seem sufficiently important to command premium prices for eastern wines.   And those alert to the cost factor cannot help noticing that, while a certain amount of European oak is coming to this country at exalted prices, a great deal more good American oak cooperage material, new and reconditioned, is sent back to European wine regions annually, and has been for years (15).

*Finishing*

The final steps do not differ greatly from procedures elsewhere.   The length of the aging period depends on the winemaker and market demand. There is blending to achieve various objectives: type, style, consistency from year to year, and so on.   There is a last check for stability and brilliance, then a tight polish filtration with final addition of $SO_2$.   Total $SO_2$ may vary from under 100 mg/L to as high as 300 mg/L depending on the type of wine and the determination of the winemaker.   The whole range of filter types and filtration materials is in use, including, of course, final membrane or sterilizing pad filtration for wines with a sweet finish and wines in which malo-lactic fermentation has been inhibited or has been incomplete.

A slightly sweet finish for purportedly dry wines, white as well as red, is very general and is a response to market demand, real or fancied.   Small wineries catering to tourist or other transient trade find that somewhat sweetened wines are generally preferred, no doubt because many such customers do not yet think of wine as a staple food beverage.

**Sweetening.**   Since virtually all eastern wines are fermented out dry, this means sweetening back just prior to bottling, often to the disadvantage of good wines better left dry.   Sweetening usually is done with sugar.   In some wineries, this is accompanied by a downward adjustment of ethanol to a previously determined level ranging from 11.5 percent to 12.5 percent by volume, using reserved amelioration "credits."   This is done when the winemaker, having calculated the desired sugar/water amelioration, introduces the full amount of sugar prior to fermentation but withholds a portion of the water.   By this means, the new wine achieves a higher ethanol content (say 14.5–15 percent).   The higher alcoholic content encourages bitartrate precipitation, and it is only after the has been accomplished that the remainder of the anticipated amelioration is added.   Upward adjustment of ethanol content (with spirits) is not practiced.

Nominally dry wines may contain 1 percent or more sugar. Accidental refermentation is guarded against by various combinations of high $SO_2$, membrane or sterile pad filtration, and, in some wineries, sorbate. There are no truly sterile bottling installations that I know of in the East. Types of closure depend on the nature of the market catered to, cork finish with real leadfoil capsules being reserved for the winemaker's notion of premium grades.

### Sparkling Wine

Bottle-fermented sparkling wines are, of course, the eastern wines par excellence. They continued to dominate the market long after California had taken over the bulk of the general wine market. As recently as 1950, when the annual wine judging of the Sacramento State Fair went "international" for the first and only time, eastern sparkling wines walked off with a majority of the prizes in their class. The blind judging was conducted rigorously under the auspices of the University of California, Davis, and all but one of the judges were Californians, so that the judging was as objective as possible. The quality of the better California sparkling wines has improved vastly since then, but the best of the eastern sparkling wines still can hold their own.

The base wine is unlike that of either European or California wine, meaning little or no *V. vinifera* grapes or wine are used. The usual grape ingredients are Catawba (the juice of which is nonfoxy when handled properly, though the whole grapes are very foxy, and is not subject to browning), Delaware, which contains no foxiness, that is, methyl anthranilate, and now a newcomer, the French hybrid Aurore (Seibel 5279). The base wine is fermented and finished with great care. The pick of the crop is used, free of botrytis and other rots. The interval between picking and fermentor is as brief as possible. Fermentation is induced without delay to provide a reducing environment immediately and help to hold the use of $SO_2$ to a minimum. There is thorough protein and tartrate stabilization. Wines destined for the cuvée, or blend, undergo bulk aging for eight months to a year and a half. Blending is not done until just prior to bottling for the secondary (bottle) fermentation, with a delay of a few weeks to make sure that the cuvée itself is stable.

From then on, elaboration follows the classic bottle-fermented pattern. Bulk process installations are few in the East. Before bottling for refermentation, a closely calculated quantity of sugar syrup is added, as in California or Europe. The cuvée then is filtered closely, membrane filters commonly being used, not only for brilliance but to eliminate all possibility of carrying over lactic bacteria into the bottle. (One large winery prefers not to encourage prior malo-lactic fermentation, another encourages it; but in both cases, care is taken to eliminate lactic bacteria prior to refermentation in bottle.) An active culture of ethanol-tolerant yeast is then mixed into the bottling tank.

Here follows the first of two deviations from classic procedure. For refermentation, crown caps long since have replaced corks, as they have in California and elsewhere. They are cheaper and they provide an impenetrable seal, so that it is unnecessary to stack the bottles on their sides during refermentation, though this still is usually done. Some wineries allow the refermentation to proceed with the bottles standing up and in cases. When refermentation is finished, the wine, under its own pressure and containing yeast sediment, is left to mature for a considerable period, sometimes for several years. Natural clearing takes place, and the wine acquires the characteristic flavor from yeast autolysis that distinguishes it from wines made to sparkle by other and less expensive methods.

Here enters the second deviation. For the old and laborious method of clearing the wine of its yeast sediment by "riddling," which is still used in small operations and by stubborn traditionalists, large producers now use the so-called transfer process. The bottles are chilled to reduce pressure, then uncapped and placed in an elaborate isobarometric apparatus, which empties them and passes the accumulated wine, still under pressure, through a filter. In the meantime, the empty bottles with their accumulation of yeast sediment enter a cleaning line and are carried by conveyor to the far end of the filter. There they are again filled, this time with the brilliant, filtered wine, still holding its pressure. A proper dollop of sweet dosage is added, and the bottle is corked, wired, and labeled for market. Unlike sparkling wines made by the cheaper and swifter bulk process method, wine finished by the transfer process may have all the benefit of ripening in bottle on its yeast; and the whole tedious process of riddling has been eliminated besides. Sparkling wines finished by the old method and the transfer method are often practically indistinguisable, except for the wording on the bottle: "Fermented in Bottle" in one case, "Fermented in *This* Bottle" in the other. The one important difference between the eastern and other well-made sparkling wines is the cuvée of grapes and their wines from which it is made.

### Fortified Wines

Little needs to be said of these. They are predominantly of the sherry and port types, and the nature of these types is determined more by fabricating procedure than by the grapes used—though varietal differences are still important in the finer grades.

For material, a good deal of low-acid California bulk wine is used, blended with eastern wine. The California contribution is limited currently to 25 percent if an eastern appellation (such as "New York" or "Ohio") is to be used. The California contribution will be reduced in the future for those wines with a viticultural area appellation, in accordance with one of the many changes in the comprehensive revision of federal labeling regulations for all wines, which has been announced recently and will come into effect on January 1, 1983.

It is in the eastern fortified wines that much of the cold-press Concord with its negligible foxiness is used. The blends are sweetened and fortified with grape spirits (the eastern wineries do not distill their own spirits, as is done in California). They are then "baked," which is to say placed in special heated tanks equipped with an apparatus that introduces a constant stream of fine oxygen bubbles. The result of this combination of heat and oxygen is a darkening (oxidation and caramelization) and the general flavor characteristics of port, sherry, madeira, and other such wines, modified in varying degrees by the base material and the amount of baking. After baking, the best of these wines are aged in oak cooperage, in the case of one winery, outdoors winter and summer. To achieve uniformity, some of the large wineries have installed solera blending systems. The ports receive less baking than the sherries, only enough to develop what the French call the goût de rancio. Very little of the flor-yeast sherry type has been produced, at any rate commercially. (For further information on eastern wines and grape breeding, see *16–22.*)

## Prospects

Forecasting is a dubious business, especially so in an industry like Eastern winegrowing, which is undergoing a kind of renaissance, a renaissance that includes changes of ownership and management and drastic changes of policy in the case of the well-known large wineries as well as the widely scattered new generation of small wineries. I will be brief, contenting myself with a few oversimplified observations.

The sparkling wines will continue to be the flag carriers. The demand is backed by a secure tradition. The best of them are excellent wines by anybody's standards. The cheaper ones are sound and palatable, with more flavor character than their California counterparts. Production techniques are well established.

Though the demand for still wines of strongly labrusca character, white and red, sweet and dry, is nothing like that for the more neutral California vinifera wines, it is real and should continue, though it is likely to diminish gradually. Even so, the multipurpose *V. labrusca* grapes will continue to predominate for a long time, if only because they have important other uses besides wine. The production of Concords exceeds that of all other eastern varieties put together.

Eastern prospects for *V. vinifera* grapes and wine are not very promising, for cultural rather than wine-quality reasons. When a harvest of them does come through and the wines are well made, their quality easily rivals and sometimes excels that of their California counterparts. This applies more to the whites than to the reds, up to now at any rate. The likeliest area for them is probably the Southwest, but some microclimates that they can tolerate, and where they can be economically viable, doubtless will be found elsewhere. They will probably never be planted generally.

The new hybrids, with more hardiness and disease resistance bred into them, have much more promise. The wines of the best of them are wholly vinifera in character, though there are no exact counterparts of existing V. *vinifera* varieties. The hybrid Vidal 256 with its Ugni Blanc (Trebbiano) parentage probably comes closest to that, though the same may perhaps be said of some of the new German Riesling hybrids. As a class, the white wine hybrids are so far superior to the reds. But it must be remembered that grape breeding is an ongoing thing with wide-open possibilities.

There is a strong trend toward the use of varietal grape names, or less fanciful proprietary names (what the French call noms de fantaisie). This represents a desire to get away from such old and meaningless generic terms as burgundy, chablis, and sauterne, or else a wish to identify and set apart wines from grapes new to eastern viticulture, whether they be the new hybrids to the occasional V. *vinifera* variety. It represents pride of work-manship and, to some degree, it makes sense commercially. Unfortunately, it downgrades the very real importance of blending; and most experienced winemakers everywhere know that, with few exceptions, the quality of a wine may be improved by judicious blending. But how are conscientiously blended, and hence improved, wines to be named if varietal names become equated in the public mind with top quality? This matter of nomenclature (including the use of vintage dating) certainly has not been solved by the new federal labeling regulations and remains a very real problem for the future.

The dispersal of Eastern winegrowing (see map, Figure 3) is not tempo-rary, despite the prospect of a good deal of failure. Much of it is probably permanent, and the spreading to still other areas is likely to continue. There are several grounds for this assumption.

One is the remarkable increase of demand for wine as a food beverage during the past decade, much of it in areas where little or no demand existed previously and no wine was produced. It represents a real change in the American dietary pattern. Such regional demand stimulates curiosity about the regional production potential. Some of that curiosity translates into action. The present broad distribution of small new vineyards and wineries represents just that. Those that prove out successfully become points of further diffusion.

The character of the wines from these new areas will continue to move away from that associated with traditional eastern varieties and toward that associated with V. *vinifera* wines. Most of the individuals embarked on these small new enterprises have done so with the deliberate intention of getting away from the older varieties and exploring the possibilities of the new.   For many of them, thought of profit is secondary to the challenge.   Their prospects are further improved by the continuing emergence of new hybrids, such as those now beginning to come out of Germany, and of American breeding programs as well.   Examples of the latter are the ongoing program at the New York Agricultural Experiment Station at Geneva and the promise for the southeastern states that is implicit in the development of *V. rotundifolia* hybrids at the University of California, Davis.

Giving fancy free rein, one even anticipates a reversal of emphasis in California from white wines back to the wines they grow and make best, which are red, and the emergence in the East of a range of white wines with a fresh lightness, a fruitiness and a delicacy rarely found in California's otherwise admirable white wines.

## Acknowledgments

The author gratefully acknowledges assistance in the form of information and advice from Thomas Chadwick, Charles Fournier, Leonard Mattick, Seaton Mendall, Eric Miller, Andrew C. Rice, and from the editor, Maynard A. Amerine.

## Literature Cited

1. Hedrick, U.P. "The Grapes of New York;" State Printers: Albany, NY, 1908.
2. Wagner, P.M. "Grapes Into Wine;" Knopf: New York, 1976, p. 302.
3. Munson, T.V. "Foundations of American Grape Culture;" T.V. Munson & Son: Denison, TX, 1903.
4. Ordish, G. "The Great Wine Blight;" Dent: London, 1972.
5. Galet, P. "Cepages et Vignobles de France," Tome 1. "Les Vignes Americains;" Imprimerie P. Dehan: Montpellier, France, 1956–1964, Vols. 1–4.
6. Galet, P. "A Practical Ampelography," (translation L.T. Morton), Cornell Univ. Press: Ithaca, NY, 1979.
7. Galet, P. "Precis d'Ampelographie," 4th ed.; Imprimerie P. Dehan: Montpellier, France, 1976.
8. McGregor, R.A.; Cain, M. "California Grape Acreage, 1979," California Crop and Livestock Reporting Service, Sacramento, CA, 1980.
9. Becker, H. "Results of Interspecific Hybridization in Geisenheim (Table Wine Varieties)," In "Grapevine Genetics and Breeding;" Institut National de la Recherche Agronomique: Paris, 1978.
10. Mendall, S.C. "Prospects for Growing Vinifera in the Northeast," *Eastern Grape Grower Winery News* **1979**, *5*(2), 14–16.
11. Rice, A.C. In "Chemistry of Winemaking," *Adv. Chem. Ser.* **1974**, *137*, 88–115.
12. "Wine. Part 240 of Title 27, Code of Federal Regulations," *U.S. Govt. Off., U.S. Dept. Treasury, Bureau of Alcohol, Tobacco and Firearms, Washington*, **1979**.
13. Ferré, L. "Traite d'Oenologie Bourguignonne;" Institut National des Appellations d'Origine des Vins et Eaux-de-Vie: Paris, 1958.
14. Beelman, R.; McArdle, F.J. "Influence of Carbonic Maceration on Acid Reduction and Quality of a Pennsylvania Dry Red Table Wine," *Am. J. Enol. Vitic.* **1974**, *25*, 219–221.
15. Heller, W., Canton Wood Products Co., Canton, OH, personal communication.
16. Adams, L.L. "The Wines of America," 2nd ed.; McGraw-Hill: New York, 1978.

17. Amerine, M.A.; Berg, H.W.; Kunkee, R.E.; Ough, C.S.; Singleton, V.L.; Webb, A.D. "The Technology of Wine Making," 4th ed.; Avi: Westport, CN, 1979.
18. Cattell, H.; Stauffer, H.L. "The Hybrids;" L & H Photojournalism: Lancaster, PA, 1978.
19. Cattell, J.; Stauffer, H. L. "The Vinifera;" L & H Photojournalism: Lancaster, PA, 1979.
20. Snyder, E. "Grape Development and Improvement," U.S.D.A. Yearbook of Agric. 1937, pp. 661–664.
21. Wagner, P.M. "A Wine-Grower's Guide," 2nd ed.; Knopf: New York, 1965; p. 221.
22. Wagner, P.M. "Wines, Grape Vines and Climate," Sci. Am. 1974, 230(6), 107–115.
23. Eastern Grape Grower Winery News 1979, 5(6), 32–35.

RECEIVED July 14, 1980.

# INDEX

*Jacket design by Carol Conway.*
*Editing and production by Robin Giroux.*

*The textual material was composed by Carolina
Academic Press, Durham, NC. The front matter and
index were composed by Service Composition, Baltimore, MD. The book was printed and bound by
The Maple Press Co., York, PA.*